Gaia Servadio

Born in Italy, Gaia Servadio has lived in England for over thirty years. She has written for newspapers and magazines on music, politics and literature; she has worked for the cinema and television and is a regular broadcaster. She is Art Correspondent of the Italian paper *Corrière della Sera*. She has written fifteen previous books including the novels *Melinda, Don Giovanni, The Story of R* and non-fiction, *A Profile of a Mafia Boss, Mafioso, Insider Outsider* and a biography of Luchino Visconti.

SCEPTRE

The Real Traviata

The biography of Giuseppina Strepponi,
wife of Giuseppe Verdi

GAIA SERVADIO

SCEPTRE

Copyright © Gaia Servadio 1994

First published in Great Britain in 1994 by Hodder and Stoughton
First published in paperback in 1995 by Hodder and Stoughton
A division of Hodder Headline PLC
A Sceptre Book

A John Curtis Book

The right of Gaia Servadio to be identified as the Author of
this Work has been asserted by her in accordance with the
Copyright, Designs and Patents Act 1988.

10 9 8 7 6 5 4 3 2 1

British Library Cataloguing in Publication Data

Servadio, Gaia
Real Traviata: Biography of Giuseppina
Strepponi, Wife of Giuseppe Verdi
I. Title
780.92

ISBN 0 340 61718 7

Typeset by Hewer Text Composition Services, Edinburgh
Printed and bound in Great Britain by
Cox and Wyman Ltd, Reading, Berkshire

Hodder and Stoughton
A division of Hodder Headline PLC
338 Euston Road
London NW1 3BH

This book is dedicated to the memory of my parents Luxardo and Bianca Servadio

CONTENTS

———— • ————

ILLUSTRATIONS

Giuseppina Strepponi by an anonymous painter, 1841.
(*Museo Teatrale alla Scala; Foto Saporetti*)
The most popular composers of the 1820s and 30s:
Bellini, Rossini, Mercadante, Ricci and Donizetti.
Giuseppe Verdi aged twenty-nine. (*Foto Dalmazio, Busseto*)
Giuseppina Strepponi, an etching of around 1839.
A contemporary illustration of the final scene from *La traviata*.
The famous impresario Bartolomeo Merelli.
(*Museo Teatrale alla Scala; Foto Saporetti*)
The piano at Palazzo Dordoni where Verdi composed
Rigoletto, La traviata and *Il trovatore*. (*Foto Dalmazio, Busseto*)
The interior of Giuseppina's bedroom. (*Foto Dalmazio, Busseto*)
King Vittorio Emanuele II of Savoy, King of Piedmont,
surrounded by his heroes.
Viva VERDI, a code which meant 'Viva Vittorio
Emanuele Re D'Italia', 1859. (*Museo del Risorgimento*)
Angelo Mariani.
The interpreters of *Don Carlo*. (*Foto Archivio Storico Ricordi*)
Verdi visiting Turin to hand King Vittorio Emanuele
the result of a plebiscite. From a drawing by Edoardo Mantania
from *Illustrazione italiana*. (*Museo del Risorgimento*)

The interpreters of *La forza del destino (The Force of Destiny)*.
(*Foto Archivio Storico Ricordi*)
The barricades at Porta Ticinese in Milan during the Five Days (1848).
(*Museo del Risorgimento*)
The marriage certificate of Verdi and Giuseppina.
(*Museo Teatrale alla Scala*)
Giuseppina at the time of *Un ballo in maschera (A Masked Ball)*, 1858.
(*Museo Teatrale alla Scala; Foto Saporetti*)
Verdi and Giuseppina in Russia.

Filomena 'Fifao' Verdi was re-named Maria when she was
adopted by the Verdis. (*Cassa di Risparmio of Parma and the Credito su
Pegno of Busseto*)
Teresa Stolz as Aida.
Clara Maffei, 'Clarina'.
The church of San Marco in Milan, during the first performance
of the Requiem Mass. From a drawing by Pessina,
etching by Centenari. (*Museo del Risorgimento*)
The same Requiem Mass performed at La Scala. From
a drawing by Tofani, etching by Baldi. (*Museo del Risorgimento*)
Giuseppe Verdi in 1887. (*Obbiettoivo Due*)
A photograph of Teresa Stolz. (*Foto Saporetti*)
Giuseppina aged seventy-five.
(*Museo Teatrale alla Scala: Foto Saporetti*)

Endpapers The interior of La Scala Opera House, 1858.
Drawing by Bonamore and Tofani. (*Museo del Risorgimento, Milano*)

INTRODUCTION

Donna son io, signore, ed in mia casa.
I am a lady, sir, and in my own house.

LA TRAVIATA, ACT II

If it were simply that Giuseppina Strepponi became Verdi's wife, I would certainly not have devoted so many of my ever-decreasing years to writing her biography. She was an intelligent and cultivated woman. She was a gifted writer; her correspondence demonstrates an agile hand and mind. She was also a voracious and acute reader; when studying Shakespeare or Byron, Calderon or Cervantes, she kept a dictionary by her side; with Maupassant and Balzac she had no such problems, having read and spoken French from her childhood.

Had she merely been Verdi's wife, I would have found it difficult to spend a year and a half on research and many further months writing her story. 'Peppina' herself certainly added to my difficulties. Giuseppina Strepponi did all she could to cover her traces, to blot out certain events of her life – those events that were not in keeping with the image of respectability she managed to create. But facts cannot always be concealed and, with the help of letters and documents, and a continual effort to understand, much has come to light. Not everything, however. Various people before me have worked on Verdi documents and in so doing have found details concerning the life of Strepponi (by the way, what an ugly surname!). Some of the musicologists who have guided me were indignant about the obstinacy with which Giuseppina managed to conceal elements of her past.

One of these scholars, to whom I am extremely grateful, is Maestro Giampiero Tintori of the Museo Teatrale alla Scala who urged me thus: 'Whatever you do, write the truth. Whenever people talk about Strepponi, they seem to think they must say nothing.' And he told me how Giulio Ricordi, the music publisher, heard terrible rows within the walls of Palazzo Doria and the house at Sant'Agata. Giuseppina, therefore, was not as acquiescent in old age as she has been made out to be. She was not the great friend of Verdi's mistress. On the contrary, she was enraged by the humiliating ménage à trois that was maintained for so long.

Maestro De Angelis, who was the first to lay hands on the birth certificates of two of Giuseppina's illegitimate children, also declared that he was irritated by the aura of sanctity that the married couple managed to cast around them, an aura which Italy of the Risorgimento had sanctioned, thus creating one of the many ambiguous icons of Italian history. When he announced his discoveries in a lecture, he was subjected to protests and insults; he was up against a kind of national brainwashing. Perhaps the assumption of genteel respectability was a necessary element of nineteenth-century patriotism: the relationship between Verdi and Giuseppina had become a symbol and so the veneer of decorum was not just of their own making.

Verdi himself, of course, was able to rise above such considerations. All his strength, his passionate temperament, found vent in his music. But Giuseppina hardly opened her heart in her letters, many of which were cryptic or written almost in code. She was not exactly a Cosima Wagner, but she remained a spouse, a mere spouse. I do not think that she had much influence on Verdi – he was far too strong a character to be susceptible to another personality. Nor do I believe that his music would have been fundamentally different had there been another woman by his side. All the same Giuseppina tried to direct the progress of his life and his art; at Sant'Agata she would sit in silence, almost hiding behind the door that connected her room with Verdi's, and she would listen with discerning appreciation to the musical phrases that emerged from his piano.

In the early years, when Giuseppina was a kind of ambassadress for Verdi, Giovannina Lucca, the music publisher's pushy wife, tried to exploit her, but even then Giuseppina did not influence Verdi. Indeed it was he who ended up by swaying her, and the Luccas disappeared from Giuseppina Strepponi's life. Giuseppina's role was a feminine one; she adapted to things, accepting the decisions taken by her companion, later her husband. In fact she had no choice in the matter: all her cards were stacked on that man whom, right from the beginning, she had helped to succeed in the great operatic world. But with Verdi's help, Giuseppina set out to destroy that now unseemly past, which they both felt was not befitting to the dignity of a famous composer. In so doing, however, they reduced themselves to being cardboard cut-outs, because in remodelling their past, the Verdis appeared unreal, becoming nineteenth-century icons, quite removed from reality. Thus in most biographies of the composer, Giuseppina Strepponi appears as an irritating woman, her husband's docile shadow, sharing his triumphs and setbacks. She called him 'Verdi'. She was 'La Peppina'.

But this is the story of a different Giuseppina, a kind of Violetta Valéry, a *traviata* who does not die of consumption but who is redeemed and lives on to the mature age of eighty-two. In one sense, this Giuseppina-Violetta, who made a name for herself in the musical world, who struggled to attain a position of her own, does die because she gives up the stage to become a different woman, Signora Verdi. It is the drama of women in the nineteenth century – and not only in that century. A Violetta, not a Marguerite Gautier and not even an Emma Bovary – although Giuseppina Strepponi is a kind of emblem of the nineteenth century in Europe. Thus this story is typical of a certain European milieu of the last century.

It reveals to us Milan, the Milan of canals and the gardens of aristocratic houses running down to their banks, of the nobility taking the air along the water's edge; the humble Milan of Verdi's early days, the bustling, rowdy Milan of Via dei Filodrammatici with all its little shops, its offices belonging to the theatrical agencies and impresarios. One such shop belonged to *Sciûra* – the Milanese for *Signora* – Giovannina Lucca who spent her day sitting at the door, her large shape on a small chair, her hat full of ribbons, waiting for the composers and musicians to pass by; sooner or later everybody congregated there. At the Caffè dei Filodrammatici opposite La Scala deals were settled; a little further along contracts were exchanged; the less important agents did not even bother to keep an office; everything took place in the cafés. In this scenario, opera was the hub around which the life of the city revolved. It was cinema, television and literature all rolled into one.

In the eighteenth century opera had been an entertainment for the upper classes, if not for the Court alone; now it had reached the bourgeoisie. Partly because the bourgeoisie itself had only just appeared in Italy. From 1815 onwards because of Rossini, opera had acquired enormous popularity. The protagonists of this world were superstars comparable with Elvis Presley or the Beatles in our day. A successful singer became a symbol just as Marilyn Monroe did a century later; people would buy prints with portraits of Giuditta Pasta or Maria Malibran, two beautiful champion singers. But there were other favourites such as Caroline Ungher, Giuditta and Giulia Grisi, Napoleone Moriani, Giorgio Ronconi and Luigi Lablache, all celebrated singers who could indulge in any kind of caprice. For example, lifting pieces from one opera and singing them in another. And like film-stars, they earned more than composers – and directors. The singers could make an opera a hit, and without a great name it was difficult to stage a new work. Nonetheless every season offered at least two new works, since an impresario who failed to do so was not worthy of the name. Here again opera was like the cinema a century later; novelty was of the essence.

To become a successful impresario was one way to be accepted socially, but there were more casualties than successes within the industry. Alessandro Lanari was considered one of the great impresarios of the century, along with Domenico Barbaja, Vincenzo Jacovacci and Bartolomeo Merelli, who was perhaps the most famous of them all. Of the four, Barbaja, who was half-illiterate, was possibly the most brilliant and in fact died a very wealthy man. When he was just the owner of the Caffè dei Virtuosi opposite La Scala, he launched a drink known as the Barbajada – hot chocolate with hot cream – which the Milanese took to with delight, particularly in winter.

Barbaja ended up managing the San Carlo in Naples at the height of its glory; he kept race-horses and a collection of paintings in the somewhat garish palazzo he built at Mergellina to his own design. The famous contralto Isabella Colbran ditched him to marry Rossini: Barbaja knew her too well, he would never marry her. (In fact Rossini was to regret his decision.) Barbaja used to talk of himself in the third person, raining down insults and abuse on his own head – 'That beast Barbaja!' – but also boasting he was richer than Croesus.

Lanari, who plays an extremely important part in our story, ruled over the Pergola in Florence; Vincenzo Jacovacci handled the Roman theatres – in particular the Apollo – for all of forty years. Merelli was born in Bergamo like his friend Donizetti with whom he studied composition, also writing a few librettos. They were more or less contemporaries. The son of Count Moroni's administrator, a handsome man, lively and intelligent, Merelli was keen to get ahead; he was arrested as a young man on suspicion of theft but was later released. This episode is not at all clear; there was no proof against him although the police kept him in prison for six months which left a mark on him. After becoming an inspector of the imperial theatres in Vienna, in 1826 Merelli opened a theatrical agency in

Milan, and later in Paris. As an impresario, he was assigned to La Scala and the Cannobiana. He had a villa at Lentate where he led the life of a *gran signore*, throwing parties, keeping race-horses, just like Barbaja; however he differed from the latter in his shoddy stage-sets and organisation. This was to be a source of contention between Giuseppe Verdi and Giuseppina in later years.

Almost all the female singers passed through the impresarios' beds – a routine, just as it was for actresses. There was no contract that did not correspond to a fleeting (or not so fleeting) liaison. And just as the impresarios exchanged singers on the stage, they were equally ready to swap them in bed. No female singer – not even Malibran – was said to have escaped Merelli's embraces. This was perfectly normal – quite as normal for the ambitious singers as it was for the impresarios and agents who would then engage them. It was normal also because the impresarios and singers would find themselves travelling together for months, on exhausting journeys, staying at small hotels, far from their families. There is nothing strange in the fact that the young, ambitious and poor Giuseppina Strepponi passed from one bed to another. The doubts that posterity has as to the father of her second and third children, were probably secretly shared by Giuseppina herself. The impresarios and agents were of course all married, generally to people from the music world, to sisters of famous basses, to aunts or cousins of music publishers.

As a young woman Giuseppina was promiscuous. Illegitimate children were not at all rare in artistic circles, where women met many men (most other women at the time were unlikely to meet more than a few in the course of their whole lives). Furthermore hardly any acceptable contraceptive methods were known; for example, we find that George Sand had two children by different fathers and her lovers included the poet de Musset, the poet's doctor, Chopin and her lawyer. But George Sand was a passionate mother which could not be said of Giuseppina.

La Scala was not just a site for performances, but a social meeting place. Some boxes hosted men of note – today we might say cult heroes, men like Vincenzo Monti, the poet, Silvio Pellico, a future Risorgimento hero and fashionable writer. Even Lord Byron on a visit. In the foyer people gambled or observed the beautiful ladies as they talked through their noses (a fashion of the time among the Milanese aristocracy), accompanied by their *cavalieri serventi* who wore cravats with great looping knots. At La Scala or the Ducale of Parma, those in the first and second tiers could count on a discreet sitting-room at the back of each box, where people would eat sorbets, court the ladies, play with tarot cards. Stendhal, who rented a box in the third tier at La Scala for the whole Season, remembered hearing a cry from one box of gamblers: '*Ti te set un cojon!*' ('You are a cretin!') while from another box came the cry: 'Silence! Silence!' The respectable people would meet up at the theatre, eat, play, dance, flirt, gossip, even during the performance. This maddened the romantic Berlioz, who had dreamed of finding a genuinely musical, attentive public at La Scala: some hope!

The boxes were owned by noblemen; the bourgeoisie could only rent them. The theatres opened for two seasons. There was the Carnival Season, which at La Scala began on Christmas Day and ended on 20 March. In general the *Impresa* (the enterprise or firm) put on two serious operas, one specially commissioned and the other new to that theatre. There followed the Autumn Season which began on 11 August and finished on 30 November, with two semi-serious or comic operas one of which was expressly written for the theatre, and a serious one which could be part of the repertoire; this was obviously the less demanding season. The parterrre at La Scala cost three Austrian lire, the gallery one lira and fifty cents; the nobility had their private boxes. There were no seats in the parterre, but for an extra 80 lire one could hire a chair for the whole season; otherwise one remained standing.

The audience would listen, but only up to a point: the performance always began with a barrage of slammed doors, with outbursts of laughter; questions and answers would be hurled from one box to another and the theatre was lit up from within the boxes even during the performance. When the famous aria – or romanza, or cavatina – began, a religious silence would fall, to be broken by thunderous applause and demands for an encore, which were unfailingly granted. In the winter the curtain would rise at seven-thirty, in summer an hour later. Usually the performance began with the first act of an opera, which was followed by a ballet lasting about an hour and a half, and then the second and third act of the opera. The performance would end with a comic ballet or a dance. An evening at La Scala thus lasted from five to six hours – not counting the gambling, the gossip and the excursions into the foyer.

The theatres belonged to the Governments, which found them useful. Indeed Austria encouraged music, hoping that it would work as a substitute for political adrenalin; this encouragement lasted until the Italians – and Verdi in particular – began to use opera for political purposes, because all other vehicles of expression had been stifled. What could be more powerful or more popular than opera? When Rossini, as early as 1815, had written the hymn 'Rise, Italy, the time has now come!' spelling out a very patriotic message, there were not enough bourgeois to welcome the message.

There were several auditoriums in Milan: in the evening everyone went to the theatre, the noblemen escorted by their valets, the ladies concealed from view in coaches with the family coat-of-arms. Behind the Royal Palace stood the Cannobiana which, like La Scala, had been built by Piermarini, and the Carcano was at Porta Romana. The Foro Bonaparte which took the name of Piazza Castello after the fall of Napoleon, had become the meeting place for the rising middle classes of Milan. Amidst its spreading trees, there stood an amphitheatre, and although it had never been completed, sea-battles were staged there, drawing huge crowds.

There were seasons when La Scala was beaten by other theatres but it was still the real goal for all composers and performers, just as it is today. For example, the Ducale of Parma, founded by Marie Louise of Austria, gave prestige to her authority; the San Carlo in Naples belonged to the Bourbons, while the Apollo and the Argentina in Rome to Prince Torlonia; since the sacerdotal government could not openly concern itself with sopranos and dancers, this was a matter to be handled in other ways – and not in public. In the early nineteenth century, the centre of opera had moved from Bologna – the university and intellectual centre of the Papal State – to Milan, which had become the new capital of the Napoleonic kingdom. The attraction was due in part to the fact that La Scala had the gambling monopoly. But there were still other great theatres in Venice, Florence and Naples – and with the theatres came the agents and the impresarios.

Even though the Papal State did not tolerate permanent theatres in Rome, it was strangely open-minded, and such slapdash impresarios as Jacovacci flourished there, perfectly reflecting the atmosphere of the city (just as La Scala might be said to stand for Milan: more high-minded, more serious, and indeed more Austro-Hungarian). Many new operas by Donizetti and Rossini were staged there, *La cenerentola (Cinderella)*, both text and music, was put together practically overnight, because the Vatican censors had turned down the libretto previously submitted. On the contrary Verdi's *A Masked*

Ball, which was inadmissible in Naples even with the variations proposed by the librettist and composer, was allowed to go ahead in Rome.

In Naples the political atmosphere was stifling, and although Giuseppina Strepponi and Giuseppe Verdi were often tempted by the city's pleasant weather and sociability, in the end they always decided against setting up home there. The management of the San Carlo was absurdly inept and agreements counted for nothing, the King feared opera and mistrusted culture. This had not always been the case with the Bourbon family: previous generations had patronised music at the San Carlo, even when comic opera was irreverent towards those in power. But in the last declining generations, the family were happy to wallow in ignorance.

We have a rare list from the 1842–43 Season concerning the frequency with which composers were performed in various Italian theatres. The list gives us an idea of musical tastes and fashions in Italy at the time. In eighty theatres, of which nineteen were in Rome, eighteen in Lombardy-Veneto, sixteen in the Kingdom of Sardinia, twelve in the Two Sicilies, ten in Tuscany and eight in other areas, fifty-nine staged operas by Donizetti (with eighty-two performances of eighteen operas); twenty-two by Bellini, eighteen by Luigi Ricci, fifteen by Rossini – whose fortune with the public was in decline. They are followed by Mercadante, a Neapolitan composer, Pacini and Nicolai, with twelve, nine and seven respectively. Last on the list, Giuseppe Verdi was performed in only three theatres.

Milan was the centre of opera business; it was then a city of some 150,000 inhabitants: it exported silk to most of Europe, and the city's commercial activities were in continual expansion: despite this, twelve per cent of its inhabitants worked as 'attendants': Milan swarmed with valets, butlers, servants, cooks, grooms, porters and coach-drivers who served both the aristocracy and the newly wealthy bourgeoisie. The military classes and the Austro-Hungarian bureaucrats too were accompanied to La Scala by pages and waited upon hand and foot in the palazzi they occupied in the centre of town. Inns and restaurants abounded, and at the Hotel Europa one could choose from 140 dishes, headed by risotto and Milanese tripe. Fashionable travellers stayed at the Reichmann in Corso di Porta Romana with a reading-room and a smoking-room, and at the Hotel de la Ville in Corso Francesco. It was a small but splendid town, the jewel in the Habsburg crown, and then the capital of Napoleon's Cisalpine Republic. Where the Sforzas' palace had once stood, the French had built the seat of the vice-regal government, later occupied by the Imperial Viceroy, the Archduke Regnier. The façade that looked onto the Piazza del Duomo was elegant, but the interior was even more impressive, with its wealth of marbles, its staircase, its inlaid floors and Gobelin tapestries on the walls. The ceilings had been frescoed by the Directoire painter Andrea Appiani. In its music-room, with its columns supported by shapely caryatids with veiled faces, Napoleon appeared in the guise of Jupiter. The ceiling was frescoed with the apotheosis of the Emperor, whose image, of course, had been swiftly removed.

In Milan one finds a plethora of cafés; the 'conspirators' used to meet at the Caffè Cova, like those in *A Masked Ball*, conspiring half in earnest, half in fun. The cafés were watched over by Austro-Hungarian spies and were the centre for the Carbonari, the secret sect which plotted revolts; opera was the gazette of subversion. Verdi, like Rossini before him, became the promoter of the ideal of Italian unity; maybe with a touch of cynicism: patriotism was good box-office. Indeed, when success smiled on him, Verdi abandoned the 'Risorgimento' line.

It was in the cafés that the Seasons were decided, and there were several wine-shops, elegant ones like the Mazza, the Biffi and the San Quirico and intellectual ones like the Bagutta, the Caffè della Cecchina and the Caffè della Peppina; the De Cristoforis and the Accademia had their regular customers too. The Caffè Martini, at all hours, was a meeting place for composers, librettists, singers, players, choir-masters, prompters, choreographers, dancers, mime-artists, impresarios and theatre-agents. Sir Charles Santley, an English baritone, described how these places were crowded with celebrities but also with impatient young singers. At the Caffè Martini, his account continues, the agents appointed by impresarios who were on their travels, would meet the singers on the look-out for contracts: the Milanese agencies drafted all contracts, not only those for Italy, but for the Americas and Europe. At the cafés, in the theatres, in their boxes, people would discuss the singers and composers, and – after the arrival of the Austrians – the news in the *Gazzetta ufficiale*: all other newspapers had been banned, although twice a week, the *Gazzetta di Lugano* reached Milan, with the news of what was happening abroad.

'Abroad' consisted of that part of Italy which was not an Austro-Hungarian province, as well as France and Germany. Curiosity about the other continents was limited to folklore. Little was known of England, a mysterious, severe land, remote and extremely fascinating. England was the real protagonist of the century: not only had the country become rich with its Industrial Revolution and its colonies, but the Tories had managed to get the upper hand over the Whigs. The English workers presented a people's charter to the Parliament; they were claiming the right to vote for every adult, something unheard of in the Italian states. Separated both physically and politically from the Continent, rich, and well-protected by its powerful fleet, England had become fashionable. No man could appear in public in Milan without bowing to the English fashion. Ties had to be knotted *alla Byron*, and top hats and tail-coats were de rigueur. The wasp-waist obliged men as well as women to wear tightly laced girdles, and hair was romantically curled with red-hot irons. English literature was the very height of fashion, Byron was a star, a kind of pop hero pursued by girls who tore strips from his tail-coat to keep as souvenirs, although in Venice he found himself upstaged by the young Rossini.

It is as well to point out that opera did not consist only of music; the libretto was extremely important too – it is no accident that even today the name of the librettist precedes that of the composer. Felice Romani, for example, was a poet of the first order, a highly cultured and clearly likeable man; we find him working with Feliciano Strepponi, Giuseppina's composer father, and with Gioachino Rossini; he became Giuseppe Verdi's Roman friend. Verdi himself had a great respect for the text. He himself tinkered with the librettos but he could never get the rhymes – librettos were all in verse; Giuseppina did so too, and with good results, as can be seen from several snatches of dialogue in her handwriting.

As the operas were composed and sold, the institution of censorship in the various States – an institution that was not impervious to bribery – flourished alongside it. The music publishers did good business, even though copyright protected neither them nor the composers. Ricordi was the great name, and then Lucca (who had begun as a clerk in Ricordi's workshop), Fabbricotti and Cottrau. At the heart of this activity were the composers, even if they were not always the best paid.

In twenty-six years Gaetano Donizetti composed sixty operas: this enormous output gives an idea of the continual demand there was from each theatre for new works. It is thus no wonder that composers borrowed arias and overtures from their own compositions which had been performed elsewhere. Verdi passed off as new works, operas that were merely patched up or had been done in a different language. At the heart of this activity were the librettists like Solera, Piave, Ghislanzoni, Cammarano and Boito, all interesting men; they could be said to be the writers of the Italian novel, which otherwise hardly exist in the eighteenth and nineteenth centuries. Italy's true literature in the last century was in fact the operatic libretto.

It is no accident that opera imported into Italy the literary masterpieces of Northern Europe, as well as the plays that were being staged in Spain, Paris and London. It might of course be remarked that in France people were in the habit of reading; the only honest answer to this is that the comfortable bourgeoisie of Italy were lazier, preferring 'to be told' the story rather than to read it and reason it out for themselves. The same is true today: instead of reading the classics, people prefer adaptations for theatre, cinema and television. Operas were so popular that as soon as a novel or drama made its mark – it was snatched up by the musical world and recreated as an opera, often in several versions: Silvio Pellico's *Francesca da Rimini*, for instance, inspired many operas, now forgotten. Victor Hugo's works were ransacked, and he often complained of the exploitation of his dramas by the operatic stage, because the public then lost interest in the plays themselves. Schiller and Shakespeare were subjected to this form of popularisation as well, just as today films or television versions are made from the classics. John Rosselli remarks in *The Opera Industry in Italy* how composing an opera, particularly in the first half of the nineteenth century, was what we would today call journalistic work, carried out quickly, on commision. Provided that the libretto itself was ready, the composer often wrote the second and third acts during the rehearsals of the first. Verdi did his orchestration on the spot, turning up with the piano score, divided between voices but not orchestrated.

The Italian middle classes were in any case urban, and thus more inclined to meet in theatres than to stay at home and read in the evening. The Northern European bourgeoisie possessed land and estates. If their equivalent in Italy had similar possessions, they made quite sure not to live in them: they loved their city houses. The comfortable classes in search of either entertainment or information found both in the librettos. The libretto is thus a source of poetry, of ideas, of great plots. A good libretto was considered essential – Rossini's are excellent – and in a certain sense it was Verdi who 'ruined' the craft of the librettist, with his (and Giuseppina's) constant interference. Verdi wanted the text to serve the music; up till then the music had served the text.

The libretto was written in Italian, a language which, despite the divisions, barriers and customs-houses, was used throughout the country. Or rather, it was used by the upper and middle levels of society: the aristocracy and the bourgeoisie – and also by the Jews – as in Austria where it was the Jews who, after the fall of the Austro-Hungarian Empire and during its decadence, kept the language and the arts alive, and who for this very reason encountered hostility and later persecution. Napoleon had opened up the ghettos, but after the Restoration they were once again set under surveillance and the tiny Jewish community of Italy found itself persecuted as before. This was another reason why the Italian Jews were all solidly in support of the Risorgimento. Like my grandfather, who was born in 1857 in Ancona – in the Papal State – and who was called Cavour. And his sister, born in 1860, Italia.

One point needs making about Verdi: although the century was intensely anti-Semitic, although Verdi was surrounded by people who never spared some anti-Semitic remark – like Giuseppina and Piave – and although his hated publisher (Lucca) was either Jewish or of Jewish descent, never did the composer utter a word which could be interpreted as racist. Not only that but he contributed to a fund in support of Dreyfus. He even wrote a letter to a priest, Canonico Arfini, asking him to stop with his 'stupid persecution' of a Jewish pupil.

Although the poor people of Italy spoke incomprehensible and fragmentary dialects, just as there were some different languages and strange hybrid mixtures in the Austro-Hungarian Empire, it is important to realise that Italian was a national language. Even before Dante, it was being used inventively by Cielo d'Alcamo and served a world which, despite political divisions, enjoyed a cultural and spiritual unity. This unity is not always easy to understand, particularly for non-Italians. It derived from an aesthetic sense: by way of example we may note how Gothic architecture came from the south of Italy and was immediately taken up by the north; the lines of Alberti's Ideal City range from the Duchy of Urbino to Naples with the great sculptor and architect Laurana. Opera, in this sense, continued to give a cultural, linguistic and social unity to an Italy that was otherwise politically disunited.

Our story also tells of salons, places that do not exist nowadays since they no longer have any reason to. But the nineteenth-century salon had an important role, both politically and socially. There one met the most important people of the age. Singers were rarely to be found in such places, as they were usually on their travels, and, unless they had 'made it', were considered somewhat 'demi-monde' – with the exception of those who had married dukes and marquesses, like Sophia Löwe and Maria Waldman. It was in the salons that the composers found their librettists and sometimes their inspiration. When he had achieved success – certainly not before – Giuseppe Verdi was invited to Countess Maffei's house, and it was in her salon, which we would today describe as intellectual, that he found his political creed, his future librettists and quite a few of his lovers. It was several years before Giuseppina Strepponi, now Signora Verdi, was to be admitted to Casa Maffei. When she could visit it, the salon no longer held any attraction for her, nor for Verdi – and nor for other people. Times had changed.

At Casa Maffei we meet Liszt in the company of Comtesse Marie Flavigny d'Agoult, visibly pregnant with the future Cosima Wagner. The appearance of the couple caused a slight stir of shocked scandal among the Milanese, but little more. Contessa Maffei reacted merely with a certain boredom to the attention paid to Liszt. As Balzac entered Casa Maffei, the Countess greeted him with the cry: '*J'adore le génie!*' He was accompanied by a dwarf – actually a cross-dressed page. Or rather, a young female lover of his, of horrendous appearance, who imagined that by dressing as a man she would be able to pull off the George Sand trick. The Comtesse d'Agoult herself published her writings under a male name; dressing as a man or using a man's name was a symbol of modernity, of aristocratic Bohemianism. Balzac caused a certain consternation with Cavalier Andrea, the husband of Clara Maffei, who had been born as early as 1798: 'Dear Clarina,' the Cavaliere wrote to his younger wife, jealous more of his reputation than his honour:

Should you not see me at two o'clock, go with Signor Balzac to Hayez's studio, passing by less frequented streets so as not to be observed. Now, my dear Clarina, I would like you to pay a little attention to me and reflect calmly on my words . . . All eyes are on this famous foreigner. Everybody knows that he spends many hours at our house . . . my reputation is entirely Italian . . . You alone are the object of his attention therefore and if Signor Balzac's visits were to confine themselves to the hours of the evening, I would not stir from my inertia and send you this long letter and indeed I would feel very pleased that my wife is able to entertain such a celebrated man. But in this gentleman's conduct I think I can recognise quite a different aim and the experience of thirty-seven years makes me fear that he is trying to abuse your good faith and your enthusiasm for his writings.

Prince Poniatowski, who kept a salon in Florence, was a professional singer – likewise his family, performers of Rossini and excellent musicians; Count Mario of Candia, husband of Giulia Grisi, was part of the singing aristocracy and wrote a book which was published in London. Like the aristocracy, the world of the theatre was considered a sinful one, the singers were reputed to be whores or courtesans – and almost invariably they were. But while the aristocracy was forgiven for its sins, the singers were not. Princess Cristina Belgiojoso, who was an inveterate and original sinner, looked down on Countess Maffei because she considered her husband to be a reactionary and, with many friends in prison and spies around, the Princess considered Clarina Maffei's patriotism risible. Of course the Princess's sympathy had been with France.

At the beginning of the century, Napoleon was engaged in his second Italian campain and he had proclaimed the Cisalpine Republic which included most of Emilia, Romagna and Lombardy. Milan became the capital, first of the Republic and then, with Napoleon's increasing folie de grandeur, of the kingdom. Profoundly secular – indeed a declared enemy of the Church – Napoleon had introduced into Italy the first taste of radicalism that Italy had had in centuries; he had brought in new laws, the Napoleonic code, the classical Lycée and the Italian flag. It was Napoleon who opened the Conservatoire; before then music could only be studied at home with the help of expensive tutors or in the orphanages with the clergy and he transformed the antiquated Italian educational system. Public education for girls, however, was not yet contemplated; a few years later they would be allowed access to the Conservatoire, but only for singing and harp-playing.

But at the same time he was sending out of Italy coffers of gold, collected by means of massive and unpopular taxes, and also art treasures such as the Mantegnas from Modena and the Veroneses from Venice. Although he had inflicted terrible taxes on his Italian possessions in order to finance his continual campaigns, Napoleon had been the only person ever to give Italy any semblance of unity.

The French had given power to the local governments, even though they had to account for their every decision. At the same time they had wrested many privileges from the aristocracy, handing over posts of responsibility to the middle classes. Thus in northern Italy the power of the bourgeoisie was born.

On 18 May 1804 Napoleon had been proclaimed Emperor; the Cisalpine Republic was transformed into the Kingdom of Italy and Napoleon crowned himself as its king the following year, with the iron crown that had belonged to Charlemagne. The event was celebrated with a Te Deum and an allegory performed at La Scala; Niccolò Paganini and the celebrated ballerinas profoundly moved both the Milanese and the French soldiers. Despite his division of Italy into ridiculous principalities – for example, his sister Elisa, the wife of a Corsican officer, became the Princess Baciocchi of Lucca – Napoleon remained a hero to the young, even after his fall. Between the autumn 1814 and June 1815, while Napoleon was on the isle of Elba, negotiations were under way in Vienna: the grandees of Europe were parcelling out the continent with the aid of maps. Beethoven, pianist to Prince Metternich, the Austrian Emperor's prime minister, played for the congress members while the Prince persuaded the world that Italy was nothing more than a geographical expression – an irritating remark that was to remain famous.

The Congress of Vienna restored dukes and monarchs to their old Italian thrones, absurd characters who seemed almost to have stepped out of Viennese operettas. In Florence the Lorenas returned, in Modena Francis IV; Marie Louise, daughter of the Austrian Emperor, widow of Napoleon, was destined for the Duchy of Parma, Lucca went to Louise Bourbon, while Lombardy-Veneto returned to its status as an Austrian province. Vittorio Emanuele returned to Savoy – his realm was called the Kingdom of Sardinia – and the Pope to Rome. The sovereigns of the Restoration introduced rigorous censorship. Everywhere newspapers and journals were suppressed, printing-shops were closed and publication permits became difficult to obtain. Cafés, clubs and public squares thus took an important role as places where people could discuss matters and news could be exchanged. Life, on the other hand, became more boring.

In Milan, the Austrians seemed to want to support the arts. Stendhal appreciated this when he returned to Lombardy in August 1814:

Setting out from La Scala I take Via Santa Margherita, I pass respectfully in front of the police who can do whatever they wish to me, for example make me leave within two hours! I look at the new prints in the shops near the police station and if there is anything by Anderloni or Garavaglia I restrain myself with difficulty from buying them. Then I go into the Piazza dei Mercanti and from there the Piazza del Duomo. When my eyes, which were previously bent in artistic contemplation of the prints, have taken their fill of pleasure in admiring this marble castle, I follow the Via dei Mercanti d'Oro and the living beauties I find there distract me from those of art: but the sight of the Duomo and the prints has rendered me more sensitive to beauty and more insensitive to material interests and to all ideas of dejection and sadness. I make my way to the letter-post, where the women go to collect their letters in person, because the servants are all in the pay of their husbands or their lovers, I go via the Piazza del Duomo to the Corsia dei Servi, where around midday one regularly finds one or more of the twelve most beautiful women in Milan.

He ended up staying in Milan for seven years.

After Waterloo and the defeat of Napoleon, people mourned for the lost unity of Italy; consolation was found in a new vision of things, in disillusionment, melancholy, Romanticism. Whereas the rationalists of the Enlightenment had loved the Graeco-Roman world, the Romantics exalted the Middle Ages and Gothic art. It was on this basis that they chose their librettos and texts, that they coloured their notes. Whereas the former had lived in the clear light of day, the Romantic preferred darker tints, mysterious landscapes. The rationalists had placed their faith in progress; the aftermath of Waterloo, the collapse of all ideals, had left young people with a hankering for melancholy. For those seeking an ideal – the eternal quest of the man of culture – Italian unity was an uplifting, arousing dream. Napoleon had given a first taste of such possibilities, a unified republican Italy; despite all the abuses of power, the crippling taxes and the wars, with Bonaparte the country had entered the modern age. The notion of unity had emphasised to the Italians the existence of an enemy – in politics where there is no enemy, one has to be invented. And what better enemy could there be than the Germans? Which, in nineteenth-century Italy, meant the Austro-Hungarians, those people who had lorded it over the country too often and for too long. It was not true, of course; the Habsburg Empire governed its southern provinces with a rigidly honest bureaucracy, whose lessons endured until Milan was hit by the cyclone of Craxi and his minions.

This is also a story of travelling. Theatre folk were constantly on the move, taking with them cart-loads of costumes, clothes and scores. The companies made their tortuous way by carriage across the Apeninnes, or took the ferry to cross the Po. The quickest journeys were by sea; from Naples the Verdis set out for Genoa, Civitavecchia and Leghorn. But such crossings were by no means tranquil – nor indeed were the stomachs. The wardrobe followed in a convoy of carts and had to set off in time from one theatre to another, from one season to another. From Naples to Milan, by land, there were five customs-posts to be passed – all corrupt, slow and suspicious. Whenever Verdi and Giuseppina went to Genoa, which became a habit with them during the winter, their destination lay in the Kingdom of Sardinia – the house of Savoy – which was slightly more liberal, if rather more provincial, than the Empire of Franz Joseph. Austria tried to cultivate its southern kingdom; it valued Milan, its southern capital, and Trieste, its most important port. It laid great stress on the policy of entertainment: opera was therefore encouraged, it served to distract, to arouse passions. So long as it steered clear of political argument.

After Rossini, Italian opera had turned to Romantic themes and kept well away from politics. In this way it had nothing to fear from the censors; indeed, it served the regime by acting as a worldly and artistic sop. Musicians like Donizetti had even been forced to abandon the management of the San Carlo in Naples and later the same theatre was to lose Giuseppe Verdi. The police had a point: opera was like a powder-magazine, just waiting to go off. A keen music lover, the revolutionary thinker Mazzini wrote an essay on the potentialities of popular songs; no longer believing in the Carbonari, Mazzini founded *Giovane Italia*, the Young Italy, a clandestine republican group of the extreme left. In 1837 Mazzini arrived in London, where he was to live as a famous exile for many years. Many singers and composers – Verdi included – went to meet him during their operatic travels.

The journeys also took the opera companies to all the great musical centres of Europe, Vienna and Paris; London too became a goal since wages there were extremely good, much higher than in Italy. Paris with its two opera theatres, the Opéra and the Théâtre des Italiens, was a centre of attraction, but compromises had to be reached with the French: they always wanted large-scale ballets in their operas, and their orchestras were as arrogant as they were atrocious (little has changed!). In Paris there reigned a claque which could be hired at a steady rate; Italy had its factions, but such a highly organised claque was curiously enough a Parisian prerogative. However, Paris offered freedom, both socially and intellectually. In Paris one could meet writers, composers, librettists, singers. The city had salons that the rest of Europe tried to imitate: it was possible to meet Berlioz and de Musset, Rossini, Lamartine, George Sand, Victor Hugo. Flaubert too went to the literary dinners held in a private room at Magny's, complaining that that kind of life was making him too effeminate.

Giuseppina was born in Austro-Hungarian territory and spent her youth under the double-headed eagle of the Habsburgs. Apart from the brief, stormy period under Napoleon, so did both Giuseppe and Giuseppina's parents. Verdi was also born a subject of the Emperor, and remained so until three years after his birth when Parma became the duchy of the Emperor's daughter Marie Louise, Napoleon's widow.

Giuseppina Strepponi, an ideal protagonist of this century, was born in 1815 and died in 1897. As a famous singer, she conquered the stage and, for a short while, she led the life of a performer, first as a soprano and then as *primadonna assoluta*, travelling through the duchies and the small kingdoms, taking her place at Court, in the great houses, in the palazzi, the inns, the small hotels. The companies travelled from one hotel to another; sopranos and tenors, basses and contraltos ran from their bedrooms to appear on stage, revered by frenzied audiences. A soprano might marry a prince but Countess Giulia Samoyloff, great beauty and a queen of the European salons, was excluded from receptions at Court for marrying the famous baritone Pery, a handsome man who had sung in Verdi's *I Masnadieri*.

At the time of this story, Italy emerged from the trauma of the Napoleonic period only to find all its hopes dashed by Metternich and the Restoration that was agreed at the Congress of Vienna. At the time of Giuseppina's birth and the 1814–15 Restoration, the situation in Italy was as follows: the Viennese emperor returned to Lombardy, the Bourbons to Naples, the Austrian grand duke to Tuscany; Venice was no longer a free republic but a province of Austria, and Genoa had become a dependency of Piedmont; nor was Piedmont yet a wholly Italian power. Besides the new feeling of *italianità*, the middle classes found it irksome to cope with eight separate states each with tariff barriers, individual coinage and measures. These states ruled like old-fashioned absolute powers, including the Papal States and the Kingdom of Naples (often referred to as the kingdom of the Two Sicilies); Naples, which had been Europe's most populous and cultivated city in the sixteenth and seventeenth centuries, became one of its poorest. The Bourbon regime was corrupt and backward. Secret societies grew up in Naples like mushrooms: their intent was to overthrow the regime which was under the thumb of the Austrians (who had exacted exorbitant fines from the Neapolitans). The secret societies of the Carbonari flourished everywhere, the common enemy being the Austrian regime and the common hero Mazzini, a Genoese who today we would call left-wing. The powers who inflicted the Restoration dictat on Italy found an excuse in Metternich's notorious 'geographical expression' quotation. It was far from the truth.

The Romans had united Italy into a confederation in the third century BC and when Cicero wrote about *Italia* he meant what we call Italy today: Italy was therefore an older national – if not political – concept than either France or England. Dante, in the thirteenth century, pleaded her case:

> *Ahi serva Italia, di dolore ostello,*
> *nave senza nocchier in gran tempesta,*
> *non donna di provincia, ma bordello!*

> (Alas, servant Italy, hostess of suffering,
> a ship without a pilot in a great tempest,
> not a provincial matron but a prostitute!)

It is easy to dislike the nineteenth century, particularly its latter half, with all its hypocrisy and sham. It seems much more remote from us than does the eighteenth century, a more enlightened period – and less hampered by bourgeois values. People were on the defensive, because the bourgeoisie was in the ascendancy and they made a show of being respectable and Catholic, champions of the Family and of the State. It was the Italian bourgeoisie that unified Italy, not the aristocracy – and it is impossible to talk of a popular movement.

The intellectuals, the musicians, the singers and the composers, found employment with the middle classes as they emerged in northern and central Italy – no longer with the Courts; they therefore expressed the vocations of the bourgeoisie. The rise of the middle class was much slower in Central Italy (where indeed we find opera but no composers or singers), which was in the hands of the Church and, in the south, alas, it coincided with a criminal class, the Mafia; it hardly produced music: Bellini – a Sicilian – flourished in Milan.

So the key to this story of Giuseppina Strepponi lies in that unloved middle class, in that unloved century, with all its clashing contradictions – a century no less turbulent than ours, plagued by cholera, rebellions, revolutions and wars. My point of view is of course a modern one: I live in our own troubled times, and see Giuseppina through twentieth-century eyes – and I see her as Violetta. I have therefore called this work of mine *The Real Traviata* because Giuseppina was led astray – *traviata* – by her century in more ways than one.

1
LODI'S WERTHER

Feliciano Strepponi, follower of Voltaire. Lodi. The family,
the Conservatoire in Milan. Marriage to sixteen-year-old
Rosa Cornalba. After Giuseppina, other children are born.
Maestro di Cappella in Monza. Assistant director in Trieste.
Giuseppina also as a student at the Conservatoire in
Milan. Career and death of Feliciano.

---•---

Quest'è l'immagine de' miei passati giorni . . .
This is the image of my past days . . .

LA TRAVIATA, ACT III

Little money, great hopes. Feliciano Strepponi, Giuseppina's
father, born in Lodi in 1797, was a young Werther and, like
Werther, wore yellow shoes and a blue frock-coat. But Feliciano
was a Mediterranean Werther. He imagined himself already an
acclaimed musician and dreamed of becoming . . . of becoming
what? A great impresario, before whom even Barbaja would turn
pale, and who would carry off all the most beautiful singers, even
Giuditta Pasta.

He also dreamed of becoming the most highly acclaimed musician
in the land: the theatres would clamour for him. He would receive
letters from all over the world. But above all he hoped to dazzle his
family; his parents and his brother, Francesco, who was already a
musician. He would astound them with the first opera he composed,
with the palazzetto he would buy in Lodi . . . With its narrow
streets flowing into the large rectangular Piazza del Duomo, Lodi
was a small town which offered splendid surprises: the façades
of the buildings with their ochre plaster had the elegance of
time-honoured wealth, the brickwork churches – all testified to
the remoteness of marble and stone. Lodi was discreet, it did not
flaunt its jewels openly, but disclosed them pearl-like, one after
another. The church of the Incoronata, where Feliciano's brother was
Maestro di Cappella and played the organ, might pass unobserved. But

when one entered, the church revealed its Renaissance friezes and magnificent paintings. The sacristy was a masterpiece of Lombard rococo, with an added touch of Austrian flavour: Lodi was after all subject to Austria until it was conquered by Napoleon.

It was in Lodi itself, in 1796, one year before Feliciano's birth, that Napoleon managed to defeat the Austrian garrison, thus ensuring his entry into Milan and French dominion over Lombardy. For a few years, until the fall of Napoleon and the peace of 1814, the city was named in streets and squares all over France and the Cisalpine Republic – a custom of the French with their battle-victories. '*La bataille du Pont de Lodi*', also mentioned by Stendhal, was soon forgotten, however, with the advent of the Congress of Vienna. And the monument that had been erected to General Bonaparte in the large Piazza della Vittoria – which still bears the name of that victory which took place on the River Adda – fell under the pick-axes of the Habsburgs who had returned to rule.

But no, Feliciano did not want to buy a palazzetto in Lodi, he did not wish to remain there. He wanted to go to Milan. After all, what on earth could an acclaimed composer like Feliciano Strepponi ever hope to accomplish in that small market town with its damp climate? Too near Milan to exist in its own right, too far to become part of it.

A faithful Bonapartist like everyone else in his family, Feliciano had come to the public eye when he conducted the solemn Te Deum in the Cathedral to celebrate the return of the Emperor in 1812. He was only fifteen, was studying at the Conservatoire in Milan and was thought to be extremely talented and precocious. He aroused the admiration of his fellow-citizens – and also of Rosa Cornalba, the sixteen-year-old girl who was in love with him. At that time, people married young, especially in Lodi, where there was nothing else to do, other than sit in the cafés, go for strolls, visit the town clubs or make love. But Feliciano had not yet finished his studies at the Conservatoire in Milan.

The citizens of Lodi had erected that clumsy monument to the Emperor – alas; not the General any longer, the Emperor now ... Even Napoleon had been warped, corrupted by adulation, by his own propaganda. Two years after the glorious Te Deum – after the Emperor had been deposed dragging down with him Feliciano's dreams and hopes – Feliciano married Rosa to an organ accompaniment provided by his elder brother, Francesco.

Rosa's family – the Cornalbas – had no money, her dowry was

practically non-existent, however they boasted some noble blood, being relatives of the Barberini, a papal family: indeed they would call their youngest daughter Barberina, after that famous surname. The witness at their wedding was Feliciano's sister, Giovanna, who taught at the local school; the Strepponis were the sort of family that today might be described as intellectual and secular in tendency. They were a lively group, they spoke foreign languages, they read and debated all the matters of the day – even politics, warily. They were liberal – *Volterriani* – but despite this, it seemed as if they were all destined to work for the Church, particularly after the fall of Napoleon; for a composer or organist, there was no other choice.

However, for his exams at the Conservatoire, Feliciano had performed according to his highest aspirations: he had written an opera for which he won a special composition prize. But, although he tried to find employment in the capital, all he managed to obtain was a job in Monza, a provincial town north-east of Milan – and worse still, he was to work with the clergy.

One day he thought, he would like to take Rosa to Milan in a carriage drawn by a pair of horses and with his own personal coachman in the English style. He would show her the illuminated stores and cafés, the little shops along Via dei Mercanti where the private sedan-chairs passed, emblazoned with the liveries of the noble families, the Belgiojosos, the Trivulzios, the Littas: in the evening, carrying their excellencies to the opera, their pages marched alongside bearing torches. Maybe they would have a valet and a compliant maidservant, too, one day. The hairdresser would powder his wig for the evening – for wigs were still in fashion, despite Napoleon's disapproval.

Rosa Cornalba was beautiful and petite, with a thin waist and white hands like a ballerina's. Her tiny nose was in marked contrast with the prominent feature that protruded from Feliciano Strepponi's face. Their children, Feliciano thought, would inherit their mother's nose and their father's intelligence. However, their first child, a daughter, was identical to her father, not only in her liveliness and eagerness to learn, but in her outsized nose and large dark eyes. She was born in September 1815 and was baptised in the Cathedral with the names Clelia Maria Josepha but was immediately called 'Giuseppina'. After Giuseppina, in 1817 the next child to be born was Davide Carlo Cristoforo, the only son; a year later Maria Teresa was born, followed by Maria Antonietta in 1819. The youngest,

Barberina, who was thirteen years younger than Giuseppina, was born in Monza.

After leaving the Conservatoire in 1820, Feliciano in fact moved to Monza where he spent seven more years working as Maestro di Cappella. As a result he had hardly any time to visit Milan, the all-important agents, the Caffè Martini. Yet it was only in Milan that this Mediterranean Werther in his threadbare tail-coat had any hope of finding somebody to buy his opera, or rather his operas, which he continued to write. He needed to find a great libretto, he needed to befriend a famous librettist and that you could only do in Milan – certainly not in Monza, nor Lodi.

To go to Milan meant to meet everybody, to share the new ideals, the new musical trends. At one of the cafés, Feliciano met the famous librettist Felice Romani, who had written a libretto for *Francesca da Rimini*, from the novel by Silvio Pellico. Feliciano had also met the author himself at La Scala. Silvio Pellico was a man who came from the enlightened upper class, a revolutionary who was said to be a Carbonaro, like Feliciano. And also like the young Giuseppe Mazzini, who had just been arrested in Genoa. In fact, despite censorship, people always managed to keep abreast of things: a great revolution which took its impetus from France was shaking Europe, overthrowing the regimes set up by Metternich.

In July 1830, the common people and the middle classes took to the streets in Paris to protest and Louis Philippe d'Orléans, a liberal who was linked to the Carbonari, thus took over from Charles X. On the other side of Europe, German and Polish students took to the streets but where Metternich and the Tsar were in control, there was no hope of change. Many were forced into exile, including Chopin, and Paris was the place that drew them, the new liberal city of Europe.

The rebellions were soon put down by the Habsburgs. In Milan the Austrian police arrested several friends of Feliciano Strepponi: the writer Silvio Pellico was condemned to death. The sentence was considered an outrage: besides, the secret meetings, the plots hatched in cafés and boxes at La Scala, were seen as little more than an excuse to get together. Other conspirators managed to escape. For Milan it was a black day, the boxes at La Scala remained empty. A report read: 'Universal mourning for the extremely tragic catastrophe of the sentences that are to be pronounced tomorrow to various members of the principal families implicated in political affairs.' Later the death sentence was commuted to twenty years in prison. Feliciano had been sheltered from spies, plots and arrest by the fact that he lived between Monza and Lodi. Milan had become a city all too rarely frequented.

In spite of the political upheavals which affected the musical world, Feliciano's world, life went on – and so did opera. He made his début in Turin, at the Teatro d'Angennes, with *The Bachelor Husband*, an *opera buffa* which opened the Season. The critics were quite positive; besides, during all those months Feliciano had befriended the writers and editors of the musical journals who were all-important in the industry. The musical journals were tolerated by the different regimes but some, such as *Il Conciliatore*, had been closed by the imperial police. Discussions became ever more clandestine, the liberals began to conspire. With no hope of reform, revolution seemed the only way to change. The secret societies, so important in operatic plots, began to proliferate in the real world as well. Many masons who had become liberals, like Feliciano and Felice Romani, organised the Carboneria, which was inspired by the associations of coal-heavers (*carbonari*). In this political climate, full of tensions, the various regimes preferred opera buffa. Indeed the next opera that Feliciano composed was for Milan and it was an opera buffa. *Who Does thus, Does Well* was staged at the Teatro Re; this was an important opera house, which stood between the Duomo and La Scala and took its name from Carlo Re, a puppeteer and ex-shoemaker.

To have an opera staged in Milan, meant that Feliciano had arrived. In some seasons La Scala was eclipsed by other theatres; for example, in 1830–31 the Carcano, with two new operas by Bellini and Donizetti outstripped La Scala, which by way of new works only had an opera of Strepponi's and another by Luigi Ricci.

In this orgy of theatres, Feliciano forgot all about Monza, the Cathedral and its cantatas and Te Deums; he had rented two rooms in Milan between the Corso della Porta Orientale and the Lazzareto. But his continual absences from Monza were the cause of grumbling among the priests and Feliciano risked losing his job. Rosa was furious. Feliciano might delight in musical twirls and arpeggios, in cabalettas and duets, but the family had to eat and money was short at home. Feliciano claimed that it would soon be flowing in, because the opera circuits now embraced the whole of Italy, the courts of other countries, the world . . .

Rosa who, by now, was the mother of five children, had few chances of leaving home. She would have liked to join her husband in Milan, from time to time, so that she could have bought those new hats she had glimpsed in the illustrated fashion gazettes, the bonnets pulled close around the cheeks with flowing ribbons or the fine muslin dresses, Directoire-style. But she simply couldn't afford such things – nor new divans, chairs for the drawing-room or clothes for the children.

Feliciano, however, bought himself new clothes. How could he not? When he did the rounds of the cafés and the theatres, or called on the impresarios and the primadonnas; when he went to the Milanese salons which began to be open to him, it would have been unthinkable to turn up without an English-style top hat. Rosa was getting both fed up and angry while Feliciano was getting annoyed and bored with Rosa. He preferred the company of singers, those eternal wanderers he had learnt to love. He enjoyed being with agents, impresarios, people who knew the world, who had never even set foot in Lodi or Monza. At home the person Feliciano got on best with was Clelia, or 'Giuseppina' as she was known. When he returned to Lodi from Monza or – as was more usual – from other places where he had been trying to get an opera together or had been meeting some impresario or librettist, Feliciano would play music with the girl.

Giuseppina was a born musician, a true Strepponi; she played the harpsichord beautifully, studied hard, was eager and dedicated. She also practised with her aunt, a teacher, who taught her to read and to write, both in Latin and Italian, and with her cousin Luigi, another musician. She learnt foreign languages with ease: a little German was indispensable, with the Austrians everywhere. But everyone in the Strepponi household had always had more than a smattering of French, and Giuseppina knew it even better than she did Italian. Rosa instead spoke dialect and did not get on with her daughter, maybe because there was too close a bond between Feliciano and Giuseppina.

Nobody was surprised when the church authorities in Monza decided to sack the young Maestro di Cappella. Although Feliciano had always been careful, they certainly could not tolerate his latent radicalism. Besides, Feliciano had received an excellent offer from Trieste. Maestro Farinelli was asking him to be his assistant director at the Teatro Grande. This meant leaving the sacristy with its priests and good women for ever, and going to work in an opera house, where he would engage singers, conduct an orchestra, and work with the people he cared for most: theatre folk. And, above all, it meant a move to a capital city, leaving foggy Lodi and the provincial

Monza for the Empire's most important port. Trieste, a mercantile and cosmopolitan city, had practically been created by the Austrian monarchs: a wealthy class was developing there, a lively bourgeoisie who went to the theatre and craved for novelties.

The Teatro Grande, unlike the others in Italy, belonged to the municipality; however, this did not mean that the Governor of Trieste and the Chief of Police, both musical dilettanti, were prepared to leave it to its own devices. They were always ready to censor any libretto that 'stank' of subversion. Massimo d'Azeglio, future Prime Minister of the Italian nation and the son-in-law of Manzoni, the writer, said: 'The Austrian government governed Lombardy for many years by means of the Teatro la Scala; and it must be admitted that for a time it managed it well.' The same could be said of the provinces of Trieste. The Teatro Grande was part of the European circuit which included Vienna, the San Carlo, La Scala, Florence's La Pergola, the Comunale in Bologna, La Fenice. The Imperial family often visited Trieste, whose geographical position between the Balkans and Austria made it of vital importance. Feliciano would be able to stage his operas there, the great Habsburgs would have a chance to appreciate them: his Bonapartist and then Mazzinian faith had begun to dwindle. By now his name was becoming known in musical circles all over Italy. He composed songs and arias for concerts, he wrote some symphonies; the Te Deums and Requiems now belonged to his tedious past as a Maestro di Cappella.

The Strepponis went to live in a spacious flat in the parish of Santa Maria Maggiore, which looked onto the Piazza Piccola. It was only a few minutes' walk from the Canal Grande and the port; in the roadstead, boats of all types and nationalities were anchored, flaunting all the new flags invented at the Congress of Vienna. People walked up and down the port, selling water, fruit and hot soups, calling out their wares in a medley of different tongues, Slavonic and Teutonic, Latin and Hungarian. The area around the port was always bustling and lively, ablaze with the colours of different national costumes. Along the aristocratic Corso, the wealthy citizens paraded in their tricorn hats, which had come back into fashion, some even with pigtails. The Bonapartists, the Carbonari and the liberals sneered. Above and beyond Trieste, the Alps were visible, and when the wind of the Bora swept the streets, the Strepponi family would wrap up in their shawls and veils and go out. The salt air did them good. It was wonderful to live all together, for Giuseppina to be able to practise music with her father; for Rosa to be able to go out in the evening with a well-respected husband; to buy at last those bonnets, those cushions she had so desired.

At the bidding of Maestro Giuseppe Farinelli, Feliciano had to compose two operas which Maestro Francesco Basily, the censor at the Milan Conservatoire, had written in other versions. As already mentioned, it was quite common to re-work librettos or successful stories. In 1828, therefore, Foppa's comedy *Sargino (Love's Pupil)* was staged and enjoyed a discreet success. In 1830, Feliciano returned to Turin with *Love and Mystery*, but he wasn't well served by his singers. The great break came with the melodrama *Gli Illinesi*, with a libretto by Felice Romani, the famous poet who had written for Donizetti, for Bellini and Rossini. To compose music for verses written by that intelligent man who Feliciano had met in Milan, who had two degrees, who was also a well-known man of the Left, was a great opportunity. After the success of *Gli Illinesi*, Romani – by now a real friend, provided Feliciano Strepponi with a second comic libretto, *L'Ullà di Bassora*, this time for La Scala.

For La Scala! Many aspired to become fashionable composers for La Scala; Gioachino Rossini had retired to France at the age of just thirty-one. His place had been taken by Vincenzo Bellini (1801–35) and by Gaetano Donizetti (1797–1848); it was with their music that Romanticism came to opera. The libretto plots were taken from Walter Scott and Friedrich Schiller, or even Shakespeare, now seen through new eyes. Madness, early death and illness became vital ingredients for the success of an opera. There were few sopranos who were spared the cavatina of 'Casta diva' ('Chaste goddess') from Bellini's *Norma* which would later become Giuseppina's pièce de résistance. Bellini, a man of elegance, adored by women and consumed by passion, had a musical style that Feliciano imitated. His ethereal looks, the mystery that surrounded him, were themselves magnets. Donizetti, the other creator of the new Italian opera whose music was just becoming fashionable (Feliciano was present at his first success, *Anna Bolena*, in 1830) composed almost mechanically. A few years later, when Bellini was dying, Donizetti was all the rage with *Lucia di Lammermoor*, another of Giuseppina's pièces de résistance. A good friend of Donizetti's, Feliciano Strepponi hoped to pursue the same kind of career; not only as a composer, but as an impresario, a musical inspector. Feliciano was considered an excellent *concertatore*, he knew all about the orchestra, about phrasing, about voices. Soon he was attracting to the Teatro Grande good performers, new operas, and Trieste's orchestra was getting well-known.

It was during the rehearsals and then the performances of Feliciano's operas in Trieste that Giuseppina had occasion to see and study two of the most famous singers of the age, Giuditta Grisi and Carolina Ungher – the latter had sung in the first performance of Beethoven's *Missa Solemnis* and Ninth Symphony. Grisi was a soprano and Ungher a contralto; they were both extremely beautiful and surrounded by rival entourages. Their stay in Trieste was a major event.

Giuseppina – and her father too – had decided that her future lay in singing. It was not an easy decision to take, since she also played the piano superbly. A singer's life, from her observation of Grisi and Ungher, seemed to be a marvellous one in all ways. Wherever the two primadonnas went, they were showered with flowers, jewels, poems, and declarations of eternal love from princes, dukes, marquises; opera singers in the nineteenth century had a monopoly over dreams. After this glimpse of the possibilities that the profession offered, Giuseppina decided to break off her general studies and devote herself solely to music and singing. For Feliciano and for Giuseppina too, there was only one Conservatoire – that of Milan, which now took female pupils, although they were segregated from the males. During the course, they had to read 'some historical books' and 'treatises on the arts'.

Feliciano took his daughter to Milan and presented her personally at the Conservatoire: after all, he had been a model student and Vincenzo Federici, his composition teacher, was bound to help him. He did not feel well, Feliciano had difficulties with his breathing and, at times, felt faint. Maybe he was overworked. Giuseppina would have gone to live as a paying-guest with friends of Feliciano's. But there was just one problem: it was November 1830 and since Giuseppina was born in September 1815, she was over the enrolment age for students. However, Francesco Basily, who knew the Strepponis well, made an exception to the rules and accepted her as a candidate for the entrance exams – something he had refused to do two years later for a pupil in exactly the same situation: young Giuseppe Verdi from Busseto, near Parma, just a few months over the age-limit, was turned down by the Conservatoire; it was something Verdi was never to forget. She passed. Giuseppina Strepponi, now known as 'La Strepponcina', had demonstrated 'to an eminent degree the requisite qualities for an excellent musical disposition . . .'

Thus Giuseppina entered the Conservatoire and, what was more important, moved to Milan, the great capital so dear to Feliciano's heart. He was in Milan, too, rehearsing his opera *L'Ullà di Bassora* at La Scala. The opera's librettist, Romani, introduced Feliciano to Alessandro Lanari – the greatest of all librettists introducing him to the greatest of all impresarios! At the time, Lanari managed the Canobbiana, a smaller theatre than La Scala, built at the behest of Marie-Thérèse of Austria. As Feliciano met Lanari while working at La Scala, it is more than likely that the composer would have brought the impresario to hear his daughter's voice, and that he would, anyway, have introduced the two.

L'Ullà di Bassora was first performed on 20 September 1831, with Grisi, Badiali, Galli and Winter in the lead roles; it was well received, though it was not a total success. It had a further fifteen performances and there is no doubt that Giuseppina, who had now been at the Conservatoire in Milan for one year, was present at many if not all of them; she was thus beginning to breathe the air of La Scala. Her singing teacher, Pietro Ray, who also came from Lodi, accompanied her to La Scala, pointing out faults and virtues of the voices on the stage: Maestro Ray thought that Giuseppina's future as a primadonna was assured. She had great talent, Pietro Ray told Feliciano.

At sixteen, she was pretty, petite like her mother, but highly intelligent. Her hair was tied behind her neck with a large bow, while corkscrew curls hung down beside her cheeks; her eyes were large and grey, under dreaming eyebrows, and her mouth was thin, and well-drawn. She was judged to be 'very advanced in her studies', as was to be expected with her family background, and she continued to cultivate her gift for languages with further study at the Conservatoire.

Of all the children she was the only one who spent much time with her father, whose interest she shared. By now he was her greatest critic and also the person Giuseppina most wished to impress with her achievements; she wished to reward him for his faith in her. She would have liked to have the good looks of Maria Malibran or the Grisi sisters – Giulia and Giuditta not only sang like angels, but were extremely beautiful. Of course she dreamt of singing in her father's operas, of being able to bring them to an unrivalled success, a triumph. Although graceful, Giuseppina was cursed with Feliciano's nose, which she tried to hide by letting her hair hang loose and never allowing herself to be seen in profile. She was only a young girl, of course, and took little interest in politics, despite the fact that in Milan people talked of little else, however wise it might have been to avoid the subject. She did not go to cafés – such places were exclusively male enclaves. But nobody, not even her father, explained to her the traps of her profession, the difficulties she would encounter, the fact that being a female opera singer, was almost synonymous with being a courtesan, a prostitute, a *traviata*. Of course her mother had told her nothing and Giuseppina, living alone in Milan, was finding things out for herself.

She had sometimes caught sight of Papa sitting at the Martini in the company of a dubious lady, 'a singer'. With his hair cut short in the English fashion, he really looked like a gentleman. He coughed and often felt sick, but by now he was truly launched. With an almost successful opera at La Scala, a number of friends in musical circles, all the contacts he could wish for, just one thing was missing to crown his career and his life: money. He thus decided to transform himself into an impresario, that figure who, as we have said, was as powerful as the Hollywood producer. We have no details of the exhausting year Feliciano spent on long journeys, putting together companies, setting up seasons.

He was pale and thin, he felt very weak – the Strepponis were physically delicate: he could not therefore work both as an impresario and with the theatre, so he left the Teatro Grande although the family remained in Trieste. Feliciano had invested the earnings that in those months of steady work had ensured the family a certain level of comfort. But it turned out to be a disaster, the enterprise failed entirely and he found himself in inextricable debt. Forever travelling, desperate, agitated and feverish, Feliciano returned to Trieste in time to die. By Christmas he was tormented with fever, and on 13 January, Feliciano, not quite thirty-five years of age, died of encephalitis after a long period of delirium. He knew he was leaving a young wife and five children alone in the world and without a lira – or worse, with a heap of debts.

Giuseppina, who was in Milan, did not make it to Trieste in time to be with her father in his last moments. The body was taken to Lodi where Giuseppina joined her weeping mother, brother and sisters. In the Church of Santa Maria Maddalena in Lodi, his brother Francesco conducted the 'elaborate and solemn' requiem mass composed by Feliciano when he was only twenty.

2

AGENTS, LOVERS AND IMPRESARIOS

Giuseppina graduates with honours from the Milan
Conservatoire in autumn 1834. First concerts in Lodi and
opera début. The impresarios and the theatrical agent
Camillo Cirelli. The opera seasons and praise from the
music critics. First child.

Godiam, fugace e rapido
È il gaudio dell'amore . . .
Let us enjoy life for swift and fleeting
are the pleasures of love . . .

LA TRAVIATA, ACT I

Two weeks after Feliciano's death, friends in Trieste organised a
concert at the Teatro Mauroner to help the Strepponi family.
Rosa Strepponi with five children, all still to be educated, had been
caught unprepared by this sudden death. Feliciano had always
seemed so full of life, even though his health had noticeably
deteriorated over the last few months. The modest proceeds of the
concert barely sufficed to pay the rent of the flat and to organise
their return to Lodi; what point was there in remaining in Trieste
without Feliciano, without work, without the Teatro Grande? Rosa's
brothers, who were music-lovers if not musicians, helped the widow
by continuing to pay for Giuseppina's education at the Conservatoire
until the end of the year. However, by June 1832, Rosa's financial
situation was so precarious – bills seemed to arrive from everywhere,
all the time – that the Conservatoire in Milan received a letter from
the Royal Provincial delegation of the Lodi district: the widow had
been forced to sell her furniture and her husband's clothes, it said;
one of her daughters, Maria Teresa, had been taken in by the city
orphanage: the situation was truly desperate.

Given the circumstances, Giuseppina, for all her talent and

will-power, would not be able to continue her studies in Milan unless she obtained a study grant by special concession. The Director of the Conservatoire, then known as the Censor, was still Maestro Basily and he supported her application to the Governor. Obviously he was not offended by the fact that Feliciano, his ex-pupil, had set to music some librettos for which he himself had already composed music:

> Owing to the recent death in Trieste of her father, a Maestro composer of music, this family is now in direst poverty and her widowed mother whom as a result of the proceeds of a Performance expressly for her benefit, was able to pay the fees for her daughter's current academic year, will thus be obliged to withdraw her and cut short her course of musical instruction and her career which shows every sign of being a successful one, to the honour of the Establishment and to her own advantage and that of her poverty-stricken family.

For two years Giuseppina studied as a free pupil, at the expense of His Majesty's Imperial Government; where she lived and with whom, we do not know. We can however draw some conclusions as to the quality of her voice, and its vibrant resonance: it had a Callas-like quality rather than a Joan Sutherland one and was backed by a musicality and dramatic feeling. That she was a model student is clear from the Conservatoire's registers on the day she left, 25 September 1834: 'After the usual grand Performance, on which she appeared in various pieces, she was awarded a prize and distinguished herself in everything. Categories of study: Singing and harpsichord.'

Although short, she had grown extremely pretty; the oval of her face, the slope of her neck emerging from a beautiful low-cut neckline with a wisp of silk veil in the Directoire style, her white shoulders, her wide-set eyes, serious but sparkling, were all signs of promise: it would not be difficult for her to become the focus of dreams for huge audiences. Giuseppina was the incarnation of the Bellinian diaphanous heroine, a romantic damsel in melancholy distress, and at the same time the agility of her trills and her verve gave her a potentiality for comic roles as well. In fact she made her début at the Philharmonic Institute of Encouragement in Lodi, her native town, with an aria from *L'elisir d'amore* (*The Elixir of Love*), with 'full orchestra accompaniment'. The city gave her an exuberant reception. 'Strepponi received universal acclamation, a just tribute to the various gifts that nature has bestowed on her . . .' She also sang the cavatina from *Norma* 'with a piano-forte [sic] accompaniment performed by the amateur Sig. Dott. Pompeo Griffini' and 'Serene on my behalf' from *La sonnambula*. 'Her extremely agile voice and well-chosen models' were observed by Cleto Porro in the *Gazzetta della provincia Lodi-Cremona* on 31 October. The quality of her voice and of her training left no doubt: the Lodi audience, keenly musical, were overjoyed at the idea of being present at the launching of a star. Giuseppina remained in her native town for a short while, staying with her uncle.

A month later Giuseppina sang 'before the flower of the citizenry' in Palace Modigliani with the orchestra of Lodi's Philharmonic Institute. Signorina Strepponi showed her vocal talents 'which have been perfected by careful training, with the result that she surprised everyone with the many and various modulations with which she enriched her singing.' The first part of the concert concluded with a symphony written by Feliciano. Poor Feliciano, how proud he would have been of his Peppina, applauded by the city he had so longed to astonish himself. This was a truly great gathering. Giuseppina was presented to the 'upper crust' of Lodi society. And it meant a great deal to her, she longed to be accepted in the salons of Lombardy. First those of Lodi, which would be followed in due time by the more important ones in Milan. For she knew that in the salons the stars sang, they became known, they met suitors, composers, impresarios and sometimes settled contracts. The article in the *Gazzetta della provincia Lodi-Cremona* informs us also that the orchestra, conducted by Maestro Stramezzi, accompanied a duet from the opera *Gabriella di Vergy*, another from *I Normanni a Parigi* (*The Normans in Paris*): and one from *Anna Bolena*, concluding with a cavatina from *La sonnambula* (*The Sleepwalker*) works by Bellini and Donizetti, the two composers of the day.

Since Giuseppe Verdi was in Lodi at the time, with his father-in-law Antonio Barezzi and a friend, it is not unlikely that he heard about or even attended the concert and thus saw the promising singer. They did not meet: Giuseppina was then far more sophisticated than the young and still unknown composer, and she was perhaps already too much a woman of the world for that respectable group of men. Portraits show her dressed in fine clothes, looking severe but not yet earning her living. So who was buying such fine clothes for her? Who was paying for her travels? It is more than likely that nineteen-year-old Giuseppina already had a 'protector', someone who provided for her and her family.

La Strepponcina made her real and exhilarating début in a full operatic performance on Boxing Day 1834, at the Orfeo Theatre in Adria. The opera was Luigi Ricci's *Chiara of Rosenberg*. It is to be supposed that she spent Christmas with her fellow-performers, agents and impresarios, rehearsing and sleeping in an inn rather than at home with her family. She was probably in the company of the agent who had undertaken to protect her, Camillo Cirelli. He bestowed more attention on her than anyone else before. He was a father figure, older than Feliciano and equally attentive to her; to the way she dressed; to her progress in the operatic world.

There had never been a real relationship with her mother, nothing to compare with the intense affection and union of interests that had bound Feliciano to his eldest daughter. It was thus natural that young Giuseppina had looked for an older person to have by her side, to help her – even though the girl already showed a strong character, without much need of outside assistance. But she was young and she knew very little about how to advance herself in her career, in the world of show-business.

Only three years after her father's death, Giuseppina made her début as primadonna in *Matilde di Shabran* by Rossini at the Teatro Grande in Trieste where Feliciano had worked. An opera half-written by Ferretti and half set to music by Rossini, *Matilde di Shabran* (*Beauty and Heart of Iron*), first performed at Teatro Apollo in Rome under the baton of Niccolò Paganini, was musically a complete mess. A true star would not have undertaken it, nevertheless, it required a fine, strong voice, and was thus ideal for Giuseppina. She thus managed to sing an important opera from the modern repertoire on that same stage that had been trodden by two primadonnas of the first rank, Caroline Ungher and Giuditta Grisi, stars who had inspired her. Furthermore, it was an important season, the Carnival Season, and the Emperor's birthday was being celebrated. The début was followed, on 12 February, by Donizetti's *Anna Bolena*, with La Strepponcina in the important role of Jane Seymour. But Giuseppina would never have managed this leap from small concerts in Lodi – almost domestic affairs – to the Teatro Grande in Trieste within the space of a few months, had she not met – probably in or around the Conservatoire – Camillo Cirelli.

Born on the 20 December 1778, Camillo Cirelli came from Brescia, a town near Milan, Lodi and Monza, that is to say the area where opera was at the centre of urban life. He was married to Elisabetta Pinotti, a Neapolitan whose sister was the wife of Luigi Lablache, a famous bass. Cirelli, who had a daughter called Giulia, had heard of Giuseppina from Alessandro Lanari, the great impresario. In fact Lanari had almost forced La Strepponcina on Antonio Bassi, Cirelli's partner who, at that time, was about to be the impresario in Trieste. He was forming a company for the Teatro Grande and providing the entire Season. So it is clear that Lanari already knew her, and it was perhaps Lanari himself who pushed her into Cirelli's arms, after having enjoyed her favours himself.

In 1831, the year before Feliciano's death, Cirelli needed new capital and announced that he was setting up a partnership with Adolfo Bassi, a wardrobist. Bassi owned stage-sets and costumes, and had made a lot of money; this gave Cirelli the chance to put on shows, to become an impresario rather than a mere agent. The name of the new agency was 'Camillo Cirelli and *Adolfo* Bassi, theatrical agents and wardrobe capitalists' (sic); dazzled by the success of such impresarios as Lanari and Merelli, Cirelli hoped to become equally important; after all he was well into musical affairs. There was in any case no dividing line between a theatrical agent and an impresario. Impresarios 'leased out' those singers they had under contract and also subleased them, thus becoming agents; just as agents organised shows and seasons, even important ones like the one in Trieste. Indeed on 9 August 1834 Cirelli signed a contract with the administration of Brescia's theatre for three years, for which he was to receive 41,000 Austrian lire. With the help of Bassi's capital and costumes, Camillo Cirelli had become an impresario, but he was not to give up his theatrical agency. However, Cirelli had hardly signed up with his native city, when at the last moment he decided to leave the undertaking to Bassi, his partner. The Brescia Administration was not amused and asked for a substantial sum to be returned. The theatre sued Camillo Cirelli: Bassi had been involved in some imbroglio.

However, the season in which Giuseppina made her début as primadonna on a very important stage was the result of a remarkable effort by Bassi, in both financial and organisational terms. Cirelli's partner, who had little experience in such matters, had hoped to stage grandiose spectacles for Trieste with singers of the calibre of Giuditta Pasta. However the sums that were demanded soon persuaded him to change his mind; this is interesting, it gives us an idea of the fees that were paid to fashionable singers at the time, clearly not so very different from the kind of sum demanded by a Pavarotti or a Domingo today. La Strepponcina, in fact, who was as yet unknown on the great circuits, contented herself with 460 florins as against the 2,666 that Eugenia Tadolini, a famous soprano, took for the same season. Giuditta Pasta had demanded 3,000!

Giuseppina's career was assured: the graceful singer had a prodigious memory and, thanks to her father and the Milan Conservatoire, an enviable technical training as a soprano lirico-drammatico. Her voice was flexible and wide-ranging, her figure nimble, her dramatic talents notable. Lanari had encountered the '*Generalina*', the little General, which was his name for the singer, because of her determined demeanour – first with her father Feliciano and then in Via dei Filodrammatici and in the boxes at the Cannobiana, La Scala and the Re. It was a small and close-knit world that Giuseppina had managed to penetrate with Feliciano's help in his Milanese days. Her friendship with Lanari was to turn into a working liaison, although it later degenerated into outbursts of rage and jealousy. It is likely that there had already been some amorous affair between the important impresario and the young student at the Conservatoire; Lanari's recommendation of her to Cirelli and his associate Bassi (whose first name sometimes appears as Antonio and at others as Alfonso), was perhaps due to this, but the Generalina's singing skills could have caused him no worries. Along with Barbaja, Lanari was the impresario who had a sense of quality and insisted on high standards. Although *Matilda di Shabran* was not a popular opera, Giuseppina was a revelation. She began to sing all over Lombardy, she was tipped as the new hope of the stage. Soon an invitation came from Vienna, where the impresario Merelli, the emperor of opera, held sway.

Giuseppina had made it to Vienna and moreover at Merelli's invitation! Vienna, the capital of the Empire, the seat of the Emperor! She sang at the Kärnthnerthor theatre in Donizetti's *Anna Bolena*: 'She did not disappoint the expectations she had aroused,' a local review stressed. At the end of April 1835, she performed the role of Adalgisa in *Norma* for the same theatre and then left Vienna on 15 May for a round of cities and roles arranged by Cirelli. In Venice, for her benefit night at the Teatro Gallo, a poem was dedicated to her – with a portrait. This was a custom with famous singers, a lithograph printed in many copies meant that there were fans who wanted to possess the image of the diva, it meant that the new star had already acquired a following. Dressed in the French manner, the now famous low-cut neckline hidden by a veil, encircled by celestial clouds, her hair beribboned and curled in the Empire mode, Giuseppina was already a star. She was only twenty years old.

As Giuseppina's fortunes changed, so did those of the Strepponi family: Rosa moved to Milan, to the Belgiojoso Palazzo, at number 105 of the Guastalla District in the parish of Santa Maria della Passione. They occupied a flat within the great palazzo: the Strepponi women used to call on the Princess Belgiojoso, proving that the family now had a good social position. The Princess's salon may have been eccentric, but she nonetheless belonged to one of the highest branches of the Milanese aristocracy, which was a rigidly closed affair. The Strepponis and the Cornalbas evidently had both the manners and the clothes required in such circles. Still attractive, not yet forty, Rosa lived with two daughters, both of whom were sickly; the third, Maria Teresa, was left behind in Lodi's orphanage. Giuseppina was now always on her travels. The boy, Davide, had moved to Pavia where he was studying medicine.

In the subsequent summer and autumn seasons, Giuseppina was part of a company set up by Cirelli which toured the Veneto – still within the Imperial circuits, that is to say – singing in Udine, Gorizia and Verona in a repertoire that included *Lucia, L'elisir d'amore, Lucrezia Borgia, Norma* and Rossini's *Mosè*. In Venice she sang at the San Benedetto theatre, and for Carnival – the most important season of the year – she was in Brescia, Cirelli's native city. In the spring of 1836 she was back in Venice, but this time at the Fenice Theatre. On this occasion La Strepponcina was asked by the famous ballerina Taglioni to write a dedication for her. The mere fact that she was including her name and a remark in Taglioni's Souvenir Album (which is kept by the Paris Opera) is an indication of the young singer's fame. Indeed her dedication precedes the page inscribed by Antonio Somma, a well-known Venetian poet who was to become manager of the Teatro Grande in Trieste and also one of Verdi's librettists, followed by pages inscribed by the composer Giacomo Meyerbeer and the bass Luigi Lablache, Cirelli's brother-in-law.

In the following months she was in Mantua, Piacenza and at the Concordia Theatre in Cremona where Cirelli had been impresario ten years or so earlier. For this reason a bond was established between Cremona and Giuseppina which was to last all her life. Cremona was near Lodi, Busseto and also Sant'Agata where Giuseppina was to live for a long time. The manager of the local Philharmonic Society, Ruggero Manna, who was also a composer, wrote several songs for

Giuseppina on this occasion. Manna was an important man, once a protégé of Princess Elisa Baciocchi Bonaparte who ruled over Lucca before the Restoration. Later on, around 1840–41, Baciocchi's son-in-law, the elderly Count Filippo Camerata dei Passionei, would become La Strepponcina's lover for a while and even a candidate for her hand. She was now safely on her way to Olympus. The contracts were arranged by her agents Boracchi and Cirelli – Bassi had been given the sack over the Brescia contract. The agency was a success and Cirelli had taken a new partner, a certain Robbia, who was lame and a former secretary of Merelli. Finally, in the spring of 1837, Giuseppina was to appear in a season of Lanari's at the Teatro Comunale in Bologna, which in Italy at the time was second only to La Scala. Lanari wrote to Cirelli:

> Bologna, 17 April 1837
> I hope you have completed the contract for a year with La Strepponcina in the way I instructed before leaving my house yesterday, which is to say for L. 19,000, on the consideration that since no commission was being paid, the L. 20,000 was abandoned. I thus hold it to be a completed transaction, and on my return the Contract will be approved and we will agree as to the other Articles . . .

Since Lanari addressed this letter to Cirelli and not directly to Giuseppina, the agent was presumably managing her affairs. By now everybody knew that they were lovers and that they shared a room whenever they travelled together.

At Bologna she played alongside the greatest stars: Napoleone Moriani, the languid 'tenor of beautiful death', who impaled himself with sublime elegance on Donizettian swords or collapsed in Bellinian swooning-fits so authentic that women fainted; and Giorgio Ronconi, the bass whose voice shook the glass in the windows. With these great singers, the Generalina made her Bologna début on 15 April in Donizetti's *Marino Faliero*, followed by *Lucia di Lammermoor* and *I Puritani* (*The Puritans*). The ovations were for Moriani but Giuseppina was honoured as well. Assuming all the glory of a primadonna, on 5 August 1837 she returned to Lodi for a concert. This time, the local newspaper did not limit itself to mere praise: it paid homage to her in the servile language of the time.

. . . Signora Giuseppina Strepponi was cradled and educated in our midst. Our Philharmonic Institute is happy to have her as an honorary member. Tripping from stage to stage she has graced many illustrious and glorious cities with her harmonious accents . . . On Friday evening the halls of the Institute were thrown open for a grand Performance. There is no need to mention her profound musical knowledge, her wide-ranging, clear and vibrant voice, her forceful and energetic singing, with its continual gradations, forever increasing in strength and modulated with trills, endowed with an expressiveness that belongs only to those on whom nature has bestowed an individual way of feeling; nor need we mention those ardent but secure traits that have served to divide the sublime from the mediocre.

The very presence of Giuseppina inspired a patriotic spirit in the townspeople, filling them with pride: she threw lustre not only on the town but on the motherland. Thus, even in this review, we find the idea of the nation associated with singing, with music.

In autumn 1838 Giuseppina was back in Cremona for the season; once again in a performance staged by Cirelli. She never stopped travelling but we know little about these journeys; we can only imagine them. First the sets and the costumes would arrive, and a few days later, the whole company, invariably greeted by the townsfolk with enthusiasm. The houses were thrown open to the leading singers, dinners and dances were organised, love-affairs were embarked on in an attempt to make up for months of provincial boredom. The town orchestra would do its best to learn the new scores – because it was important for an Impresa to bring new works – the first violin or the harpsichordist would stand in as a conductor, unless the composer himself turned up. The impresario, the agent or both, would act as directors although it hardly mattered since the singers did whatever they wanted in any case; even Giuseppina would sometimes introduce arias from completely different works, especially when she saw bored faces in the boxes and when the chatter of conversation grew too loud in the background. And so, with a nod of her head, she would give the lead to the orchestra and bring in a Bellini cabaletta for which she was famous or a scene from Donizetti that had no connection with what she was singing. Thus she would regain her audience's attention and their applause . . . There were some dandies who only came for one act; just to see the ballerinas; others would turn up at the end of the evening when the local bucks had the chance to dance with the primadonna, to hold the divas in their arms.

The season in Cremona had become an important event since Ferdinand I, Emperor of Austria, and Maria Carolina, the Empress, arrived on 23 September to hear Bellini's *Norma*. Giuseppina now played Norma herself, no longer Adalgisa. Dressed in white, her dark hair flowing loose, her frail arms outstretched towards the children she would have liked to murder in vengeance for her lover's treachery. If we think about it, the story of Norma was highly symbolic of Giuseppina's later life. Her repertoire was getting richer, she sang Rossini, the new French composer Auber and Luigi Ricci whom she knew from Trieste. Also Mercadante, a Neapolitan who was the most successful of the new Italian composers. She was paid in *svanziche* now, the Austrian currency, which was highly valued as the dollar is today.

As her career took off, Giuseppina was able to take sentimental liberties outside the bond that she had established with Cirelli; there were the gallant tenors with whom she travelled, the provincial noblemen, the music lovers. Cirelli would never be able to marry her since he already had a wife, but he served her as protector. Fleeting love-affairs were the order of the day, even more so than now, because there were so few other distractions and many people were still illiterate; opera and seduction were the only means of entertainment open to them. Although contraceptive methods of a somewhat alarming kind existed, it was easy to get pregnant. The hypocrisy of the century turned a blind eye to carnal love; it was tolerated until it resulted in swollen bellies. One could ignore and forgive all kinds of love, even make them the subject of scurrilous poems – so long as they bore no embarrassing and visible fruits. Which of course they did – all too often. The singers left a trail of foundlings in orphanages all over the country, and both the children and the unmarried parents were a target for contempt; so much so that the considerable number of abandoned children became a major social problem. In some states, those responsible could be sent to prison. On her travels Giuseppina kept her eyes wide open: she had to take advantage of her moment of triumph, of the legend that surrounded the heroine of romantic sublimation. She had to find a husband.

They often travelled together, though, she and Cirelli. He had moved his agency and home to Florence, which had also become Lanari's central point. When she was at home, which was rare, Giuseppina lived in Milan with her mother and her family. After all it was she who paid the rent on the Milanese flat. She might find a husband in Turin, the elegant capital of the Savoy kingdom, where she was to sing for an important season. From August to October 1837 she was engaged for the splendid Carignano Theatre with the impresario Vincenzo Giaccone, to whom Lanari had contracted her. But she realised she was pregnant.

At around the fifth month of her pregnancy, obviously tired and weak, she missed a few performances. Like many people in the business, Lanari had no idea of her condition and she had no desire to inform him as yet; he was so angry at her defections that he refused to speak to her. In a letter dated 29 August, Giuseppina answered '. . . now that you are speaking to me again, I am sorry to have to turn down the Carnival having left negotiations for Parma and other theatres in Italy as well as London . . .' Unlike most sopranos she dealt with her correspondence personally, using a fluent and cultivated prose style. On this occasion she was writing directly to Lanari, that is to say not through her agent, and was concealing the fact of her pregnancy. She was also using the opportunity to emphasise her success, vaunting a host of requests from theatres abroad. 'As you and everyone told me, the season in Turin is excellent, and having had the good luck to meet with approval, no other woman but me is so desired by the public, and I will have to take all the work upon myself: so I find it absolutely necessary not to commit myself with anyone, though if my intentions had been different I would definitely have favoured you.' This too was an excuse devised to prevent Lanari, who had her under contract, from engaging her anywhere else for the next few months: she knew that before and after the birth it would have been impossible for her to sing. She had already begun to develop her own literary style, which enabled her both to say and not to say things, and which makes it necessary for us to read between the lines. She probably talked in the same way; it was always essential to interpret what Giuseppina said because she was far from the innocent young thing she seemed to be.

In the same letter, Strepponi concluded coquettishly: 'I cannot give your regards to Cirelli because he is not here. I will give him your regards in writing.' As if to emphasise that she had passed to better things . . . and men. On 16 September, Giuseppina wrote again to Lanari, from Turin, confirming that if he wanted to engage her for Ancona, she would demand 6,000 francs and 'an entire benefit evening, expense-free'.

Such evenings were very popular with the singers, as they were extremely lucrative. The star would perform a selection of pieces from his or her repertoire, taking liberties that nowadays would make us shudder, sticking pieces together, Reader's-Digest fashion, changing notes and registers and then receiving a shower of presents from the public. Gifts, flowers and money would be hurled onto the stage, with the risk of hitting the ushers or even the star in person. And then – at the end of the performance – which was known as an *Accademia* or benefit evening – the primadonna would pass round the room with a basket in which she collected further donations. And, on the way out, the audience had to pass a box for any last small offerings. There was no chance of the spectator escaping his obligations. There were scenes of sheer frenzy when an admirer in a box hurled a bag of gold coins at Giuditta Pasta and hit a servant on the head who was seriously injured. The star herself was delighted – both at the size and weight of the gift and the fact that it was not her head that had been in its path. All these gifts were a way of expressing gratitude to the heroes and heroines who acted out the dreams of Italians in the nineteenth century.

Now that she was visibly pregnant, invitations at Court stopped arriving. Although the oppressive kings of Savoy were detested by the patriots, Giuseppina gave no thought to politics; that was the last thing on her mind. Like every successful singer, she was on the side of officialdom; when she visited other kingdoms, she would never disdain an invitation to Court if it arrived. And since the sovereigns were fond of opera and liked to enjoy themselves, invitations to court did arrive especially if one was part of a reputable company; worldly success was thus guaranteed, of however precarious a kind. Nobody was fooled though: invitations were extended to those who were riding high at the time, and female singers were sought because they were considered to be of 'easy virtue'; indeed often the ladies of the court were not present at such 'after-dinner' gatherings, where the conversation was free and easy.

From her Turin lodgings, Giuseppina was busy writing to Lanari; this time her 'friend Cirelli' was by her side. 'He would be very pleased to enter into a partnership with you for the opening of the theatre in Venice . . .' Giuseppina was trying to involve her lover-protector in Lanari's business affairs by getting herself leased out to Cirelli. She was particularly keen to do so because her agent had agreed to recognise the baby she was about to bear, and to give it his name. She stopped singing in the first week of December 1837.

The baby was born in January, in Turin, the capital of the Savoy

kingdom and was brought into the world by no less a person than
the royal obstetrician. The child was registered as 'Sterponi' and
baptised in the church of Sant'Eusebio, in the parish of San Filippo;
in the register of births and baptisms, 1838–41 no. 9, we read:

> In the year of the lord 1838 on the 16th of the month of
> January at the hour of five-thirty in the evening in the parish
> church of Sant'Eusebio, town of Turin, a child of male sex was
> presented in the church, a child born on January 14th at the
> hour ten-thirty in the evening in the district of this Parish, the
> son of an unidentified father and of Giuseppa Maria Clelia
> Strepponi, a singer by profession, domiciled in Turin; the child
> was baptised, in consideration of the risk to life, by Collegiate
> Surgeon Luigi Garbiglietti at home, and the names Camillo Luigi
> Antonio were imposed, the Godfather being Luigi Vestri, actor
> by profession domiciled in Turin and the Godmother Signora
> Antonietta Darselli, maiden-name Dupin, a woman of wealth,
> domiciled in Turin, represented by Sig. Camillo Cirelli. The birth
> was reported by Signor Luigi Vestri.
>
> Signed Luigi Vestri and Parish Priest Andrea Crosa.

There was nothing shameful in the fact that Giuseppina and her
companion had brought a baby into the world. The only thing
that mattered was that in the last months of pregnancy she had
sung rarely and badly. The baptism was almost a social affair,
as the names of the godparents indicate: the godfather, a famous
actor in the Royal Sardinian Company and a childhood friend of
Giuseppina's; the godmother, the wife of a great choreographer and
daughter of the tenor Domenico Donzelli. When Camillino, as his
mother was to call him, was only two months old, Giuseppina sang
in a concert and was immediately received back into the great opera
circuits. The child was sent to his father in Florence, where – with
the help of Lanari who had been apprised of the facts, and who had
great experience in such problems – a nurse was found for him. It
is strange that Giuseppina did not think of sending her baby to her
mother and her sisters who were in Milan, and it is even stranger
that she did not want him with her.

3

PRIMADONNA ASSOLUTA

Another contract with the impresario Lanari. The
impresario's *Memoirs*. Giuseppina in Rome and her début
at the Argentina Theatre. Gossip, letters, quarrels: an
unwanted pregnancy. Merelli and cholera sweep Milan.
Giuseppina's sister Maria Antonietta dies of consumption.
Triumphs: Giuseppina becomes Primadonna Assoluta.
Return to Florence. Birth of Sinforosa.

——————————— • ———————————

Un sol colpo vi torria coll'amante il protettore . . .
You'll lose lover and protector
at a single blow . . .

LA TRAVIATA, ACT II

Strepponi made extremely intelligent use of the stage, a natural
actress, a perceptive interpreter of dramatic roles and a gay
coquette in comic ones. It was her dramatic presence and technique
rather than her voice which raised her to that special Olympus
reserved for primadonnas; Lanari's intention was that she should
become one of his prime properties, to be ceded or leased to all the
great theatres in exchange for precious *svanziche*. There were new
markets opening up in North and South America where opera was
becoming popular. It is worth recording that in 1838, Lorenzo da
Ponte, Mozart's forgotten but magical librettist, died in New York
where he had gone in search of success.

Giuseppina, small and thin, did not enjoy good health, she
overtaxed herself. After Camillino's birth, she only took a few weeks'
rest before returning to the stage, to greater acclaim than ever. To
judge from the portrait that now hangs in the Theatre Museum of
La Scala, her pregnancy had endowed her skin with an extra lustre.
But on the other hand, with age and knowledge, her eyes had taken
on a veneer of cynicism. Her family situation (if we can so call it)

could hardly make her happy – Camillo Cirelli was sixty-three, an old man, and from protector was becoming a protégé; he had not succeeded in his attempt to become an impresarió of the calibre of Lanari or Merelli. After working as inspector-general of the Imperial Austrian Theatres Merelli had managed operatic events in Paris, St Petersburg, Berlin and London. In the autumn of 1836 he assumed control of La Scala, thus introducing a cosmopolitan atmosphere and new fashions. Merelli dominated opera in Milan and everyone wanted to meet him – including Giuseppe Verdi. Cholera came and went, carrying off the poet Leopardi amongst others, striking the cities, most oppressed classes through ignorance and reaction, almost like a metaphor for their condition. The epidemics rekindled Giuseppina's religious faith – a faith that was mainly manifested by obsessive prayers, bargains struck with God by means of candles and costly masses. With death everywhere, people were frightened; they stopped going to the theatre and small businesses failed.

As Giuseppina's fortunes grew, so did her needs; Maria Antonietta was very ill and Barberina's health was so precarious that there were fears for her future too. The calls on her charity from members of her family only seemed to grow. Giuseppina's brother Davide was studying medicine at the ancient university of Pavia and not yet earning his own living; the family who looked after Camillino were a source of expenditure which she shared with Cirelli. Medical treatment for her sister – treatment *in extremis*, since there was little chance of saving Maria Antonietta from consumption – the great enemy of young women in the Po valley – was costly. And above all there was her own extravagant lifestyle. When she returned to Trieste, in the Carnival Season 1836–37 for Buzzola's *Ferramondo*, Giuseppina travelled with her own maidservant and new clothes. 'Constantly interrupted by the most flattering signs of appreciation,' she felt a star. On 23 February, with Giuditta Grisi, Giuseppina was Juliet in Bellini's *Capulets and Montagues*. 'Faced with such a strong rival,' wrote *Il Pirata*, 'Mademoiselle Strepponi surpassed herself and with surprising emulation challenged her otherwise dearest Romeo for the palm.' The audience was ecstatic.

Musical journals like *Il Figaro*, *La Fama* or indeed *Il Pirata* from which we have quoted also specialised in gossip, not always of a musical kind, just like *Hello!* or the *Daily Mail* in our own day; they concentrated on the famous, often singers, whom the public enjoyed seeing dragged through the mud. Indeed in February 1839, Giuseppina herself was driven to protest, against Signor Regli, who had published an article about her and Cirelli. After her triumphs, instead of caring for her health, Cirelli, who passed himself off as her husband, exploited her by making her perform too often and taking a cut of her earnings. Indeed the correspondent of *Il Figaro*, having heard Giuseppina sing the role of Nina in Coppola's *Nina Mad for Love*, gave a note of warning: 'A pity that this talented young woman should sing for so many consecutive seasons, with the serious risk of weakening or damaging that clear and pleasing voice of hers.'

At this time too Giuseppina was again portrayed in lithographs with her hair hanging loose, in imitation of Nina's madness, and with the oval of her face and her long white neck, she personified the Romantic heroine. Like Lucia of Lammermoor, Nina also goes mad after being forbidden to marry the man she loves, and although Coppola's delightful opera precedes Donizetti's, they are both in the grand romantic tradition.

Engaged by Cirelli, she moved to Mantua. The gala evening in June, procured for her 'a hail of verses and flowers'. But *Il Figaro* continued with its warnings: 'La Strepponi whom we believed wanted to rest from the continual glorious labours she has sustained in so many theatres, has now rushed off to Piacenza ... We hope that this excess of activity will not prove fatal to her ...' In Piacenza with Ricci's comic opera *Adventure of Scaramuccia* and Donizetti's *L'elisir d'amore*, she fully revealed her gifts as a performer of opera buffa. She mantained her correspondence with Lanari who discussed engaging her again. At the end of August and in September she was in Cremona for *Lucia* and *Norma*; everybody wanted her to sing the latter. *Il Pirata* commented (4 November 1837) '... the applause was for Strepponi alone. She is always good, always capable, vivacious.' Before she could sign a contract with Lanari, she had to go back to Turin, a city which reminded her of bad times, of her pregnancy, because she had been engaged by the impresario Vincenzo Giaccone. She opened at the Carignano Theatre with Auber's *The Deaf Girl from Portici*, an opera which surprisingly was not well received. 'The cultivated Turin audience had had more than enough of Auber's extremely learned music,' wrote *Il Figaro* and it was swiftly replaced by Donizetti's *The Madman at the Island of St Domingo*. 'Strepponi sang excellently,' commented *Il Pirata*, 'and was warmly applauded, especially after her cavatina and the rondeau, pieces that are not actually part of the opera score, but which were inserted in accordance with well-known customs.'

Lanari's latest contract, drawn up in Venice, duly arrived. This time she was treated as a *primadonna assoluta*; the paper bearing the letterhead 'Sig. Alessandro Lanari, the impresario of the Grand Theatres' underlined some points that were to become important: 'in the case of sickness (which may God prevent) after eight days the fee will be suspended, and will not become due again until such time as the above-mentioned Artist is able to resume her services.'

The locations were yet to be agreed but Lanari could, according to the contract, sub-contract or lease her out to whomsoever he chose, but not overseas and not in Milan which was under the aegis of Merelli. However the Generalina was not going to accept this: 'Since Sig. Lanari, possibly by mistake, has omitted to say that I may be sub-contracted outside Italy, I have taken it upon myself to add this in both Contracts.' And that was not all: Giuseppina asked to be paid her monthly wages in advance.

The singers were 'sub-contracted', 'leased out' or 'sold' in much the same way as Hollywood stars were bartered among great producers. Someone like Lanari would pay a monthly salary to whole companies and various singers. A few years before the events we describe here, Lanari had had ten principal singers under contract, as well as six secondary singers, fourteen dancers, a choreographer and the ballerina Carlotta Grisi, sister of the two famous singers.

Giuseppina's new contract with Lanari was hailed as a mark of ulterior success: 'The outstanding primadonna assoluta Giuseppina Strepponi has been engaged for a year by the theatrical contractor Alessandro Lanari,' wrote *Il Figaro* on 7 February 1838. It also announced that the tenor Napoleone Moriani and the famous baritone Giorgio Ronconi were to be featured. In March 1838, Peppina had to go to Milan, probably for her sister Maria Antonietta's funeral. There was hardly any bond between these two sisters; unlike Barberina the youngest, Maria Antonietta, who was excessively plain, had received hardly any education. While Barberina was regarded by Giuseppina almost as a daughter, the soprano had little in common with Antonietta who felt no interest in musical matters. But Antonietta's death distressed Rosa, not only because she felt guilty towards her neglected daughter but because she felt she had failed all her children as a mother – she had probably found a man for herself, although she still lived in the apartment paid for by Giuseppina who, after all, and in spite of all her successes, was still in her eyes only a glorified 'traviata'.

Giuseppina wrote an affectionate letter from Milan to Lanari who was in Rome for the Carnaval Season but she wanted confirmation 'since, having been persuaded in my own interest and out of self-respect to accept two concerts at the Court in Piedmont next Lent, it will be impossible for me to make my trip to Venice. I shall be in Rome on 3 April at the latest and since, as you know, I need very little time to prepare a new Opera I hope that the good Lanari will not censure me for such a short delay.' While in Milan, she added, she had been to La Scala to see Mercadante's *The Promise*, a successful opera of the day in which she was later to perform. 'You must say a thousand kind things to dear, good Unger and the tenor of Fashion [i.e., Napoleone Moriani] . . .'

On 7 March *Il Figaro*, prompted by Cirelli, published the news that before going to Rome, Giuseppina was to give a special concert for the Court in Turin; but because of her new contract with Lanari, 'she was unable to accept the generous offers made to her by Signor Laperte, impresario of the Royal Theatre of the Grand Opera in London.' The intention was clearly to advertise the fact that she was also in demand abroad and by other impresarios as well. '. . . Without risking the accusation of being presumptuous,' La Peppina wrote to Lanari from Turin, in March, 'I can frankly state that I found universal and highly flattering favour.'

We have a wealth of information from this period, thanks to the discovery of Strepponi's letters to Lanari, a discovery made by the musicologist Marcello De Angelis. Despite all her pleas that they should be destroyed, the impresario conserved them with religious devotion. They would come in useful later and he knew it. Lanari also wrote his *Memoirs*, in which he gives his own version of the relationship between himself and Giuseppina, a relationship which was to turn acrimonious:

> In February 1839, this lady was offered to me by the Cirelli Agency for a year. As I had a high esteem for her, I engaged her, granting her the fee she requested, which amounted to 212 thousand Austrian lire and I immediately placed her before the eyes of the world at the Gran Teatro Argentina in Rome, together with artists famous throughout Europe, Moriani and Ronconi. She was accorded an enthusiastic welcome in this theatre and thus the name of Strepponi once more began to resound favourably.

Lanari's *Memoirs* continue: 'In Rome there was a reciprocal desire on both my part and Signora Strepponi's to draw up a new contract:

Strepponi's wish was that I should raise her to the level of the great artists, which in fact happened; and my wish was to derive some profit from her, as I did with other virtuosos.' This contract covered two years from March 1839 to March 1841 which were to be crucial in Giuseppina's career and life.

Together with Cirelli, Peppina arrived in Rome as a primadonna, feted and honoured. For all its bigotry and its chaos, the capital of the Papal States was extremely beautiful. The climate, so much better than that of the Po valley, suited Giuseppina; she felt in top form. The Argentina was re-opening after refurbishment and was now under new management. Lanari had thus been called in, as an impresario famous for his grandiose stage-sets and the quality of the singers he engaged. Unlike the great theatres of the North, the Argentina felt no compulsion to include the usual two obligatory new operas. There was no completely new work, no opera commissoned from young composers or popular musicians. But it was probably on this occasion that Ronconi and Moriani spoke to Giuseppina Strepponi of Giuseppe Verdi, a composer from Busseto. He had been supposed to make his début at the Filodrammatici in Milan with *Rocester* (sic), with a libretto by Antonio Piazza, but there had been problems. However, the young Maestro was now about to leave Busseto and there was talk of a new opera from him for the spring of the following year. The two singers had a score for piano and voices. People generally respected Giuseppina's musical knowledge, her taste and intuition; she was someone whose opinion was consulted.

With expectations running high, Giuseppina Strepponi made her début at the Teatro Argentina in *Lucia di Lammermoor*. It was a success. But in *La Rivista teatrale*, on 21 April 1838, the critic Tosi commented thus: 'Signora Strepponi (Lucia), who is new to our stage, starting from the cavatina, taken from some score we can but guess at, demonstrated a melodious and limpid voice, accompanied by a good singing method and a perfect pronunciation.' The writer criticised the musical substitutions that Strepponi had made but went on to say that it was not until the duet that the primadonna's true worth became clear: 'Thus Strepponi's vocal merits revealed themselves to far better effect in the beautiful duet with Edgardo. The applause that this young and talented singer received during this piece was not only due to her singing method, but was also a tribute to her expressiveness, her soul and the outpouring of passion to which she abandons herself wholly at the moment of leavetaking from the man to whom Lucia had devoted all her love . . .'

On 3 May there followed Bellini's *Puritani* under the title of *Elvira Walton* – no puritans could coexist with cardinals under the Roman sky! The same critic, even more enthusiastic about Strepponi, wrote:

Do you wish to hear a fresh, limpid, wide-ranging voice, singing that is expressive, animated, well-reasoned, free from those supposed embellishments that are always accompanied by a thousand grotesque mannerisms and contortions of the neck? Do you wish to enjoy singing that is all spontaneity, accuracy, symmetry and totally lacking in those so-called effusions that torture the refined ear, and demonstrate the absurdity, awful taste and dramatic ignorance of those who perform them? Finally do you long to hear someone singing in the Italian school using a perfect Italian diction, not forcing you to experience our tongue mangled and the simplicity of Bellini's sublime notes betrayed and maltreated? If this is your desire, go to the above-named theatre and listen to Signora Strepponi in this opera. This young singer who has no need to fall back on false convulsions and swoonings in order to cover her failures and to gain the Public's compassion, but who has added to her value by uniting true artistic feeling with great commitment, this singer – we repeat – has succeeded in demonstrating that the tokens of favour obtained in *Lucia* were but a tiny portion of what was due to her.

Peppina was becoming the herald of a new style of performance; her way of moving on the stage was less rhetorical than what the public had been used to, and was closer to today's taste. And she was slender, unlike the typically gross nineteenth-century soprano, she was pretty, she was the embodiment of Romanticism. Cirelli had left, she was alone to enjoy her triumphs and she felt happy, very happy. Everybody was in love with her and she, maybe, was also in love herself.

'Tender, gay, sublime and melancholy according to the circumstances, there is no sentiment of passion that she did not express stupendously in the interesting but challengingly and difficult character of Elvira. The spontaneous and unanimous applause that was accorded her in all the scenes in which she appeared, was not a tribute, as it sometimes is, to the power of coquettishly sparkling eyes, or to a shapely figure, but to her uncommon merits . . .' So great was the success that the same version of *Lucia* with Strepponi, Moriani and Ronconi, that sublime trio of superstars, was transferred to the Apollo Theatre on 19 April, together with Donizetti's *Pia dei Tolomei. La Rivista teatrale* continued in its praise: 'The general feeling of continual and growing admiration for Strepponi is shared by everybody.' At her benefit performance, in the cavatina from *Norma* 'Strepponi offered us new enchantments of all kinds. The room echoed as much with applause as with voices enraptured by such extraordinary singing skills.' The company was covering itself in glory, reviews spoke of audiences in ecstasy. Giuseppina 'was sublime'.

At this stage Giuseppina took a lover who, so it would appear from her own words, made her pregnant. Cirelli, who was in Florence, had to be told: he did not take to Giuseppina's new pregnancy kindly, in fact, he was furious. He thought that the father was somebody he nicknamed 'the Sergeant'. Many of the biographers of Verdi point to Merelli as the father of this child while the most recent accuses Napoleone Moriani, the tenor who was singing with her in Rome. But when we find an 'M' designating a perfidious lover who broke things off rather than face up to his responsibilities, it is clearly Raffaele Monti, a tenor who would be Alvino in Verdi's *Lombards* and who had sung with Peppina in Turin. Indeed his full name – 'the fiancé Monti' will appear later in a letter found by De Angelis among the Lanari correspondence. But, to be truthful, it is unlikely that Giuseppina herself was sure who the father of this child was. It would be no surprise to discover that Merelli was an occasional lover, although more at the outset of her career, not at this stage. Her summons to Vienna, for example, was probably a reward for performances that were not only musical in nature. It would have been an honour to share the bed of Merelli, so powerful a man, a leading figure in the opera world of the day, it would have been a medal to pin to her famous neckline, certainly no disgrace. As for Moriani, Giuseppina was also likely to have had an affair with so famous and fascinating a tenor.

On 3 May all three of the stars took part in a concert at the villa of the Princes Massimo, given in honour of the Grand-Duke of Tuscany and a member of the royal family of Saxony. In Rome life drifted by pleasurably; in those days the singers spent their time in fabulous palazzi and beautiful gardens with rose-bowers on the banks of the Tiber; gentle breezes blew from the Tyrrhenian sea, keeping the sky a gentle turquoise and sweeping away the humidity.

Rome was then a small town of some 120,000 inhabitants, almost all, princes and cardinals, bureaucrats, prelates and mediators: an abominable world from the human point of view but redeemed by its marvellous climate. The ruins of the Roman aqueducts, the marble columns, stood out against the Italian pines, the city was like the country and the country was like the city, the salons of the Papal aristocracy, of the Colonnas, the Torlonias, the Boncompagnis, opened their doors to singers, affording glimpses of unimaginable art treasures. 'On 19 June the performances at the Teatro Argentina in Rome came to an end,' wrote *Il Pirata*, 'amidst enthusiastic acclaim and the three "champions" Strepponi, Moriani and Ronconi went to Florence. As soon as they arrived, they were invited to the brilliant performance that Prince Poniatiowski gave in his palazzo on the 25th of the same month to honour the Duke of Lucca, brother of H.M. the King of Naples, the Princess of Syracuse and many other persons of high rank.' Giuseppina sang the by now famous cavatina from *Norma* and perfomed a duet with Moriani.

The company performed *Lucia* at La Pergola which was packed to bursting point, with queues outside for tickets at any price. The singers were called back on stage twenty times to take a bow. The audience also went crazy when Giuseppina appeared in the mad scene, her white dress and her arms stained with blood. 'And so Strepponi distinguished herself more and more,' wrote Lanari in his *Memoirs*. Next she sang in Leghorn, which was a busy port, together with Ronconi; for August and September Lanari ceded her to Cirelli for Cremona 'with no profit', the impresario specified. Not only Giuseppina's voice was beginning to show signs of strain, but the singer herself was exhausted and finding it increasingly difficult to bear up under her pregnancy. Cirelli took care to write to Lanari from Brescia that *Norma* was a colossal success. A partner of the impresario had written saying the exact opposite. When she returned to Florence, her voice was strained; Pietro Romani, the conductor who worked for Lanari, informed him that the situation was alarming: 'Strepponi is always ill, and suffers from coughing-fits on stage that are pitiful to see.'

At the beginning of November, Romani wrote again informing Lanari how the Florentine performances were going: 'in the first act Strepponi was seized by such a coughing-fit that she had to leave the stage before concluding it.' In Florence Giuseppina moved in the salons which had been barred to her when she had been less successful. It is unlikely that she took Cirelli along with her, although he still played an important part in her business affairs. Giuseppina spoke good French, a language which was widely used in Florentine society; she knew some Spanish and, as a subject of the Austro-Hungarian Empire she could get by in German. She had a vague grasp of English, a language not yet fashionable although it was the language of Shakespeare, Walter Scott and Byron. Translations were scarce at that time, and texts had to be read in the original. She moved well in the sophisticated Florentine world, she could maintain a conversation, she knew when to remain silent and when to express an opinion, she knew how to kiss His Eminence's hand, how to curtsy to Their Excellencies. Spending time in Florence was also a way of keeping an eye on Camillino and the family with whom he lived.

The day after Christmas a concert was given in honour of Liszt, who performed a fantasy on Rossini's cavatina from *Tancredi*, and improvised on a theme from *La sonnambula* which Giuseppina had performed that same evening. She too received lengthy applause. Singing in a concert for Liszt, the most fashionable man of the time, gave her a certain pleasure. But this social success was bound to be short-lived; when her pregnancy became evident the elegant salons would no longer be so enthusiastic to receive her. Despite what certain aesthetes may say, maternity is never graceful, especially for those who experience it.

Around this time, unknown to Giuseppina, Bartolomeo Merelli began to bargain with Lanari to get Giuseppina transferred, but no agreement was reached until the end of the year.

'I will thus take on Moriani, Strepponi and Ronconi Giorgio for Spring 1839 at La Scala, beginning on the second Sunday after Easter and ending around July 1st,' wrote Merelli to Lanari on 3 December 1838, 'performing five times a week and three or four operas . . .' One of the new operas that Merelli had in his programme was Verdi's *Oberto*, and he was thinking of Giuseppina and Moriani as the lead performers. In the meantime, difficulties arose with Lanari. Giuseppina did not dare to confess a second pregnancy so soon after the first, and she wanted to exploit all possibilities to earn money. She was aware of the deleterious effects of this pregnancy, which she was continuing to pass off as yet another illness. When she began to skip performances and to try to go back on her word, Lanari was stirred into an angry exchange of letters. But when her pregnancy was fully visible, Giuseppina, who had taken the lead role in *Norma*, *La straniera*, *La sonnambula*, in December sang again in *Lucia*. Lanari, back in Venice, was informed by his partners that Giuseppina had become a major star; in *The Promise* she aroused 'the fanaticism of the public'. He replied to her letter in which she finally confessed to her pregnancy – a secret she could not keep much longer. The impresario assured her that she could count on him, but in the meantime she should procure some medical certificates to justify her 'illness' and thus her absence from the Fenice in Venice in which Lanari had booked her. 'In November,' Lanari continued in his *Memoirs*, 'I am informed by Strepponi of a misfortune that has befallen her. The misfortune was that she was pregnant, and she besought charity, sympathy, pity, that I should not ruin her, as I could well have done. At Carnival Strepponi was to appear at the Alfieri Theatre in Florence. There she performed *La sonnambula* and *The Promise*. The latter opera aroused the public enthusiasm, the Theatre was always packed full, at the height of Carnival . . .'

After learning of the real nature of her illness, Romani, the conductor, started teaching the soprano Amalia Mattioli the part that the Generalina was supposed to sing in Venice. He also begged Cirelli – and here we see that Giuseppina's agent had a real power with the press – to persuade the musical journals to write up La Mattioli so that 'when la Fenice sees Amalia Mattioli' turn up instead of the diva Strepponi they were expecting, they would not complain too much. 'This morning Cirelli told me about Peppina's true condition,' continued Romani in a letter to Lanari, 'he told me that you had suggested he should confide in me and that I would find a way to get a legalised certificate, I will try to do so . . . I observed that Strepponi causes such a stir that any opera done without her would be rejected by the public . . . In Florence we cannot say that Strepponi is ill, the public knows that she is pregnant, they can see it, but they applaud and without her I am certain that it would be a real fiasco.'

Merelli had been told nothing of Giuseppina's pregnancy but fortunately the contract had not been signed as yet. 'When on 15 April you are not in good form, as I believe your "indisposition" will continue and will already have been announced at the Fenice and so everything will have been settled . . .'

According to Giuseppina's calculation, her baby was due in mid-March; she confided in Lanari's partner. 'Strepponi is an enchantment,' the latter wrote to the impresario. But she looked tired. 'I would let the board of directors in Venice know what Strepponi's illness consists of, but I would tell them only on the last day of Carnival.'

In mid-January 1839 Cirelli returned to Florence after a long absence; he had kept away from Giuseppina, being angry with her for bringing into the world this child of uncertain provenance. He found her extremely depressed. 'Having made the necessary calculations,' he informed Lanari in a letter which, as usual, was full of deceit, 'you can count on Peppina appearing on stage in Milan on 30 April.' They would arrive in Venice ten days earlier 'by which date I believe she will have made a full recovery.'

Letters went to and fro; despite all the borders they had to cross, they reached their destinations promptly. They could always prove useful to the police: singers were often used 'politically'. Since these letters were read by the censors (just as phone-calls today are tapped), certain people would be referred to only by their initials or nick-names as we can see by the use of 'M' or 'the Sergeant' referring to the probable father of the child Giuseppina was shortly to give birth to.

While Giuseppina was busy building a barrier of certificates to conceal the real cause of her absence from the Fenice stage, a rival singer was writing letters in which she accused her of not singing 'because she is pregnant', and asking to be engaged in her place. Merelli wrote: there were rumours that Strepponi was five months pregnant. 'If it were so, what would I do?' He should keep his calm, Lanari replied 'since it must be mere chatter, because I know nothing of this and I should know.' The contract with Merelli had been postponed anyway. Everything depended on the date of conception which no one, least of all Peppina, was sure about.

Cirelli realised that there were doubts about 'the mistakes she made in Rome after my departure', he wrote to Lanari on 26 January 1839. Maybe her calculations were wrong and he was the father of the expected baby. 'Indeed I flatter myself it is so. Enough, I have forgiven her! She was seduced by the treachery of another. May God forgive him . . . I flatter myself in saying that I am the father, that the Sergeant left nothing but ignoble filth. If you knew how he treats her now! She should have expected it . . .!' The Sergeant, he wrote, had behaved 'like a real murderer, abandoning the wretched woman to herself, refusing to see how much she had suffered, and the shame he had covered her in before the world, as if the poor victim had never existed, and after betraying her in spite of the most ardent promises.' The more Cirelli tried to convince Lanari that he himself was the father, the less he believed it. The impresario had seen or suspected nothing; he never poked his nose into other people's business, 'and I would be glad if it would be an error of calculation.' Of course it is most unlikely that Lanari would have been oblivious to what his superstar was doing during her triumphant season in Rome.

As she was short of money, Giuseppina tried to draw her February salary a month in advance: the pre-natal expenses were considerable and apart from everything else, she was unable to sing for at least one month. Strepponi gave birth and the theatre had to close because there was no time to replace her with another woman, since it was almost Carnival Thursday. Romani managed to procure the medical certificates which would save Lanari from having to pay the fines imposed by the Fenice for Giuseppina's absence. They were signed by doctors who were careful to make no mention of a pregnancy; furthermore Romani assured Lanari that 'dog doesn't eat dog, undertakers get on together'.

The baby was born on 9 February 1839, not mid-March as expected: she was either early or, as Cirelli hoped, she was his daughter, not the Sergeant's. 'Peppina has been happily delivered,' Cirelli wrote on that very same day, 'the error in calculation is so large that it puts my mind at rest. However, the rancour remains in my soul . . . Enough, I am not yet dead . . .' If he, Cirelli, had not been there to assist Giuseppina who knows what might have happened! 'Enough! God will give him his just deserts . . .' It was true: in the moment of need the only person who had come to her help was the elderly lover, whose protégée she continued to be. The baby was given the name of Sinforosa Cirelli. Thus, although with a certain reticence, the elderly agent-protector recognised her.

Before arriving in Venice, Cirelli wanted to be sure that Lanari would not make the exhausted Giuseppina sing for more than two consecutive evenings – in the past Peppina had performed *Norma* (*Norma!*) for five nights in a row. On 28 February, in Florence, after nursing her baby for almost three weeks, Giuseppina Strepponi left Sinforosa on the foundlings' turnstile at the Ospedale degli Innocenti. With detachment and, in effect, breaking the law, Giuseppina had discarded her baby. But every possible father had turned Sinforosa down, even Cirelli, who had helped her but would not produce any money for Sinforosa's survival. So many of Giuseppina's colleagues were doing exactly the same, abandoning these wretched babies, that she did not feel guilty. There were hundreds of institutes, kept by nuns, which specialized in giving shelter to foundlings – and a surprising number of those 'Innocents' resulted from the sins of the primadonnas, the stars of the nineteenth century. But those sins in effect were obstacles: a career for a woman was paved by swollen bellies and parental responsibilities. It was easy to condemn, but Giuseppina was alone, her old lover whom she betrayed, who was short of money and had already a little boy to care for, did not want to support another child whom – he rightly suspected – was not his own. Her decision was final: she could not go back on it, the law would punish her were she to be discovered as the mother who abandoned her offspring. But Giuseppina, who was cunning, allowed herself a possible way out by giving the baby a token with which somebody – herself maybe – could recognise Sinforosa later; something which was unmistakable, half of a coin, an object which belonged to the choreography of opera. She hung on the baby's neck a string with half a coin. The other half would fit perfectly. Lanari describes it thus: 'On Thursday 28 February at 11.45 p.m., after ringing the bell, the baby was left with a half-coin attached to a strip of ribbon and a piece of paper glued to it which declared the baby had been baptised. She was judged to have been born on the 26th of that month and was baptised *sub conditionem* with the above name of Sinforosa Cirelli.' It is unlikely that Giuseppina ever saw her again, although Sinforosa was to die in a mental hospital in 1925.

Immediately after the birth, Romani tried to get Giuseppina straight off to Venice and 'if Cirelli hadn't been there I would have made her go at once.' He also stated that: 'Cirelli really messed me up.' On 4 March, while Giuseppina was in Venice, the baby was given to a certain Vincenza Cecchi of Santa Maria della Serra to nurse. Seven days later, the child was 'returned' to the Ospedale degli Innocenti and on 12 March it was the turn of Monna Orsola Pasquini of the Santissima Trinità of Traversagna, in the province of Massa, to nurse her. On that very same day, oblivious to poor Sinforosa's destiny, Giuseppina started singing again, at la Fenice. *Il Figaro* commented: 'The primadonna Signora Strepponi, having recovered after a short rest in Florence from a slight indisposition, raced to Venice, where she performed in *The Illustrious Rivals*. Thus did she answer the calls of the Venetians . . .' She should have played the title role in *Lucia di Lammermoor* as well, but Ungher had taken it over.

Almost two years went by – and the reader must excuse this chronological leap – before Monna Orsola received the payment due to her not from Giuseppina but from Luisa Stefani and her husband, who acting on Giuseppina's instructions, declared the child to be their daughter. According to the records, 'They were her true and legitimate parents, living in the district of Santa Felicità' in Florence. They went to the Ospedale degli Innocenti, the one decorated by della Robbia, professing their regret at having abandoned the infant and their wish to take her home. To prove the truth of their affirmations, they brought with them a half-coin which matched the one the baby had been wearing when abandoned, saying they had baptised the child on 28 February 1839, giving her the name Giuseppa Faustina and that the baptism certificate was to be found in the church of San Giovanni. This reveals the astuteness and also the perseverance with which Giuseppina had covered her tracks as a mother. The only discrepancy was that the child had been registered at the Ospedale degli Innocenti with the surname of Cirelli and this is what gave away the true story behind Sinforosa-Giuseppa and destroyed Giuseppina's alibi.

Lanari lost out in terms of money:

Here it must be noted that Strepponi, apart from the days during which she remained inactive on account of her unavoidable confinement-period, was always paid. Meanwhile Strepponi's fame grew even greater, primadonna at the Fenice for Lent 1839. Primadonna assoluta at La Scala in the following spring, for which I ceded her to Merelli with a profit of 2,000 Austrian lire.

Finally Giuseppina had made it to Milan for the Carnival Season! She would be singing with Moriani and Ronconi, the great trio again! She was to appear with the greatest opera company of the day, in the most important opera theatre, in performances under the management of Merelli, an impresario who was less acute but more prestigious than Lanari. But after the birth of Sinforosa, her abandoned, forgotten child, her career began its downward path, the cruel depression that had tormented her occasionally in the past, was to return with increasing regularity. And her voice would never be the same again.

4

THE ENCOUNTER
OF HER LIFE

Giuseppe Verdi as a young man; he marries Barezzi's
daughter; he goes to Milan for *Oberto*, a Merelli
'production'. Giuseppina's début at La Scala; she meets
Verdi. Arguments with Lanari; the Austrian police
intervene. Serious depression. To Verona and then to
Rome for the impresario Jacovacci. Another 'happy event'.
Nabucco causes a furore.

È strano!
Saria per mia sventura un serio amore . . .?
How strange it is!
Would it be by any chance a real love . . .?

LA TRAVIATA, ACT I

While Giuseppina was enjoying a life of triumphs, of endless
social gatherings, of applause, travel and crowds, not so far
away from where she was born a young man was emerging in the
world of music. Born in Roncole di Busseto, a hamlet in the province
of Parma, on 10 October 1813, Giuseppe Verdi came from a poor
family, his sister was deranged and his parents aloof. But he was not
the boorish peasant's son of legend; on his mother's side there had
been a good deal of music. The Verdis had been landowners and
when he later acquired the estate of Sant'Agata, Verdi was buying
back land that in the past had been owned by his family.

He had started the hard way, first learning music from the local
priest and then studying in Busseto, an elegant town clustered
around the great castle of the Pallavicini. Handsome, enthusiastic
and sparkling with energy, he would walk from his home in Roncole
to Busseto which was a few miles away. His great musical talent
was recognized by one man, Antonio Barezzi, a local merchant in
whose house he went to live in 1831. He gave singing and piano

lessons to Barezzi's only daughter Margherita who was gentle and good-looking. The two young people fell in love and became engaged – but before attempting marriage, Verdi aspired to be properly educated. He received a grant from the Monte di Pietà in Busseto but he was not accepted by the Milan Conservatoire so he studied privately with Vincenzo Lavigna, helped financially by Barezzi and soon realized that he could not hope for success in the provincial backwaters where his talent was stifled by intrigue: Verdi was not much loved by his native townsfolk, his career was hampered in Busseto. In June 1834, when Busseto's Maestro di Cappella died, Verdi was refused the post which went instead to a mediocre local musician. 'I clearly see that I cannot be as useful as I would have liked to be to this unhappy town of mine.' In 1836 Verdi married the pretty and ambitious Margherita and, in the same year he composed the opera *Rocester* which he hoped to have staged in Parma and which was probably 'absorbed' later into *Oberto*. For their honeymoon the young Verdis went to Milan and then settled in Busseto where he worked for the local music school and the Philharmonic Orchestra.

In January 1838, Giuseppe Verdi was back in Milan on a 'business trip'; Margherita stayed behind as she was expecting her second baby: the first, Virginia, was less than a year old. While in Milan he went to La Scala and one evening pointed out Giuseppina to Marianna, his sister-in-law, stating that people talked about the soprano as the mother of a baby she had had with Merelli (a rare piece of gossip from his lips, and in any case incorrect: as we know, there were two children, but Merelli had nothing to do with either of them).

His first compositions for voice and piano, *Sei romanze*, were published by G. Canti of Milan and during this visit there was some talk about staging his opera *Oberto* but, in fact, he was a rather late starter in the struggle for the high ground of the operatic world.

Tall, with dark smooth hair on a high forehead and thoughtful eyes that gleamed with resentment, Verdi was extremely handsome. He was both shy and self-confident, with a touch of provincial awkwardness; he had travelled very little and had no languages, except perhaps some French which the educated classes of Parma all spoke. Back in Busseto the young couple's joy at having had a little boy turned into grief when, in August 1838, Virginia died. He left his job in Busseto and in February 1839, back in Milan, the Verdis settled in a small apartment near Sant'Ambrogio.

Once again I undertook the journey to Milan, taking with me the whole score all in perfect order, having gone to the trouble to extract all the singing parts, entirely by myself . . . In the end everything was arranged for spring 1839. In the event I was to be doubly fortunate, to have my work staged at La Scala for the benefit performances on behalf of the Pio Istituto and to have four truly extraordinary performers: Strepponi, the tenor Moriani, the baritone Giorgio Ronconi and the bass Marini.

He also published some new Romanze which were well received; on 22 April, Verdi wrote to his friend Giuseppe Demalde, living in Busseto: 'My score is still under wraps, but it is not dormant. In secret, I can tell you this; it should be performed at La Scala with Moriani, Ronconi, La Strepponi and La Kemble. I cannot guarantee it, but I can hope . . .' The singers were given the score and rehearsals began at La Scala.

But if things for Verdi were going well, for Merelli the season was not so good, everybody fell ill and Merelli complained to Lanari as one impresario to another: '*I Puritani* (*Puritans*) was performed again last Saturday, and more successfully on Moriani's part; however he did not sing the last part in the duet with Strepponi: the following Sunday Ronconi was ill . . . last night Strepponi was indisposed . . .' So the impresario had to forget all about the benefit performance. Reminiscing later on in life, about *Oberto* and those early years, Verdi recounted. 'After sharing out the parts and after just a few singing rehearsals, Moriani fell seriously ill . . . so everything was held up and there was no longer any chance of staging my opera!'

But for Giuseppina, her début at the opera house she had visited so often and which had always been her highest aspiration – was a great success. She was now twenty-four and at the height of her fame. She sang in *Lucia* and *I Puritani* but her real triumph was *L'elisir d'amore* (*The Elixir of Love*) for which she was recognised as a great actress and received offers from other impresarios; so she turned down Merelli's offer for 40,000 lire a year plus expenses for travel and lodging: she felt that both Merelli and Lanari were exploiting her and told Lanari she did not wish to be booked again in Milan.

But she had talked about Verdi's music with admiration. 'One evening on the stage of the theatre, the impresario Merelli had heard a conversation between Signora Strepponi and Giorgio Ronconi, in which the former spoke most favourably of the music of *Oberto*.' Merelli thought about it again: maybe the young composer's opera

was worth staging after all. Verdi was 'truly stuck' and was getting
ready to go back to Busseto when 'one morning a servant came to
me from La Scala and brusquely asked me: "Are you the Maestro
from Parma who was to give an opera for the Pio Istituto? Come
to the theatre as the impresario is asking for you . . ." And so I
went.' Merelli suggested a few 'adjustments' that could be made
to fit in with the libretto. 'I had to modify the music in some parts
for motives of tessitura and to write a new quartet. Merelli himself
suggested its dramatic position and I got Solera to compose verses
for it: this quartet turned out to be one of the best pieces of the opera!'
Solera was a celebrated librettist and a poet, famously lazy but able.
'Young, unknown, I happened to meet an impresario who dared to
stage a new work without asking any kind of underwriting . . . taking
the risk of covering all expenses out of his own funds, he offered to
divide with me half and half the money that he would get . . .' Verdi
was burdened with debts and had a young family with him; at that
time Giuseppina became a kind of lucky star for him.

In some versions it was she who spoke to the powerful impresario,
in others Merelli 'picked up' Giuseppina's comments about Verdi
and *Oberto*. Verdi's later account is not to be taken as absolutely
true. Giuseppe and Giuseppina met one another during preparations
for *Oberto*, she was the celebrated primadonna, much respected in
the operatic world thanks to her reputation but hampered by her
notoriety; he was the unknown composer whose score of *Rocester* had
impressed her in Rome and whom she recognized as a musician of
talent – as well as an immensely attractive man. Verdi appealed to
Giuseppina not only because he was sincere but also because he was
uncontaminated by the world of opera, as well as being cultivated
and direct. He shared Giuseppina's passion for English literature,
particularly Shakespeare seen through Romantic eyes. Surprisingly
enough for two Roman Catholics, they were both avid readers of the
Bible. Above all the primadonna and the unknown composer had a
great bond between them: that of music. They spoke and understood
the same language – a language that, to judge from people's letters,
was more familiar then than Italian grammar. It was thus natural
that a flame sparked between them. It is difficult to say with what
intensity because Verdi's biographers are uncertain on this point and
the two protagonists did all they could to confuse them.

As soon as the Verdi family had moved to a better apartment at
Contrada San Simeone, near the ancient church of Sant'Ambrogio,
tragedy struck for the second time; Verdi's son, Icilio, fell ill and

died of pneumonia on 22 October 1839 aged one year and two months. 'The poor little boy, languishing, died in the arms of his totally desperate mother.'

Margherita, whom Verdi called Ghita, did not attend the long awaited première of *Oberto* on 17 November 1839; desolate, she could not bear to dress up for the theatre and pretend to enjoy herself. But between one act and the next Verdi, who loved her, ran all the way from Piazza della Scala to Via San Simeone to hug her and to tell her that all had gone well, that the opera was a success – or almost.

All the performers originally designated had gone; amongst the replacements were the tenor Salvi who was to have an affair with Giuseppina, the bass Marini, and the English soprano Mary Shaw. As was then the custom, the composer of the opera sat in the orchestra. There were fourteen performances of *Oberto* and it was neither a success nor a fiasco but two foreign journals wrote about it in ecstatic terms. Merelli commissioned Verdi to write three further operas.

By then Giuseppina was far away from Milan, from Verdi's life, and if there had been a love-story between them, the composer had forgotten all about her. In any case, both Strepponi and Verdi each went to great lengths to construct fictitious versions of their lives omitting whatever struck them as inappropriate – whatever might have caused scandal in the prevailing nineteenth-century morality. Their individual accounts are often contradictory: at times this might be due simply to the erratic memory of old age, confusing dates and events, but more often it was the result of a conscious intention to change the truth. Had he been unfaithful during the build-up to *Oberto*, Giuseppe Verdi would have denied it later: how could he ever have confessed to an adventure with a celebrated singer, when he was living just a stone's throw away with a young and grief-stricken wife? So when did he and Giuseppina first get to know each other? In a letter that she wrote to Verdi on 3 January 1853, Giuseppina used the word '*conoscenza*' literally 'acquaintance'. 'I thank you for having thought of me in the first day of the new year and the eleventh of our acquaintance.' Unless she was mistaken, which is unlikely in the case of a woman so devoted to her man as Giuseppina, their acquaintance came about in 1842, the year of *Nabucco*. But acquaintance is perhaps not the same as first meeting; after all there can be no doubt that Giuseppina met Verdi in Milan in 1839, when they began the rehearsals of *Oberto*.

Conoscenza is thus used in the Biblical sense unless we think that

the couple was so determined to blot out their past that they wrote
lies to each other, in order that the prying eye of posterity would not
learn anything about them, which, I am afraid to say, is a possibility.
If we are to believe Giuseppina's letter, they were perhaps already
in love in 1839 although platonically; it was enough however to fill
Verdi with guilt. But they loved one another physically in 1842 with
Nabucco.

Although Giuseppina was at that time considerd a superstar,
she was aware that her vocal powers were beginning to fail. Her
health was not good, she was unhappy about her situation and she
suffered from attacks of depression. When she heard that the tenor
Adolfo Nourrit had committed suicide in May 1839, she wrote: 'In
adversities of fortune, there are only two roads to follow. End one's
life like Nourrit [who drowned himself], or with a bullet through
the brain, and never stoop to cowardice before anyone.' And yet
an important man like Solera, who had partly re-written *Oberto* and
was to be the future librettist of *Nabucco*, was singing her praises:

> The finest gifts of nature, which continual training has raised to
> the level of greatness; thus in both serious roles and comic ones,
> she made one forget many famous singers who had preceded
> her. Gifted with an extremely sensitive soul, she knows how to
> insinuate herself into the audience's ear with both her singing
> and her expression. Cultivated and lovable in society, an excellent
> daughter and sister, she has generously assumed the responsibility
> for the whole of her family, and her younger siblings are educated
> at her expense at the best schools. Milan is yearning to hear
> her again.

Temistocle Solera, the author of this description which appeared in
La Strenna teatrale europea, was a likeable man who had composed a
couple of operas himself. He came from Ferrara, was a little younger
than Verdi and had long horizontal moustaches and a pointed
D'Artagnan-style beard. He was an adventurer, womaniser and
spendthrift; he travelled in Egypt, Paris and Spain, plying his hand
at all sorts of different trades; he was a kind of nineteenth-century
Hemingway and had published a book of patriotic verses which had
been highly acclaimed. Solera was a patriot, a nationalist whose
father was locked up in the Austro-Hungarian prison of Spielberg.
It is thus no wonder that Solera's librettos were infused with a
scarcely veiled sense of patriotism. Solera who knew the Generalina

perhaps too well, continued informing the readers that she would be free from her contract with Lanari in 1841 when she was to return to the Milanese stage. Milan's eagerness to hear her again was only too understandable after her success in *I Puritani* and Donizetti's *Pia dei Tolomei*.

> Great in *Lucia* and more surprisingly, truly great in *Elisir d'amore*, it is only just and natural that she has left a deep and lasting impression on us. Who did not weep to hear her sobbing in these scores, and especially in *Lucia*, on the first evening of which (not to mention her later performances) she was called back on stage twenty-three times? And who did not bask in her laughter in that endearing divertissement by Romani and Donizetti, *Elisir d'amore*? Find if you can a more lively, more bizarre, more lovable Adina, a more moving Lucia; and deny if you can the rarity of singers who are able to adapt so well to both serious and playful roles.

This article makes it clear how versatile – and intelligent – a singer Giuseppina was, with a wide-ranging, limpid and exquisitely modulated voice. Once her engagements in Milan were over, Giuseppina went back to Lanari in spite of what she had said: Lanari was an excellent impresario to be associated with and she knew it. 'In summer Strepponi came back into service in my theatres, and more precisely at Senigallia; she started to complain of an indisposition which lasted until we reached Venice . . . as her Cirelli asserted, and so she began to say she needed a rest.' Thus in two cities she was replaced by an understudy who, by Lanari's account, cost a great deal of money. 'It was in Lucca that Strepponi truly felt her voice to be failing her and asked for two months' repose, which I could not grant her on account of my own obligations . . .' The impresario was forced to allow several days' leave, a disaster for his Season.

It was probably at this time that Giuseppina suffered the interruption of yet another pregnancy, whether a miscarriage or an abortion, we do not know, but the latter is more likely for she could not possibly face another confinement. If a biographer is allowed to be bold, and to think aloud – and this is precisely what I am doing in this matter – it would be tempting to think that this pregnancy was due to Verdi – and this would explain a lot of subsequent guilt which they both felt; but of course, neither would have left a trace, a hint of it. We cannot even be a hundred per cent sure that Giuseppina was pregnant. 'I thought of engaging a good primadonna to stand in for her when necessary, this was Bertolini whom I had already summoned to Verona, but Strepponi called on me and recommended Zamboni to serve as her understudy.' Although Bertolini was already on her way and Zamboni, according to Lanari, was not very good, Giuseppina managed to get her way, assuring him that by Carnival Season, she would have recovered. It was typical of the theatrical world that Peppina wanted to be replaced by an inferior singer thus ensuring that the audience would miss her.

And so she was off again on her travels with the Lanari company which included the same excellent singers as before, Moriani, Ronconi and others. They set off in great carriages, followed by the wardrobe. The costumes and scenery came after, under the management of Isabella, Lanari's sister and the wife of the librettist Francesco Guidi. The trunks contained the wigs and elaborate clothes – it was not unusual for the same costumes to be used in more than one opera as well as much of the scenery, which was grandiose, unlike today's meagre stage-sets. Sometimes the coaches arrived late so improvisation was called for. On this trip, Lanari's company performed at small but important opera houses in the provinces, but also in Florence, in Venice and Lucca. When Giuseppina was in Venice early in 1840, she sent Verdi her own portrait with a laconic and mysterious dedication. This is significant because it means that the young composer was in her thoughts; she would have never sent him a picture of herself if there had been no stronger bond between them than that of an off-stage acquaintanceship.

The arrival of an impresario of Lanari's calibre, with a company that was recognised as one of the best in the world, including a star like Strepponi, created a stir. Long before the arrival of the company, there would have been animated discussion of the anticipated season and the rehearsal-period would be followed by dinners, involving the entire city. People would 'steal' the new tunes, young ladies would try to obtain a score with a new aria so as to be able to play it in their own drawing-rooms.

Some of the company would be accommodated in hotels, uncomfortable local inns, while the stars would often be put up by the local gentry, who would throw open their houses for the occasion. Many gentlemen would aspire to sleep with the primadonnas. If a singer like Giuseppina had to stay for any length of time in one town, a small flat would be found for her; a maidservant who was part of

her retinue, would wait upon her and would look after her wardrobe
and wigs and also deliver love letters and flowers. Invitations would
arrive thick and fast.

During the run of the Seasons, successes were celebrated like
national victories. On the other hand fiascos could be almost fatal
as on the occasion when a bench hurled from the fifth tier just missed
an impresario and, less seriously, when a cod-head struck a wretched
tenor in mid-aria. Even Lanari could expect a public revolt were he
not to deliver the quality that his reputation had come to guarantee.
Cirelli, who had been working in Cremona, joined Giuseppina that
winter and – in Lanari's view – started making trouble by persuading
Giuseppina to turn down the compromise of singing four evenings a
week with the excuse of a new illness; which was announced in the
posters under the dubious name 'morbid lassitude'. Lanari could not
understand Giuseppina's behaviour. She missed performances, she
was devious, she was no longer a friend.

'Having two consecutive performances to do,' Giuseppina wrote
from Verona to the impresario on 2 February 1840, 'and not feeling
in the best of health, I notify you that I will not be able to attend
the rehearsal this morning. Signora Zamboni, the understudy, will
stand in for me as well as she can.' Cirelli had persuaded her, noted
Lanari: 'Strepponi was swayed by Cirelli, the father of one of her
illegitimate children, and she even refused to do four performances
a week although I asked it as a favour to settle the outstanding
obligations she had towards me.' Cirelli informed the manager of
the Verona Philharmonic Orchestra that Peppina would not be able
to keep her engagement. Lanari thus decided to sue her.

On 20 January five doctors, who had undoubtedly been bribed,
concluded that Giuseppina really was suffering from morbid lassitude and that 'as a consequence the Board must ask the Signor
Impresario to fulfil his obligations . . . by solicitously procuring
another primadonna capable of carrying out the performances that
Signora Strepponi will be unable to give.' Cirelli and Strepponi, who
were sharing the same room at a hotel in Verona, often argued.
Cirelli accused her of infidelity and sometimes beat her. Indeed,
at one stage, the hotelier's son found the couple engaged in fierce
argument. Strepponi threw herself at the young man's feet, begging
him not to leave the room, as if she was afraid of Cirelli's behaviour.
'This morning, by order of the Board, we visited the primadonna
singer Signora Strepponi,' wrote Dottor Giuseppe Dalla Vedova
in January 1841. He was the medical envoy for the Board of the

Verona Philharmonic. 'She showed the following symptoms: feeble, unsteady pulse, irritating cough, and she complained of pain under the sternum which extended to the shoulder-blades, a phenomenon which we believe related to the others, and which is the cause of what happened on the evening of the 12th.' Cirelli had clearly beaten her black and blue.

However, the impresario, on receiving the medical certificate, stated that he did not consider the doctors' diagnosis to be valid. Dismayed by the threat of legal action, Giuseppina wrote to Lanari: if she were to continue singing she would certainly forfeit both her voice and her health. 'No law, no authority can force me to continue in an exercise that destroys my health.' She proposed that they should proceed to reduce her salary on account of her absence. Lanari counter-attacked by saying that he expected Giuseppina to sing in Florence where she was booked unless they both were to come to some arrangement for which she was to take a four months' period of rest 'starting from Lent'. In any case he was to be indemnified for his financial losses. But at this point the 'Signor Commissario Superiore di polizia' turned up – with officially stamped papers and documents which 'drag Cirelli into the matter too . . . I suppose there must be some misunderstanding and so as to clear it up I beg you to call on me instantly . . .' Strepponi wrote to Lanari. Alessandro Lanari answered the very same day (14 February) stating that he would come and see her at once.

She replied with admirable sangfroid, since the cards were certainly not in her favour at that moment. 'If it is your desire to take the matter to the law-courts, do as you please, you will find me ready for anything . . . But if, putting an end to all unpleasant altercation, you should choose to agree to my wishes and those of Cirelli (both of us are sorry to see a twenty-year-old friendship destroyed), I assure you that I will come to some accommodation.' The impresario agreed: he too wished to conclude things without the police, the law-courts and legal fees. But on one point he was adamant: Giuseppina was to honour her contract and sing in Florence, 'the government of Tuscany demands it'. Appeals and entreaties were already pouring in from Florence where, on her last appearance, Strepponi had been a phenomenal success. The Marchese Torrigiani, manager of Teatro alla Pergola, was furious. Giuseppina was in her hotel room in Verona together with Cirelli. Maybe she was ill, maybe she was not, perhaps pregnant, or beaten up by her man but she threatened to leave, to disappear.

'I am convinced that Strepponi is trying to get round you more from caprice than real necessity,' wrote a certain Magotti to Lanari on 16 February. The singer was getting a very bad name for herself. The management of the Pergola was not to be trifled with; at this point Herr Schnitzler, the Police Commissioner in Vienna, was called in. The Austrian legation transmitted a Sovereign dispatch to the Venetian and Milanese government, forbidding them to issue a passport to Giuseppina Strepponi except for Florence. She was a prisoner; she had to go where she was contracted to perform. But apart from her weakened voice and her exhaustion, there was another reason why Giuseppina did not wish to go to Florence – an affair of the heart.

She had in fact made her peace with Raffaele Monti and wanted to join him rather than sing in Florence. There had definitely been a break-up between her and Cirelli on account of Monti who was the father of her second baby, the one who had been left behind in Florence as a foundling. That is why Cirelli was so jealous; to lose Giuseppina meant losing his principal source of livelihood. Boracchi, Cirelli's partner who was in Milan, wrote to Lanari: 'I flatter myself that by now the Strepponi business will have been settled and I would be interested to hear the result. Cirelli has not written, which makes me wonder whether there might not be trouble, her fiancé [sic] Monti may be the cause. I wish there were an end to all this and that our friend would return to his senses. Things done in the heat of the moment can be forgiven . . .' But on 8 March, Peppina and Cirelli were still furious at each other. On the other hand, they had reached a peace settlement with Lanari, and the Pergola granted her a rest period until 15 May.

Giuseppina from Florence, 12 March: 'If there is still a box free in a reasonable position for this evening I beg you to let me have the key,' she wrote to Lanari. 'You would be doing me a great favour . . .' The love affairs of Peppina were the talk of everybody. 'Yesterday I had a letter from Milan,' Moriani wrote to Lanari from Vienna:

where they tell me that Strepponi is in very poor health and she never leaves the side of that old scoundrel. I care little that she is together with a rogue, but I am most pained to hear that her health is not good. I would be grateful if you could tell me more, maybe by now she is in Florence, I won't ask you to give her my best wishes because they would not be accepted. If you have anything to say

on this subject you can put it on a loose sheet together with the
letter . . .

How many of these loose sheets by which gossip was passed on from
one city to another have been lost! It is unlikely that the 'rogue'
Moriani is referring to is Cirelli whom he had known forever, who
had always been by Giuseppina's side; he was referring to Raffaele
Monti, whom he disliked. In Florence Peppina was no longer the
toast of the salons and Prince Poniatowski, who snubbed her, stirred
up a quarrel between her and Carolina Ungher, a valuable colleague.
She felt abandoned.

Monti was not with her and her working relationship with Cirelli
was rekindled. Peppina sent him to Lanari because she wanted to
return to Milan in order to follow a treatment prescribed by Doctor
Moro, the medical officer at La Scala. It is quite possible that
this new indisposition, which had caused her to miss a number of
performances, was due to yet another pregnancy – not a miscarriage.
According to Verdi's latest biographer, Mary Jane Phillips-Matz,
a baby girl, registered as still-born in the parish of Santa Maria
della Passione on 22 March 1840, might have been Giuseppina's
third child. Having recovered, Peppina was able to return to the
stage and meet her obligations towards Lanari: 'I am glad that
the war between you and Peppina is at an end, and with honour
on both sides,' Moriani wrote to the impresario. The tenor was
in Milan. '. . . she has talent and knows how to get ahead, and
would be even more acclaimed and adored if that disgusting lame
Devil did not impede her career with his bad advice, and did not
make her so despicable in the eyes of society.' The lame man was
Boracchi, Cirelli's partner.

Giuseppina went back to Rome for the Carnival Season where
she had had such a success but this time without Cirelli. She could
not have had a better reason for going to Rome, for Donizetti,
the composer of the day, had written a new opera. But she
immediately fell ill with measles. And the rehearsals for *Adelia*
carefully co-ordinated by Donizetti himself, had to be postponed
as a result. Peppina was getting a reputation for unreliability but
the public still wanted her.

When she met the Maestro at the end of 1840, Giuseppina had
already performed as primadonna in thirteen of his operas. We have
no evidence of their meeting before this date although Donizetti knew
her father Feliciano. In 1838 he wrote from Naples saying that he

knew 'nothing about Strepponi' and talking about her father's opera
Gli Illinesi. But now their friendship became so intimate that the
composer dedicated his new opera *Adelia* to her. Gatti, the biographer
who was acquainted personally with both Giuseppina and Giuseppe
Verdi, wrote of a love affair between the soprano and the composer
of *Lucia*. Donizetti anyway rarely missed a chance with a woman
and besides a female singer would hardly have lost the opportunity
to 'try it on' with him; to be the lover, even if only occasionally, of
the greatest Italian composer of the day was a major opportunity
for a singer – especially one who had performed his works to great
acclaim. The dedication of *Adelia* to Strepponi was in fact a very
special mark of favour. This also helps us to understand why Verdi,
to whom Donizetti had always been extremely generous, later bore
him such a grudge. There was undoubtedly a bond between the
primadonna and the successful composer, who died of syphilis
seven years later. Even if, as is medically possible, Giuseppina was
not infected, her body suffered. There are grounds for suspecting
that Giuseppina's brief encounter with Donizetti caused her physical
harm: by the age of twenty-eight the singer was sterile. Not only did
she have no children with Giuseppe Verdi, but she knew she could
no longer have them when she begged him not to father any others
with different women.

The first night of *Adelia* was a disaster, partly because the
impresario Vincenzo Jacovacci had sold more tickets than there
were places. Terrible fights broke out outside the theatre; Jacovacci
was arrested and fined. It was probably not the impresario's fault:
the *bollettinaro*, the man in the ticket office and the ushers let anyone
in who gave them a decent bribe, and the première of a Donizetti
opera with the primadonna of the moment was a great event in a
torpid city like Papal Rome. This hitch did not lead to any friction
between the impresario and the primadonna. Giuseppina, in fact,
acted as godmother to one of his children.

The Roman season had not been a great success; she was depressed
and tired. When she arrived in Florence where she had been engaged
to sing *I Puritani* and Federico Ricci's *Michelangelo e Rolla*, Giuseppina
realised she was pregnant again. The father, she said, was a married
man with children. It seems unlikely that Count Filippo Camerata
dei Passionei, a friend of Lanari's, was the father, although she tried
to pin the baby to him. Peppina herself probably did not know who
the father was. Strepponi had met 'Count C.', to whom she refers in
a letter, during the fair of Senigallia back in July 1839. She stayed

at the Cameratas' palazzo while Lanari used an apartment and an office that belonged to the count. There are a couple of writers who think this baby might have been Donizetti's, but it is most unlikely, since the composer was already ill with syphilis.

Around mid-July 1841, Giuseppina's pregnancy was visible to everyone. In a confidential tone Merelli wrote to Lanari advising him not to use La Peppina at La Scala but to propose her as a mere understudy. But Lanari was fond of her, besides he had her under contract; therefore he confirmed her engagement for the Carnival Season in Milan between December 1841 and spring 1842.

When she returned to Milan from Florence, Giuseppina did not seek Giuseppe Verdi who was ill and busy composing the first of the three operas he had promised Merelli 'at eight-month intervals'; the one he was writing was a comic one. While he was at work, his two children already dead, his pretty wife Margherita fell ill. 'At the beginning of June my young companion is struck down by encephalitis and on 19 June 1840 a third coffin leaves my house! I was alone! Alone!' he recounted.

Three months after this tragedy, the comic opera *Un giorno di regno* (*King for a Day*), proved a complete fiasco. According to the journal *La Moda*, the singers, who hardly bothered to sing, got confused amidst the storm of catcalls. Thus, after the tragedy of losing his entire family, the composer now saw his hopes for his musical career fade in just one day. Later Verdi was to express his anger to Ricordi:

This same public ill-treated the opera of a sick young man, pressed by time, his heart broken by a terrible tragedy! These facts were well-known, but they proved no check to their discourtesy. I have not seen *King for a Day* since that day, and it may well be a poor opera, but countless others no better have been tolerated or even applauded. Oh, if only the public had I will not say applauded – but borne the opera in silence, I would not have found words adequate to thank them! I do not intend to blame them, I admit their severity, I accept their scorn, on condition that no-one asks me to be grateful for their applause. We poor gypsies, charlatans, whatever you will, we are obliged to sell our labours, our thoughts, our ravings, for gold. For three lire the public buys the rights to boo us or applaud us. Our destiny is to resign ourselves; that is all!

It sounds like the voice of Rigoletto himself . . .

Giovanni Ricordi, the recipient of this letter, was by then the head of the largest music publisher in Europe, with shops in Milan, Florence and London. He had started out as a first violinist, a music copyist and had learnt a lot of his trade in Leipzig, the city with the great musical tradition. Giovanni Ricordi was the first of a long line who were to befriend Verdi, from Tito, Giovanni's son, to Giulio his grandson, to the great-grandson Titino.

The disastrous reception of *King for a Day* was no defeat for Merelli who did not cancel Verdi's contract for three operas to be written at eight-month intervals: he had known even worse. Quite possibly the public had wished to demonstrate its disapproval of the impresario, suspected of Austrian sympathies, rather than the composer. There were always factions in the theatre, people hissed and catcalled for all sorts of reasons. Anyway for an impresario – or a singer – it was impossible to keep a foot in both camps, and the theatres tended to be under the influence of the 'establishment' of the time who had the power to distribute subsidies and honours. The Austrians were finding it harder to stifle the Italians' longing for independence: their presence had turned into a military occupation. Milan had lost its gaiety, 'nobody dared to breathe a word about politics'. Ghislanzoni, a future Verdi librettist and a good poet, noted that the Milanese were unable to read any news because none was printed, but the talk was of riots and bombs. 'There was a club of noblemen and a club of tradesmen. Aristocracy and trade regarded each other sullenly . . . the fashion for moustaches and full beards came up against pertinacious and obstinate opposition.'

Peppina, who was in a state of advanced pregnancy, found Milan intolerable. Her days of triumph seemed far behind her. From Bergamo, where she had fled, she wrote to Lanari in almost desperate tones (20 August 1841), 'I thank you, my dear Lanari, for not leaving me without news of yourself. You know that when one's fortunes are low, as mine are, it is nice to see that one has not been abandoned by everybody . . .' She wanted to go and work abroad, while Lanari had urged her to remain in '*la bella Italia*'.

'You are right to say *bella Italia*, but for me the idea of little work and good pay – you can see that it is an enticing one . . . and anyway I need, if possible, I need to get away from places that have painful associations. I have been treated too cruelly, under the excuse of love, and am wretched from the injuries that have been done to me in the past!' Then she went on discussing the father of the baby she was expecting. Could she be referring to Count Camerata? To Raffaele Monti? Probably neither. 'Enough, I do not wish him ill, because he has a family, and I am not so wicked as to desire his ruin, as he has wrought mine. Enough, let us not talk of melancholy topics, in a year's time I shall be calmer, because I shall perhaps be numbered among those who are no more.'

She was about to go to Trieste and Genoa, but she feared that the impresarios there might not grant her any rest-periods, 'the friend who offers his services and not merely in words is, as ever, that good man Cirelli.' So Cirelli was back in Lanari's and Giuseppina's lives; in the latter case now as a mere friend, agent and . . . nurse. He was getting old, and was often sick himself. Talking about the Count Camerata, she continued: 'The C. C. assiduously writes the kindest of letters but despite my condition and my poor health he does nothing to spare me from singing right to the very last moment, whereas in Trieste he could have relieved me of at least a part of my labours by arranging some form of assistance. Or, failing that, if only he had written to me a line that might have allowed me to hope for proof of real friendship, in my hour of need.' The Count, it would seem, had not sent her a single lira or svanzica, and was offering her no support whatsoever; but the fact that he remained in touch with Giuseppina suggests that he believed the baby she was bearing was his.

When, in the same letter, she refers to a soprano, she reveals the intrigues of the operatic world:

I understand what Ronzi writes to you. Her second fiasco in Venice is not enough for her; she wants to continue and make a target of herself in Udine and now in Brescia whereas she could easily have kept her reputation untarnished, with just one daughter to think of and a comfortable fortune. She could have accepted Palermo for a good wage, and instead she chooses to come to Genoa . . . The woman reminds me of those birds that scavenge around corpses. She went to Vicenza when poor Boccabadati had two children at death's door, and what she did to her when she arrived was truly infamous!! She came to Rome, since my health demanded that I should curtail my activity! And I now find it infamous that she should try to cause alarm and to harm a poor mother such as I. While nobody seeks her on the basis of mere gossip, she offers her services at any price! Such behaviour means she is either stupid or wicked!

Giuseppina, alluding to La Scala, said that she hoped that everything was well in Milan; she was hoping to go back and sing for Merelli now that her voice – due to a certain powder prescribed by a doctor and to good rest – had improved.

In September 1841 she was in Trieste, together with the tenor Salvi, who clearly did not find Peppina any less attractive because of her advanced state of pregnancy. She was rehearsing in the theatre under the direction of Fabio Campana, the composer of the opera *Giulio d'Este*, when she heard that, in a state of fury, Count Camerata was on his way from Ancona bound for the Teatro Grande. According to the account given by the *Osservatore triestino*, his arrival was anything but noble. The elderly count had received an anonymous letter hinting at cuckoldry and had set off at once. He now burst into Peppina's dressing-room, creating a terrible scene. Salvi, the Count's rival, was proving a huge success in *Giulio d'Este*, whereas Peppina 'temporarily impeded', as a newspaper delicately put it, did not shine – nor indeed, did the composer. The reviewer declared that Peppina's voice left much to be desired. It was hardly to be wondered! Seven months pregnant and singing the leading role!

On 4 November Peppina gave birth to another girl and the very next day the child was given the names Adelina Rosa Maria Theresia Carolina by the priest Hieronimus Degrassi. The baby was declared the illegitimate daughter of Josepha Strepponi and entrusted to a couple by the name of Vianello, who lived at 58 Porta Vecchia. Like her previous offspring this poor child was abandoned by Giuseppina, but not before she had found people willing to take it in. This meant that more people would have to be paid with her dwindling resources. With so many performances having to be cancelled, she was finding it hard to help her mother and support her children. Her financial situation was worrying, despite her contract with La Scala. Giuseppina felt abandoned by everyone. This child, who was to be known as Adelina and who had almost disappeared from the records, died of dysentery on 4 October 1842 and was given a pauper's funeral while Giuseppina was busy elsewhere.

Giuseppina was nursing her sorrows, Verdi had been ill. He returned to Busseto swearing that he would have nothing to do with opera ever again. But then Milan proved too big a magnet and he had found a flat in Via dei Servi. According to a friend, he had started to 'hang around La Scala' again and to see people.

One evening as I left the Galleria De Cristoforis I bumped into Merelli who was on his way to the theatre. It was snowing heavily and he took me by the arm and invited me to go along with him to his dressing-room at La Scala. On the way we chatted and he talked to me about the trouble he was having with the new opera: Nicolai [the composer] had been commissioned, but he wasn't happy with the libretto.

'Just think,' said Merelli, 'a libretto by Solera, stupendous! magnificent! extraordinary! Grandiose, striking, dramatic effects: beautiful poetry! But that stubborn composer just won't listen and declares that the libretto is impossible! I have no idea how I can get another one at such short notice!'

'I can help you out,' I stated. 'You gave me the libretto of *Il proscritto (The Banished)*, didn't you? I haven't written a note; I'll let you have it back.'

'Oh, splendid, that's a real stroke of luck.'

As he said so, we reached the theatre. Merelli called Bassi, the poet, stage-manager, librarian, etc, and sent him straightaway to look in the archives for a copy of *Il proscritto*. He found one. But at the same time Merelli picked up another manuscript and showed it to me, exclaiming: 'Look, here's Solera's work! Such a beautiful subject, fancy refusing it like that! . . . Take it . . . Read it . . .'

'What on earth for? . . . No, I've no desire to read librettos.'

In Verdi's account the libretto, written on large sheets, was so heavy to carry that, when he arrived home, he angrily threw it on the table and the pages accidentally opened at the line: '*Va pensiero sull'ali dorate*' ('Fly my thoughts, on golden wings') the most famous line of the future opera. 'I read these lines and was singularly moved, all the more so because they were almost a paraphrase of the Bible, which I always enjoyed reading.' He read the whole libretto without being able to sleep. However, remaining firm in his intention, he took it back to Merelli, stating that it was very beautiful but that he had decided never to write music again.

'Set it to music! Set it to music!'

And so saying he took the libretto and thrust it into my coat-pocket, seized me by the shoulders and not only pushed me out of his dressing-room but locked the door in my face.

What was I to do?

I went back home with *Nabucco* in my pocket: one day one line, the next day another, here a note, and there a phrase . . . little by little, the opera was composed.

In the story of the opera, the two warring peoples, the Babylonians and the Jews, speak in the language of the chorus: an ancient tradition of the Po valley and the region around Parma, where people sing together in inns and churches while drinking or praying; but it is a custom that gives little opportunity for soloists to shine. In the dramatic clash between the two peoples, with their patriotic and choral uproar, it is easy to lose sight of the more individual themes: the drama of the Babylonese Fenena's love for the Jew Ismaele, which is opposed by the slave Abigaille, and the madness of Nabucodonosor. The lament of the Jewish prisoners was interpreted as that of an oppressed people. The year was 1842, six years before the uprising of 1848, but the opera had a revolutionary force nonetheless; a dynamic vigour that was not to be found in the operas of Bellini, Spontini or Donizetti, and which was just what the pre-Risorgimento Italy had been waiting to hear. This opera, which was to prove so important to both Verdi and Giuseppina, was completed in the autumn; the composer, sensing the effect it would have on his fortunes, took meticulous care over it.

Giuseppina was in Genoa; she was having difficulty with a Russian tenor, a certain Ivanoff who inserted pieces and refused to sing others in Mercadante's *The Promise*. Only Verdi – and later Wagner, of course – was to take a stand against the liberties that these singers took, finally dethroning them. 'The rehearsals began and this Ivanoff insisted: "I'll cut this, I'll omit that, I won't sing that!" so that instead of the first act, we ended up with a monster.' She received five curtain calls for an aria from *Saffo*, she told Lanari. She added, 'You're probably in business with God knows how many lovers!!! Lucky you, since I'm stony broke – but I'm better off like that than having Mo...s around' [a reference to characters like Monti] 'I could do with a nice present of money from somebody ... Damn! Damn!'

Verdi, in Milan, went back to Merelli and told him, with a confidence that we can only admire, that *Nabucco* should be staged during the Carnival Season of 1842. Impossible, the impresario replied. *Nabucco* would be staged, but the repertory for that season had already been settled with new operas by established composers. 'To stage a fourth opera by an author who is almost a beginner would be risky for everyone but especially for me.'

Merelli was probably thinking of the fiasco of *King for a Day*, but he had been sharp enough to sense the popular spirit and explosive force of Solera's libretto. He advised waiting until spring. Giuseppe

Verdi, who had been transformed by those months of mourning, refused: 'Either Carnival . . . or nothing . . . and I had my good reasons, since it was not possible to find two artists so well suited to my opera as Strepponi and Ronconi, whom I knew were under contract, and on whom I was relying.'

This declaration is hard to take seriously: at that time, Giuseppina's voice had failed her badly; the part of Abigaille, the protagonist of *Nabucco*, had certainly been written with her voice in mind, but when she had been at the height of her powers. In fact Merelli had even tried to prevent Strepponi from singing in *Nabucco*. 'So I sang,' she wrote to Lanari after the performances of *Nabucco*.

> Indeed, I forced myself to go on to the end of the performances . . . My health has failed completely – I earn nothing. What little money I had, has all gone on doctors, medicines, and food for myself . . . I am truly sorry not to go to Vienna where apart from my fee, I had a half evening and little work to do. I would not have been so foolish as to stay here in Milan and consume my resources if my health had not demanded it. One must bow to destiny – with the difference that you are a gentleman and I am a poor Devil.

She was lying, had she gone to Vienna, she would have been unable to do the first performance of Verdi's new opera.

She had been invited by the Superintendent of the Imperial Theatres, Donizetti, who proved faithful to her in times of trouble. The offer was an extremely advantageous one, but she had decided to stake everything on Verdi and maybe the Austrian authorities had put a veto on her, as well: 'So are they now convinced that Strepponi is not coming?' Donizetti wrote on March 20th, 1842, 'if they want Löwe, she is in Turin, if they don't want her, so much the worse for them.' In the account given in 1879, somewhat clouded by the passage of time, Verdi continues: 'Merelli, although willing to meet my wishes, was not entirely wrong from an impresario's point of view: four new operas in one single season was a great risk . . . So, what with all the yays and nayes, the hitches, the half promises, the Scala bills were posted. But *Nabucco* was not announced!'

More furious than humiliated, Verdi wrote an angry letter; the impresario, a man of greater worth than posterity and Verdi himself have ever allowed, replied to it consenting: *Nabucco* would be staged at La Scala in the Carnival Season. But as there was no money they would have to make do with the scenery and costumes that had been used the previous year in a ballet with the same title and a similar subject. 'I agreed to everything since my greatest concern was that the opera should be staged. A new programme bill was printed on which I read at last: NABUCCO!'

While fog swathed the city, the rehearsals got under way and the opera world began to chatter, exchanging gossip and rumours in the porticoes in front of the Filodrammatici, between the music shops of Lucca and Ricordi, between one club and another.

'Twelve days after the first piano rehearsals the opening performance was held on 9 March with Signore Strepponi and Bellinzaghi, and Signori Ronconi, Miraglia and Dérivis in the cast. With this opera it can truly be said that my artistic career began.' Giuseppina, with whom Verdi had rehearsed in all the run-throughs on the piano and then with full orchestra, could hardly recognise the new Verdi as the hopeful composer of *Oberto* whom she had known in the previous year. After all those tragedies, he appeared to be frigid, deeply mistrustful of men and God, he had turned into a man of stone. 'Maestro, I wish I were in your place this evening,' the cellist Vincenzo Merighi said to him on the opening night; it was customary for the composer to sit between the cello and the harpsichord.

It was a triumph, as everybody had anticipated. The first eight performances were followed by a further fifty-seven between August and September! A record for La Scala. Of the other three operas written for that Carnival Season, not even Donizetti's *Maria Padilla* could hold a candle to the wave of enthusiasm aroused by *Nabucco*: Verdi had touched an emotional chord which, shrewdly, he was to set vibrating on other occasions: the political chord, the popular chord.

A new emotion, a new utopia, was blossoming in the hearts of the Milanese. Over the centuries, the sense of the nation had been slowly growing; suddenly nationalism became an over-riding force. Diderot had defined the nation, identifying it with the soil, the language and the blood. Historical research was thus called for in order to find common roots. This need was felt with particular acuteness in the case of the Italian people, oppressed by foreign domination. The Middle Ages was the period generally favoured in a nation's search for its roots and this has a great bearing on opera. For the Germans the Middle Ages were the period in which the superiority of the northerners over the peoples of the Mediterranean had been demonstrated once and for all; and it was also in the Middle

Ages that the French and the English had laid the foundations of their nations. The Italians looked to the marine republics and the struggles of the Communes, seeing them as examples of freedom and resistance against their historical enemies, the German peoples. Thus interest grew in the purity of the language. Indeed the first books of Italian grammar were published, painters took inspiration from the past and poems and novels on historic subjects abounded. What was later known as the second Romantic generation – to which both Verdi and Giuseppina belonged – made history into a political weapon, identifying it with a new concept; that of the fatherland, '*la patria*'. For the Romantics, that is to say the middle classes and the intellectuals, the idea of giving one's blood for the fatherland became a kind of cult. It was a new religion, one that is now dead and almost incomprehensible except in the more backward countries, which are now awakening to the concept of nationhood. As a result *Nabucco*, with all its historical quotations and all its suggestions, was written at precisely the right moment. The *Gazzetta privilegiata* of Milan, describing the evening, wrote that 'with the death of Abigaille the drama ends but there was no end to the applause, which for the leading performers and for Maestro Verdi in particular, was triumphantly prolonged.'

But for poor Giuseppina the score was too demanding and, in the autumn performances, her role was taken over by that same Teresa di Giuli Borsi whom she had described in a letter as a bird of prey scavenging amongst corpses – Giuseppina would have loved to continue, but not even Verdi – 'her' Verdi – wanted La Peppina. In a letter to Antonio Vaselli, his brother-in-law, Donizetti complained about Giuseppina's voice; she had sung in his *Belisario* just a few days before *Nabucco*.

Do me the favour of jesting with Tommaso [the impresario] about the three Italian singers that he boasts of in his theatre but do so and write to me at once. La Ronzi, goodbye; La Marini, I've heard her and that is enough . . . there is only Strepponi left. Tell him that this singer caused such a stir in *Belisario* that she is the only one who never received any applause, that her Verdi did not want her in his opera and the impresa forced him to take her. She was supposed to go to Vienna but there the government decided that they did not want her . . .

The fact that even Donizetti, whose music Peppina had performed so superbly, no longer had a good word for her, proves that her voice must have been past it. Maybe he felt the slightest pinch of jealousy – but not for Verdi the man. It was Verdi the musician whom he admired and perhaps envied. Indeed, although he had been invited by Rossini to conduct his *Stabat mater* in Bologna, he delayed his departure in order to see *Nabucco*. In the carriage that took him together with Count Pompeo Belgiojoso, an excellent bass, Donizetti continued to repeat: 'It's beautiful! It's so beautiful.' Such was the success of *Nabucco* that Merelli, on the evening of the third performance, called Verdi to his office and informed him of his intention to commission the coveted opening opera for the next season from him. He was to dictate his own conditions. The clause which would have stated the amount he would be paid, was left blank.

Despite what he wrote afterwards, there can be no doubt that before *Nabucco*, Verdi must have spent much of the time tramping from one agent's or impresario's office to another; he had been rescued from this labyrinth by a primadonna who had La Scala in her very blood. In urgent need of crucial and delicate advice, Verdi now turned to his Ariadne-saviour. 'Verdi was very embarrassed and did not know what to do. Having entered Strepponi's box, he informed her of what Merelli had said and asked for her advice.' After such a colossal success she told him he could ask for the same sum that Bellini had received for *Norma*, eight thousand Austrian lire.

It was an enormous sum. *Norma* had been the highest paid work in operatic history, the opera that had brought out the superiority of the composer over the singers. No composer had ever received such a huge sum before. For a young composer, practically a novice, to ask for as much as Bellini, the great Maestro who had died at the height of his creative powers, was an act of supreme daring. Nonetheless, Merelli agreed.

It was as much Giuseppina's victory as Giuseppe Verdi's. The bold advice she had given him – and the fact that the shrewd impresario had agreed – was to bind them together forever.

5

FAREWELL TO THE STAGE

Verdi's patriotic vein continues with *I Lombardi alla prima crociata* (*The Lombards at the First Crusade*). Peppina treated in Parma by Verdi's doctor; in 1843 she performs at Il Ducale in *Nabucco*. An infernal season in Palermo while Verdi is unfaithful to her and falls sick. Italy in ferment, the atmosphere tense. Farewell to the stage.

———————————•———————————

Addio del passato bei sogni ridenti . . .
Farewell, happy dreams of by-gone days . . .

LA TRAVIATA, ACT III

Nabucco stirred the masses with its patriotic message and Giuseppina was reflected a little in its glory. In *Nabucco*, it was Giuseppina's acting powers that saved her, not her vocal ability. Already her beauty was beginning to fade and she was only twenty-seven years old. In the portrait of her at La Scala, with the score of *Nabucco* on her lap, Giuseppina appears sickly and haggard. It is clear that the anonymous and mediocre painter identified her with *Nabucco*, not because she had made the opera a success, but rather because she had paved the way for the opera and its composer. In this awkwardly painted canvas, Giuseppina is wearing an elegant dress; her hair is crowned with camellias, pointed, stiff and prophetic. They look forward to *La Dame aux Camélias*, the future *La traviata*.

The public was rapidly forgetting her. Politics were now uppermost in people's minds; there was a seething anger and a general longing for action. To Giuseppina, however, liberalism and democracy – synonymous with revolutions – were concepts that meant almost nothing. She never gave any thought to the fact that her father had been inspired by the revolutionary spirit of Napoleon. Feliciano's death was already remote, as was Napoleon himself, and in any case women paid little attention to politics, apart from a few eccentric aristocrats like Cristina Belgiojoso. The Princess Belgiojoso dressed up as a bandit, took lovers (she had even had a dead one mummified and kept him in the house for years) and insulted the Austrians as fearlessly from her salon in Milan as from the one she maintained in Paris. By comparison with Cristina, Giuseppina's contempt for the Austrians was mainly cultural.

Verdi, on the other hand, understood the tremors that were beginning to stir the idleness of the Milanese salons and realised that the nationalistic and patriotic message should be the central focus of his next opera; he was not going to fall back on the usual romantic stories set amidst Swiss or Scottish lakes.

As Verdi made his way along Via dei Filodrammatici and turned into Via Andegari, where he had taken up residence next to La Scala, people would turn and stare at him. Little attention was now paid to Giuseppina, as she passed by in a carriage, with her fluttering veils and camellias pinned to her coat-collar. The young composer owed a great deal to Giuseppina – and knew it – but quite suddenly Verdi was the man of the moment. Even in his clothes, the pale, thin man from Busseto had become a leader of revolutionary fashion, imitated by respectable Milanese society. Men began to grow Verdi style beards, barbers gave Verdi haircuts rather than English ones. There were stews, sauces and even *arrostini* 'alla Verdi'. And yet he remained so gauche: Giuseppina was to remember how awkwardly he moved amongst people, how shyly he entered her house. The Milanese salons fought over him, while Giuseppina, who had once been a welcome ornament of Casa Belgiojoso, began to be ignored. The impresarios no longer competed for her signature on a contract, there were other primadonnas, such as the beautiful Frezzolini, and the famous Tadolini – not to mention Sofia Löwe.

We do not know how Clara Maffei's salon managed to ensnare Giuseppe Verdi. There is no doubt that those sitting-rooms, still in the Directoire style, with chairs in ochre silk and stiff divans, portraits by Hayez in the dark velvet room, and engravings by Canaletto in the adjoining hall, offered the composer ideal social opportunities, given the intellectual and patriotic climate that reigned there. The salon was frequented by such people as the publisher and patriot Giulio Carcano, the librettist Felice Romani, Liszt and, in an earlier period, by Vincenzo Bellini. Later, it hosted the future prime minister Massimo D'Azeglio (who was Manzoni's son-in-law), the writers Ippolito Nievo, Giovanni Verga, Aleardo Aleardi, Camillo Boito (a writer and also the architect who was to design Verdi's *Casa di*

Riposo for old musicians in Milan) and the composer Arrigo Boito, the most celebrated of Verdi's future librettists.

Clara Maffei, with an oval face and of gaunt appearance, was Count Spinelli's daughter. Her husband, Andrea, a man with thick moustaches and a white beard, was suspected of spying for Radetsky, the Austrian General, Governor of Milan. It is more likely however that, as a hardened gambler, Maffei was easily blackmailed. Nonetheless the salon of Countess Maffei was much visited by Mazzini supporters, in particular by a robust young man named Carlo Tenca who wrote for the so-called musical journals.

'I was introduced to her in the early months of 1842. We remained on good terms for the rest of her life.' Verdi's account of his first visit to Casa Maffei and his friendship with Clara is succinct in the extreme. Countess Maffei – the title was her father's, not her husband's, so strictly speaking she had no right to use it – kept open house from the early afternoon onwards. While the discussion raged around her and some men even played cards, she would do her crochet-work and listen to all that was said. It was in Casa Maffei that Verdi met his friends and future collaborators, as well as patriots like Tommaso Grossi who, after *Nabucco*, saw the young Maestro as their spokesman, the true protagonist of Italian unity. Other visitors to the salon were Count Opprandino Arrivabene, who wrote about music along with Francesco Regli, a critic and impresario, as well as Francesco Hayez, the portrait-painter of the Lombard romantic school. These men would also meet in the clubs or the famous Caffè Cova and Martini. Usually Verdi would arrive at Casa Maffei at around seven in the evening, after finishing his work, and before going to the theatre. Carlo Tenca, who courted the Countess, described the group of close friends, how they discussed the events of the day, their quarrels over cards and their political arguments. But Andrea Maffei was too busy gambling his wife's money away and, as we have seen, being jealous of Balzac, to realise that Clara was courted not only by Verdi but also by Carlo Tenca, both of them fascinating revolutionaries. Or maybe he simply pretended not to notice because he hoped to turn his elaborate verses into a libretto for the composer to set to music. This did in fact come about eventually, after Andrea and Clara's legal separation, perhaps because Verdi felt sorry for him.

Verdi was preparing a second opera with Temistocle Solera and using the same formula that had already brought him success. The libretto, from a poem by Tommaso Grossi, described the deeds of the Lombards on the first Crusade. But the allusion was to a very different and modern crusade. It was an explosive story, written at the time when Mazzini, from his London exile, was inspiring isolated rebellions which often ended tragically with the execution of romantic young revolutionaries. As Folchetto wrote:

> *I Lombardi* was a roaring success. The common people began to besiege the gallery from three onwards, bringing food with them so that the curtain rose admidst a strong smell of garlic sausages . . .! The public wanted an encore of the quintet, but the police did not allow it. The famous chorus *Oh Signor che dal tetto natio* . . . [Oh Lord, who from our native dwelling . . .] gave rise to one of the first political demonstrations that marked the re-awakening of nationalism in Lombardy-Veneto.

In the quintet, the Lombards were shown on stage, standing in front of the Church of Sant'Ambrogio, Milan's patron saint, about to set off on their journey to free the holy places. As they stood there in front of the stage-replica of the well-loved church, the Lombards became the public itself; everyone knew what the crusade was really about: throwing the Huns out of Lombardo-Venetian territory.

Thus the public saw itself as in a mirror, with a thin disguise of medieval trappings. With Verdi a new operatic era had began; his music spoke directly to the public, presenting them with an image that reflected their own feelings. This was no longer the rarefied opera about damsels in love with princes, or music written for court theatres, Verdi offered bombastic and truly popular music. Today we have forgotten how modern Verdi was in his time; how much he owed his roots to the band in Busseto, to ordinary people singing together; how radically different his approach was from that of Donizetti, Bellini, Spontini, Rossini or Cherubini: his was truly avant-garde music. *Nabucco* and *I Lombardi* pointed the way to new artistic possibilities. Verdi had given voice to the revolt against an anachronistic political order imposed by Metternich. Without his knowing it, Verdi's easily intelligible and stirring music spoke a language of unity – a language that Italy was then yearning to hear. 'These growing pains, this fever of energy, this mania for action reveals itself in the music of the young Verdi through two elements, both of them primitive and crude: the rhythm and the violence of the sound,' as Massimo Mila put it so splendidly in *La Giovinezza di Verdi*.

Giuseppina Strepponi by an anonymous painter. At this time (1841) she was identified with *Nabucco*, the very successful opera written for her by the young Verdi. Her hair and her famous décolleté are framed by those camellias which were symbolic of *La Dame aux camélias*, the novel by Dumas Fils on which Verdi based *La traviata*.

The most popular composers of the 1820s and 30s: (*Clockwise from left*) Bellini, Rossini, Mercadante, Ricci and Donizetti. Bellini, the symbol of Romanticism, died very young and famous, in Paris; Giuseppina was a celebrated interpreter of his *Norma*. Gioachino Rossini in 1830 when he was active; he then retired to Paris almost ceased to compose altogether. Although he had met Giuseppina in Italy at the time of *Nabucco*, they only became friends when they were both living in France. There are several letters at Sant'Agata from Rossini to Verdi. Giuseppina's début as a soprano was with *Matilde di Shabran*, an opera by Rossini. Mercadante was a Neapolitan composer who feared Verdi's musical talent. Ricci, instead, performed Verdi's operas as a conductor; he was a celebrated composer as well and lived with two of Teresa Stolz's sisters by whom he had two children. The 'wives' were identical twins. Gaetano Donizetti, an extraordinarily successful composer with sixty operas to his name, dedicated one of them to Giuseppina with whom he had an affair. She had been a great interpreter of Donizetti's music.

Giuseppina Strepponi in an etching of around 1839 while she was singing in Venice; she had difficulties with her impresario and the administration of the opera house. She sent this unflattering image to Verdi with a dedication that reads: 'In the difficult path, you Venice, guide my steps'.

Emanuele Muzio was Verdi's only pupil; he was entrusted by the composer to give Giuseppina lessons in harmony in which she was weak. This was before she left for Paris in order to teach the new Italian fashion in singing and Verdi's compositions in particular.

LA TRAVIATA

Libretto di Francesco Maria Piave

MUSICA DI

GIUSEPPE VERDI

CAVALIERE DELLA LEGION D'ONORE

dell'Editore **TITO DI GIO. RICORDI** dedicata

in segno di stima ed amicizia all'egregio signor Dottor

CESARE VIGNA

MILANO

R. STABILIMENTO NAZ. MUSICALE

TITO DI GIO. RICORDI

ABOVE A contemporary illustration of the final scene from *La traviata*. The opera was composed in Busseto while the townspeople threw stones and insults against Giuseppina's windows. Giuseppina herself suggested the name Violetta – violet – for the protagonist who, in Dumas' novel, was called Marguerite. In real life, her name was Alphonsine Marie Duplessis who would be played by Greta Garbo in a film made in the 1930s.

LEFT The famous impresario Bartolomeo Merelli who gave Giuseppina her first great role and who made Verdi's fortune. He grew up with Donizetti, lived like a king but died a destitute.

RIGHT The piano at Palazzo Dordoni where Verdi composed *Rigoletto*, *La traviata* and *Il trovatore*. The portrait of his father-in-law Antonio Barezzi in the background. Barezzi, at first, objected to Verdi living with Peppina.

BELOW The interior of Giuseppina's bedroom where Verdi would have breakfast with her. Here she kept her most beloved objects, from her father's reliquary to the bust of her made in Rome in 1840 when she was at the height of her success. She died in this room.

LEFT King Vittorio Emanuele II of Savoy, King of Piedmont, surrounded by his heroes; history, as usual, lies because the King disliked Cavour, loathed Garibaldi and feared Mazzini. He himself wanted to annex the rich North of Italy only. The South was annexed by a fluke.

BELOW When in 1859 the patriots realised that the best chance for unification was under Vittorio Emanuele, they hailed him by writing his name under the disguise of Viva VERDI, a code which meant 'Viva Vittorio Emanuele Re D'Italia': so that the Austrian, the Bourbon or the papal police forces would be unable to put the enthusiastic opera lovers under arrest.

STOLZ TERESINA   DS° MARIANI ANGELO   PROG° VERI FARALLE
(Elisabetta)   (M.Concertatore e Direttore)   (Principessa d' Eboli)

STINELLI GIORGIO   MILESI PIETRO   CAPPONI GIOVANNI   FORI ALESSANDRO   ROSSA LUIGI   COTOGNI ANTONIO
(Don Carlo)   (Un Frate)   (Filippo II)   (Sost' al M° Concertatore) (Grande Inquisitore) (Marchese di Posa)

ABOVE After the Parisian flop, Mariani decided to stage *Don Carlo* properly and trained the Bohemian soprano Teresa Stolz for the difficult and dramatic role of Elisabetta. Both Mariani and Verdi fell madly in love with her. *Don Carlo* in Bologna (1867) was a spectacular success. Mariani is at the centre, Stolz on his right.

RIGHT Angelo Mariani was a good-looking conductor who fell under the spell of Verdi and became his best interpreter, but Verdi stole his fiancée. He had been Rossini's pupil who called him 'Anzulett', little angel, in Bolognese dialect.

Verdi was elected to the Parma Assembly and chosen by Cavour to visit Turin to hand King Vittorio Emanuele the result of a plebiscite in which the former Dukedom of Parma (Busseto included) asked to become part of the Kingdom of Piedmont. From a drawing by Edoardo Mantania from *Illustrazione italiana*.

I Lombardi had opened at La Scala on 11 February 1843 and was so successful that it had a further twenty-seven performances. It lit the fuse that decreed the insurrection. There was agitation throughout the length and breadth of Italy, and it was the aristocrats and intellectuals who were in the forefront. A hundred people suspected of revolutionary activity were arrested in Salerno, while in Bologna one hundred more occupied a village and took up arms against the papal army. In Naples the Bourbon government ordered the arrest of another fifty-six citizens. February 1844 was also the beginning of the reckless venture of the Bandiera brothers, two aristocrats serving the Habsburg Navy, who had founded a secret society. Baron Emilio, commander of a frigate, had deserted in Trieste and his brother Attilio followed suit in Smyrna. They both made their way down to Cosenza, mistaking the rebellion there, caused by the perennial hunger of the south, for patriotic fervour; an error that was to be made time and time again by northerners. Raising the cry for 'an independent, free, united Italy, democratically constituted in a Republic with Rome as its capital' – the Mazzini declaration, as revolutionary and provocative as possible – the Bandiera brothers sought and found martyrdom. Anti-monarchical and anti-clerical, the Bandieras and their companions were condemned to death and shot by the Austrians.

Amidst outbreaks of brigandage and also idealistic uprisings, Italy which had remained backward by comparison to France and Great Britain, was slowly entering the modern era. Although we have seen the theatre-folk travelling up and down Italy, the life of the average Italian was very different. Separated by the Apennines, the Tuscans barely knew the inhabitants of Emilia; the Abbruzzi and Marche were isolated, as was Basilicata. Naples seemed a whole world away from Rome, and Avellino was simply unreachable. The various states were connected almost exclusively by sea and this is why Palermo was more of a capital city than Florence. The Southern Apennines were infested with bandits, the Maremma with malaria. Nearly every city in Italy now wanted a new opera by Verdi and the impresarios fought for the privilege of producing one and the publishers competed to print them. Merelli, who had sold the publishing rights of *Nabucco* to Ricordi for 3,000 lire, generously giving two-thirds to Verdi whom in any case he had helped so much, found himself cast aside by the touchy composer apparently offended by some trivial remarks. But the impresario's own megalomania was also probably to blame and in any case Merelli was on the verge of bankruptcy and forced to limit his productions. Verdi proceeded obstinately along his own path, taking offence easily, never forgiving, harbouring lifelong grudges and demanding everything of everyone.

In Clara Maffei's salon, the gleaming and slightly grey eyes of the young composer lingered on the attractions of Countess Samoyloff, the Tsar's ex-lover, whose embraces could be embarrassing since they tended to cause the transfer of thick make-up. Then there was the fascinating Giuseppina Appiani, Donizetti's ex-lover, now in her forties, or the Contessa della Somaglia and also Emilia Morosini. Verdi sent the latter a note '. . . and remember that I am all tenderness, I am dying of tenderness . . .' (21 July 1842) and 'I am forever tender, passionate, and half-dead for you.' With Emilia, who was nine years older than he, there was certainly a zestful bond. In short, Peppina was rarely – if ever – in Verdi's thoughts.

He wrote letters to Giuseppina Appiani and her pretty daughters: he had never been so feted in his life and he was determined to enjoy it. 'He amused himself by sauntering forth, sometimes on foot, sometimes in a coach, having five or six at his disposal,' wrote Muzio, a young man from Busseto who had been sent to stay with Verdi by Antonio Barezzi, the composer's father-in-law. 'All these gentlefolk who court him compete to amuse him.' Discreet, faithful, genuinely dazzled by his genius, Emanuele Muzio was Verdi's only pupil. We owe him a debt of gratitude because he has left us a precious testimony in his letters, and at times, he lets slip details which Giuseppina's discretion or Verdi's paranoid secrecy would have carried to the tomb. Muzio, like Verdi, had been turned down by the Conservatoire in Milan, as a 'foreigner' – he was born in the Duchy of Parma. Barezzi had sent him to Verdi for composition lessons, after securing a grant for him from the Monte di Pietà in Busseto – just like Verdi. Muzio was a kindhearted man, he never became an outstanding composer, nor was he a great conductor, which was his life-long career taking him to Brussels, Central America and Paris, where he died in 1890.

Muzio remained with Verdi for three years from April 1844 during which he acted as his secretary, as a copyist transcribing Verdi's operas, and a shadow – a role that became unnecessary after the arrival of Giuseppina. His Maestro too felt that Muzio had 'an excellent heart, but not enough head to know the world' – unlike Peppina, who knew it all too well. He earned a living conducting, a relatively new profession, since the custom had started for the composer to conduct his own operas; sometimes there was no conductor at all and we can but imagine the results! In any case the composer or stage-manager was also expected to produce the opera which he would do as best he could together with the impresario and the seamstresses. Barezzi complained about his son-in-law's silence. Muzio replied with some irony: 'You must pity him, he is always out and about, surrounded by hosts of noble hangers-on who, it seems, would be helpless without him.'

After her appearance at La Scala, another year was to go by before Giuseppina returned to the stage. According to Abbiati, one of Verdi's first biographers, the Teatro Ducale in Parma would have preferred De Giuli who, on the recommendation of a friend, had triumphed in the role of Abigaille in Vienna, but Verdi had insisted on Giuseppina. Before tackling such a difficult score, Verdi asked Giuseppina to see his physician, Doctor Tommasini, whom Verdi trusted. This is an important detail: after ensuring that she should get the part, Verdi was making certain that she would recover her voice enough to sing his score properly. In order to achieve this, he sent her to his own doctor in Parma, the city near Busseto in his own territory. Giuseppina arrived in Marie Louise's capital all alone and stayed at the Albergo Corona, near the Steccata, the magnificent church frescoed by Parmigianino, where one of the duchess's morganatic husbands lies buried in a spectacular marble tomb. Situated just a short walk from the theatre, the Corona was used by all itinerant companies. Verdi also always stayed there (unhappily the hotel was destroyed by a bomb in World War II). She paid a few visits to Doctor Tommasini whom Verdi seemed to have trusted more than Giuseppina. He appears to have done her more good than she was to acknowledge because, having returned to Milan, she rather belatedly thanked him in her own fashion, criticising him between the lines. Gargling was certainly not the remedy for her state of physical and psychological prostration: 'Gargling helped to give a tonic to the upper part of the throat,' she wrote. 'But it brought no relief to the area where I obstinately feel weakness and hoarseness . . .' In July Tommasini replied addressing her as 'the very ornate Giuseppina Strepponi'. But the cure had, to some extent, been successful, because her health improved and her voice was now ready for *Nabucco*. Verdi had vouched for her; she wanted to recover in any case because she had other engagements which she needed to honour.

This year of inactivity was due not only to a sickness in her vocal cords but to a depressive crisis. Other doctors who saw Giuseppina, but not Tommasini, claimed that there was a risk of tuberculosis. This alarming illness which struck down so many young women – another foreshadowing of *La traviata* – was suspected because Giuseppina was visibly losing weight. She ate very little and never went out, allowing herself to go to pieces. During this period she saw Verdi frequently but almost clandestinely; he was beginning to find her advice and information about the theatrical world indispensable. They were not yet a couple, although Donizetti's reference to '*her* Verdi' is significant, but there is no doubt that the composer found Giuseppina's company stimulating, almost necessary. It was certainly more rewarding than that of Countess Maffei, Emilia Morosini, Giuseppina Appiani and all the other ladies who courted him so flatteringly. Giuseppina showed him the value of good manners, coached him in languages, brought out a certain style that lay latent in Verdi; the grand ladies would never have taught him such things because they would have taken them for granted in him anyway. Verdi was Giuseppina's salvation. She now began to long for retirement. She wanted to cut her ties with the past, with all the bickering and squabbling, the unwanted pregnancies, the continual travelling, the changes of house, the occasional bedmates and coach companions. If even that hideous Barbieri woman, who was built like a wardrobe, could get married, why not her? 'I've just heard Barbieri's wedding announced. If she has found a husband, nobody need despair of finding one.'

But Giuseppina was a woman with a past and she was tied to her past by Camillino who lived in Florence – the only child she acknowledged; he was looked after by the Zanobini, a 'good' family, and Cirelli, who was sixty-four, shared the cost of his education. She saw the child from time to time but she felt no maternal love, no need to be with him, to allow him to share her home, her life, to bring him up herself. Sinforosa, her second born, had been written off by Giuseppina in an almost clinical way, having been 'recognised' as the daughter of the Stefanis, a couple to whom she secretly paid a lump sum. Short of killing the baby, Giuseppina had done everything to erase her from her life. As for the third child, Adelina, fortunately perhaps for both mother and daughter, as we have seen she died in 1842, during that year of depression, and we dare to hope that the lonely death of this innocent child gave Giuseppina more than a tinge of sadness. Maybe the deep depression that seized her was not entirely due to the loss of her voice and to her social downfall, but to the thought of this abandoned and forgotten child. But there is no reference to her daughters in Giuseppina's letters – not once did she let slip a single word, only Camillino was vaguely mentioned as 'important business' or 'family affairs'. It is unlikely that she felt guilty though, because life had been harsh with Giuseppina and she could not have coped with her career or her health as well as her children. The responsibility lay with those men who had first slept with her and then had run off leaving her to carry the burden in spite of empty promises. No singer was a saint, she was doing just what all courtesans did, what all girls without money had to tolerate: oversexed men who were never blamed by society. How did she support herself and her family during that year when she did not sing? At home Barberina had started earning a bit of money, imitating her elder sister's ways. Giuseppina was determined to settle down although Verdi was not even a remote possibility. In fact on 26 March, she talked in a letter of marrying a man who was 'not too well-off' and had no connections with the theatre. But these were dreams.

In Milan Verdi had moved to Corso Francesco, behind the Cathedral, it was his fourth move. He had been to Vienna for the Austrian première of *Nabucco* at the Kärnthnerthor, the same theatre that had seen Giuseppina's Austrian début. But he could not wait to get back; he liked Milan. He wrote to Countess Morosini about the performance: 'It turned out successful, more so than I expected after seeing the trouble caused by a certain person there.' (He was not referring to Donizetti, as has been generally believed but to Nicolai, the composer who had turned down Solera's libretto of *Nabucco*.)

It was now Verdi's turn to be constantly on the move. A week after his trip to Vienna, he went back to Busseto and then to Parma, to see Peppina who was there to rehearse *Nabucco* with the company. On 17 April 1843 he conducted *Nabucco* at the Ducale. Parma, ruled by Marie Louise – daughter of the Emperor of Austria and the widow of Napoleon, another emperor – was the capital of the state where Verdi was born, a land that had treated him with condescension. If he was not well-received by his own people whose characteristics he shared, he could not consider himself truly established. Success in Parma meant a great deal to him.

He was not sure how long he would stay. In a letter to Count Mocenigo, on 9 April, he wrote: 'On the 14th of this month I will be in Parma, where I shall stay until the end of the month.' And then, as if he had changed his mind, he wrote from Parma to Isidoro Cambiasi on 3 May: 'I shall remain another eight or ten days.' Then, on 17

May, from Parma: 'I shall stay here until the evening of the 22nd of this month.' He was beginning to value the proximity of Giuseppina. On 25 May, he wrote again to Count Mocenigo, manager of La Fenice in Venice, with whom he was working on his opera, *Ernani*, 'You can address it to Parma, rather than Milan,' and to Antonio Poggi, on 30 May, from Parma: 'Today I'm leaving for Milan.'

Although he stayed in Parma for fifty days, Verdi conducted *Nabucco* only twice – he never enjoyed conducting – passing the baton to Nicola Di Giovanni.

Such was the success of *Nabucco* at the Ducale that it was performed twenty-two times. The Duchess Marie Louise herself attended one of these performances; she was a small fair-skinned lady, with the jutting mouth of the Habsburgs, who dressed in sumptuous silk dresses and glittering jewels. She presented Verdi with a gold brooch, studded with diamonds. He had dedicated the score of *I Lombardi* to her which indicates how far Verdi was from true political freedom. Although Marie Louise was a discreet and relatively enlightened sovereign, she nonetheless represented everything that the Italian liberals detested.

The Ducale, inaugurated about twenty years earlier, was a worthy ornament in a city that had been decorated by Correggio and Parmigianino and it had all the grace described by Stendhal. A mixture of French elegance and morbid Austrian frostiness, all white and gold, with small rooms behind the boxes, which was always the case in high class theatres, the Ducale's foyer was neo-classical in style with echoes of baroque, an ensemble of gleaming whites and sumptuous golds.

Verdi and Giuseppina were pleased by their successful time in Parma. At the end of the season, the periodical *Il Figaro* hinted at the idyll between them. This is a good example of how in those days the papers shot their little darts; although not explicit, they told all. In any case, the story of passion between the primadonna and the composer was by now a subject of gossip everywhere; it would have been absurd for the musical press not to refer to it: 'Maestro Verdi who did not abandon his fortunate creation even last night, will long remember, we are sure, this season in Parma, where he was treated with enviable solicitude, where he savoured exquisite sweets, and where he met with the frenzied applause of the whole public. Truly favoured! His life must be flowing with honey.' His 'fortunate creation' is presumably *Nabucco*, but the 'exquisite sweets' and the 'honey' were clear metaphors. So clear that Verdi lost his temper with a Milanese journalist responsible for the gossip.

On 31 May, Marie Louise was present at Giuseppina's benefit performance – attended by 2,200 spectators! The programme contained arias from *Nabucco*, an act from *Beatrice di Tenda* and the overture of *William Tell*, specially rewritten for the band of the ducal army. There were three poems written in honour of Peppina. She was once again the heroine of the day, not only had she recovered her voice but she was reputed to be Verdi's woman. She was showered with flowers and money, the Duchess gave her a necklace and she curtsied to her.

Giuseppina enjoyed a good position in Parma, she was invited to Court, sometimes with Verdi, and on her own after he had left. She spoke good French – probably better than Marie Louise who must have had a strong accent. She followed fashion judiciously and brought out her pallor by favouring dark-coloured velvets, green or dark red. On 5 June, Giuseppina, grateful to Parma for the welcome it had given her, sang gratis for a benefit evening. After Parma, Peppina made it her aim to take Verdi's music around the Italian theatres.

At the Teatro Comunale in Bologna, she stood in for Sofia Löwe, who had suddenly fallen ill. At this point Cirelli popped up again, with a letter to Lanari, saying: 'Peppina is in Bologna. If her health stays good, she will be successful, I hope.' It was in Bologna that Verdi met Rossini, a composer he admired and he was to see him again when Rossini passed through Parma, accompanied by his wife. The two men were very different in character, but they understood one another. They talked of music, of Paris, Bologna and the Teatro Comunale. Although he had lost all capacity for love, after that last coffin left his home, Verdi felt affection for Rossini.

Nine days later on 11 October, Cirelli wrote to Lanari again, making an interesting reference to Verdi: 'You will have heard of Peppina's happy success in Bologna. Please God it may continue, and she will set aside the stupid love-affairs that compromise her and will finally give some thought to her future.' Two days later, it was Peppina's turn to write to her impresario friend speaking of Verdi. 'If the well-known affair that you mention is V . . . things go well, that is to say as they went in Senigallia. You will have heard about the outcome of *Nabucco* – and I am happy about it. On Thursday, if there are no mishaps, we are to stage *Roberto Devereux*.' And she condescended to ask for news of the beautiful Frezzolini, the lucky performer of *I Lombardi*, who was taking Giuseppina's place in the public's heart.

In Bologna, *Nabucco* was performed until 26 November, although *Il Figaro* noted that Giuseppina's voice was not what it had been earlier. Verdi went off to Venice, sick, irritated and exhausted by hard work. The libretto of *Ernani*, which was in trouble with the censors, had been written by Francesco Maria Piave, who was becoming a friend. Verdi's character was such that he needed a more submissive and less lazy librettist than Solera. It was Count Mocenigo who had discovered Piave and passed him on to Verdi. He cost little and was Venetian or rather he came from a family of glass-makers living in Murano. Like so many librettists, Piave had started off at the Seminary and had earned a living by journalism and improvising verses for toasts and banquets.

Verdi was paid 1200 svanziche for *Ernani* – a large sum of money. He had every intention to become rich and then to retire on the patch of land he was going to buy. At that time Verdi had no thought of composing for future generations – opera was an object for immediate consumption and corresponded to the times; that was how it had always been written. This explains why Verdi composed for specific voices. For example, his *King Lear* was never written because there was no ideal Cordelia available, and *Otello* was written with the voices of Tamagno and Maurel in mind. The singers were extremely important. But those days were drawing to a close for Peppina.

In January 1844 she was singing in Verona while Verdi was in Venice struggling with *Ernani*, it was not far and he did not wait long before joining Peppina. Verdi 'came to Verona a few days before the first performance of *Nabucco*,' *Il Figaro* noted. Embarrassed by the fact that people talked far more often of 'them', the young Maestro told Count Mocenigo that he needed to go to Verona to hear a tenor who might be suitable for *Ernani*. Instead he stayed on for Meyerbeer's *Robert the Devil*, performed by Giuseppina. Then she returned to Milan where she started giving singing lessons in her apartment. On 28 May, she took part in a concert at the Teatro Regio in Turin and on 11 August she sang in Bergamo where Verdi joined her once again for her appearance in his new opera, *Ernani*.

The bond between them was by now very strong. He was working ceaselessly: over the next four years he staged new operas at the Teatro Argentina in Rome with *I due Foscari* (The Two Foscari), at the San Carlo in Naples with *Alzira* and he returned to La Scala with *Giovanna d'Arco* (Joan of Arc), to the Fenice again with

Attila, to the Pergola in Florence with *Macbeth*. At the same time he was preparing for London where he took *I Masnadieri* and for Paris where he took *Jerusalem* which was a re-working of *I Lombardi* for the all-important Opéra.

Whilst in Bergamo they had to take an important decision together. Since Giuseppina's affairs were going badly in Italy, and she was hard-pressed by debts, the best way for her to earn was by giving singing lessons. As she had already said in a letter to Lanari, she wanted to leave Italy which was full of sad memories. She wanted to start a new life elsewhere. Peppina had decided to move to Paris; Verdi, who wanted to conquer the Opéra, would help her and vice-versa.

Peppina wrote the first of a long series of letters from Bergamo on Verdi's behalf. Delicate in its turn of phrase, precise in its contents, the letter was designed to resolve a question with Giovannina Lucca, 'la Sciûra' – whom we have already met. Giovannina was the overwhelming and yet lovable wife of the music publisher Francesco Lucca. Verdi did not like the Luccas, but they had helped Peppina through the musical publications they controlled and now they wanted to wean Verdi away from Ricordi, a publisher who had been quicker off the mark than them. Giovannina tried to use Giuseppina as a bait, but Verdi was not a fish and his reactions were always unpredictable.

Muzio recounted that, around this time, the Sciûra turned up at Verdi's door in tears; her husband had fallen ill because the composer would not sign a contract with them. When they were in bed together at night, he did nothing but sigh. 'Sigh? Is that all he does?' Verdi laughed in her face and went on chuckling to himself: 'He does nothing but sigh!' And so, from Bergamo, Giuseppina wrote to the Sciûra:

Dearest friend, on behalf of Verdi, I am answering your husband's letter of 10 August, in which he acknowledges receipt of the preliminary contract issued on the first of the same month, approving every word in it. This is fine and on my return from Bergamo, I will play the role of correspondent, and the regular contract will be drawn up. But I warn you of one thing: Verdi intends to do as he has always done, which is to say: if both sides agree on conditions, the document must be drawn up and signed without any intervention from lawyers, as they serve no purpose whatsoever.

On 16 October 1845, Verdi signed a letter-contract with the Luccas that he was later to regret. Giuseppina had succeeded in her objective. After the months she had spent together with Verdi not only in Parma, but also travelling around the country, Giuseppina was now on her own again. She was to remain alone in Palermo for a disastrous six-month season, between October 1844 and March 1845. Not only was Verdi worn out by the quantity of work he was churning out, it is likely that they had quarrelled; otherwise it is difficult to understand why they should have stayed apart for so long. Verdi was also openly unfaithful to her and this might have been the basic cause of friction. Palermo was a prison for a Lombard like Giuseppina, accustomed to the salons and concerts of Milan. Single women in Sicily were usually regarded as either nuns or whores, and all singers were whores. The separation, which she perhaps believed to be final (no letters between them from this period have been found, although it is possible that Verdi burnt them in that final bonfire at Sant'Agata) provoked another fit of depression which proved disastrous for her.

Her performance in *Linda di Chamonix* was reviewed in the Palermo newspaper *La fata galante* in these words (30 October): 'The brillant star that presided over her theatrical fortunes now seems to be on the point of fading and thus emits only the feeblest glow; this dimness must be seen as the reason for her poor performance. Let her rest on the laurels she has won, no-one will ever forget that she sang excellently and was the pride of Italy.' Odd to find in Palermo the concept of Giuseppina's voice as having been a national symbol.

There were two opera houses in Palermo, and the crowned heads of Europe came to enjoy the music and the climate. But the island was under the tight control of Bourbon censorship; the atmosphere in Palermo, a city linked by sea with the rest of Italy, was one of repression and the Mafia. Terrible poverty reigned, together with disease and injustice. The failure of the various attempts at insurrection, which broke out with even greater frequency than cholera, gave urgency to the question of what road Italy should follow to achieve its desired unity. In the Kingdom of the Two Sicilies, however, nobody, with the exception of a few mafiosi and one or two intellectuals, gave much thought to unification. The real question was about living conditions which the Bourbon government was doing nothing to improve. The moderate liberals of both lay and clerical tendencies, as well as revolutionaries linked to Mazzini, could see that elsewhere the liberal centre was winning. Even Carlo Alberto of Savoy, a saturnine and unpopular king, seemed anxious to change his ways if not his mind, becoming more sympathetic to the arguments of the Centre. Young men continued to die in rebellions, that broke out in Rimini and Rome; political solutions had to be found.

The cause of the moderates was gaining ground over the more radical revolutionaries. Among the latter was Carlo Tenca, Countess Maffei's lover, editor of *La Rivista europea* which took over *Politecnico*, another political journal. Publications of this kind had a great following among the lay and entrepreneurial classes. It was an age in which political periodicals flourished, all making use of cryptic or musical language which everybody understood. Similarly everyone recognised that their crusade, the first crusade, was against the Austro-Hungarian empire, whose inhabitants the Italians called Germans. These political crusades were discussed at the Caffè Martini or Casa Maffei in Milan, but were never mentioned in Palermo. The Sicilian aristocracy – as is clear from the novel *The Leopard* – slept long and deep while nothing disturbed its gloomy dreams. Palermo was a mysterious, stifling city with its contrasting lights, its sounds, its heady perfumes, but also it was intensely beautiful. Even so it was small and many areas were strictly 'off limits'. An elegant lady like Giuseppina, for example, would travel in her carriage up and down Via Maqueda, alongside the elegant Marina, where the palazzi of the aristocracy succeeded each other in solemn parade, but she could never venture into the Cala, the dangerous port, the Kalsa or the Vucciria. In the palazzi at Bagheria there was dancing until the small hours among the hibiscus plants: with all those princes and barons, whose days were divided between gambling and original sin, Peppina could easily have found a husband or at least a wealthy lover. But she was depressed, to such a point that she could not even leave her visiting card in the antechambers of the palazzi. Her performances in *Lucrezia Borgia* and *Ernani* were all feeble so everyone was disappointed; the public, the theatre, the aristocracy and not least Strepponi herself.

Il Figaro wrote (30 December 1842) of her *Lucrezia* that Strepponi was 'too inadequate to sustain such a demanding role' and of *Ernani* which, for censorship reasons, was called *Elvira d'Aragona*, it said:

> Strepponi, although trained in the works of Maestro Verdi, did not arouse the slightest enthusiasm in the part of Elvira . . . and we will permit ourselves to ask a question: why that permanently distracted air, as if she imagined herself to be anywhere but on

stage, before the most discerning and intelligent of audiences . . . ? We no longer recognise Strepponi in Strepponi, that celebrated singer whom we heard elsewhere not so many years ago, always (may it come true again) overwhelmed by a tempest of applause and celebration.

Alone, with no confidence in herself or her abilities, far from her family and from her Verdi who had probably forgotten all about her, Giuseppina could see no way out. Her previously impeccable acting skills were fading fast; she was even replaced in both *Maria di Rohan* and *La sonnambula*. On 9 March she mimed *La Vestale* and the first act of *Belisario*, the opera in which she had already disappointed Donizetti. 'Signora Strepponi did not sing but merely mimed the character of Antonina, so that the beautiful finale of the act failed just as the conqueror of Vitige,' wrote *L'Occhio*. This was the ultimate humiliation.

Six months went by before Giuseppina returned to the stage, this time in Alessandria. She continued to be depressed so that for months at a time she was unable to sing or to see anyone; before eventually finding enough strength to re-emerge. In addition to her physical weakness, she was probably suffering from phases of manic depression, like Rossini.

Verdi was in Milan where it snowed continuously; he was engaged in composing *Giovanna d'Arco* for Merelli. He was also under contract with Lucca to write *Alzira*, an opera for which he had no time, no inspiration, and no desire to create. He fell ill and Giuseppina came back from Palermo to look after him – helped by Muzio who occupied the bedroom next door to the Maestro's. On his recovery, he left for Naples to stage the detested *Alzira* (of which he was to write later, 'It is my worst!'). Verdi set off alone, angry with the Neapolitans, with the Luccas who had exacted from him an opera which he did not want to write and angry with himself for having contracted to do so. As it turned out, the climate of Naples did wonders for his health and he set to work on *Attila*, dreaming of Shakespeare, King Lear, and of writing an opera on a theme that he had chosen for himself, rather than one that had been imposed on him.

On his return to Milan, he was visited by the French publisher Marie Escudier. This meeting with Escudier who, together with his brother, was to become Verdi's French publisher, had undoubtedly been arranged beforehand: it resulted in an interview which Verdi was happy to grant, having planned his début in the French musical world. Escudier described how Verdi lived in a Spartan apartment; how his eyes were blue and that he had an expression which is both 'sweet and animated'. He asked him to play the 'Ave Maria' from *I Lombardi*, and Verdi, strangely compliant, agreed. He was well informed about contemporary French music and spoke the language fluently. In the meantime Peppina was singing in Bergamo. Carlo Minocchio, the copyist at the Teatro Regio, wrote a highly garbled and misspelt letter to the impresarios in Bergamo:

> I must ask you to apply with the utmost solicitude by return of post what the artistic reputation is of Signora Giuseppina Strepponi, at present primadonna, in your theatre, now singing in *Ernani*, whereas she came to the Impresa of our theatre (which instructed me with this task) and on account of her weak constitution did not sing regularly every evening and, under the pretext of health, did not satisfy her commitments scrupulously; whatever the situation, I ask you to reply promptly, so that the Impresa can continue or withdraw from its negotiations, matters being very urgent.

But in Alessandria, which followed Bergamo, Giuseppina surprised herself, enjoying a triumph of the sort she had almost forgotten, with twenty curtain calls, lavish tributes and poems in her honour. 'After fulfilling the obligations that still bind her to the Italian theatres (at Carnival she will be in Modena),' wrote *La Strenna teatrale europea* of 1846, 'she intends to go to Paris and continue her stage career there if required, and teach true Italian singing, to propagate the art that made her so famous in the musical world.' Giuseppina was in fact about to close her career in Modena and in fine style. It happened as follows: on 26 December 1845 a performance of *I Lombardi* proved so disastrous that the public asked for the head of the impresario, Pietro Rovaglia. The disturbances reached such proportions that the police did not dare to intervene and the theatre was closed. Terrorised (the public was unhappy for many other reasons, including a tyrant duke) Rovaglia hung a bill poster announcing a performance of *Nabucco* with Strepponi. The success of the second opera was transformed into a personal triumph for Giuseppina. 'The applause never ended,' wrote *Il Pirata*. 'She was continually interrupted by acclamations and by cries of *viva* for the adagio and the cabaletta; after the performance she took five curtain calls and even the ducal court showed clear signs of appreciation.'

I Lombardi was resumed, but without Giuseppina. Since the performance had greatly improved, the impresario's head was saved. Just then the notorious Francesco IV of Modena died after a long despotic reign. Once the period of mourning was over, Giuseppina returned to the stage in *Nabucco* for the last time. It was February 1846. In January she had tried in vain to be designated the singer of the Camera Ordinaria of Her Majesty Marie Louise, Duchess of Parma. It was a humiliating attempt, not only because she was rejected but because it was definitely the wrong moment to be seen paying homage to the last creation of the Congress of Vienna. If she had obtained the position, Peppina would have happily dropped the idea of moving to Paris; it was by no means easy to give everything up and move to a new country, particularly at this point in her life. As things happened, she was left with no choice. The economic and political crisis in which Italy was now imbroiled hardly assured a bright future for a performer and a singing teacher. On the other side of the Alps lay France, a much richer, more stable and civilized country, the salons of whose capital were frequented by such people as Berlioz, De Musset and Auber; where novelists like Victor Hugo thrilled the young and where Balzac recounted the vicissitudes of a rising bourgeoisie. The opera houses were rich and the latest Italian music was becoming popular even though there were not yet voices trained to perfom it. It was no longer *bel canto*, in the manner of Rossini, Donizetti and Cherubini, this was avant-garde music, a music that throbbed with vitality.

Giuseppina had spent the last few months preparing for the difficult move to Paris where she intended to settle for a long time, if not for ever. In Milan she had been living with her mother and sister Barberina in an apartment she had acquired in Via Cerva. At that time her maternal uncle, Luigi Cornalba, was also living there together with his daughter who was Giuseppina's friend, and so was her own son Camillino, but for a short holiday, in order to see his mother before she went off on her long journey. Before leaving for Paris, Giuseppina took lessons in harmony in an intensive course given by Muzio. She was rather weak in this subject and Verdi had arranged for her to be instructed by his own pupil.

After being a sad witness to the legal separation between Clara and Andrea Maffei, Verdi was preparing to leave for London, where he had been engaged by the impresario Benjamin Lumley to write a new opera. Italian opera was fashionable in London especially since Queen Victoria had started taking singing lessons. He was overwhelmed with work: these years took their toll on his health, but he had succeeded in buying a piece of land near Busseto and a house in the town. He was now recovering in the company of Andrea Maffei at the spa town of Recoaro. Meanwhile Muzio wrote to Verdi's father-in-law making mysterious references to a certain lady whom the Maestro had entrusted into his musical care. It was 'a distinguished Signora, whom I visit every day from 11 to 1 and who urgently requires to be taught harmony in just two months while she is in Milan because she is about to leave for Paris. She has a good deal of talent and studies hard.'

With all Giuseppina's financial and psychological problems, she had never let herself go. Lanari had called her the Generalina and Verdi too admired Giuseppina's strong will power, her elegance: outwardly she continued to hold her head high. Giuseppina wore fashionable Parisian attire, she greeted people with dignity and continued to improve herself by reading European literature. Living these last few months amongst her family, she played the role of *jeune fille*; we can imagine her together with her mother, her sister and her cousin. Around this date, while she was still in Milan, her uncle Luigi died – one of the relatives she really loved – and she began to wear black, a colour she was often to adopt in the near future. Travelling by coach along the Milan canals, she would step down from her hired carriage – she certainly could not afford a private one – and visit Sciûra Lucca, that powerful woman. But despite her retirement, Giuseppina felt under scrutiny – she knew she was the subject of gossip and longed to escape from it; she hoped to leave behind a whole plethora of errors, to eradicate them by her departure. The fact that Verdi had entrusted his pupil-collaborator with the task of teaching Giuseppina harmony in order to prepare her for her own Parisian tuition in singing, is indicative of how precious she was to him. It also shows that, despite the confusion over dates and events during this period, there was a bond between the two of them which if not definitive, was important to both of them.

6

THE ROMANTIC AGONY

Giuseppina settles in Paris. The public concerts and
France of the Romantic period. Berlioz appreciated
Giuseppina's voice. Anger throughout Europe: Paris is in
tumult. Verdi goes to Florence for *Macbeth* and then to
London with *I masnadieri*; he returns to Giuseppina and
shakes off Muzio. The Five Days of Milan. The couple
retire to the country. Return to Italy, arrival in Busseto,
his native town.

———————— • ————————

Parigi, o cara, noi lasceremo
la vita unita trascorreremo . . .
Paris, my dear, we shall leave,
we shall spend our life together . . .

LA TRAVIATA, ACT III

By now Giuseppina could count on Verdi. In fact he wrote to his
publishers the Escudier brothers on 22 October 1846: 'I thank
you for what you have done and for all that you will do for that lady
I have recommended. She deserves your attention in all respects . . .'
In Paris she had rented an apartment in Rue de la Victoire, where
actors, singers and writers lived, the Opéra was close and thus the
area was known as 'the new Athens'. Barberina was her temporary
escort in Paris; she wanted to be seen to live with her sister, but after
a short while Barberina went back to Italy. From the moment she
arrived *La France musicale* had been her herald:

Signora Strepponi, through her teaching, will propagate in
Parisian society a style and a method that are in harmony
with our taste and our organisation. We are convinced that
this winter this eminent artist will be the arbiter of fashion in
the great Parisian world; her courses will be held at her house,

twice a week, on Tuesday and Friday, from three to five. There will be eight courses a month at the price of 40 francs. For three months 100 francs.

What more could she want? This was the best publicity Giuseppina could get. On 15 November Giuseppina inaugurated her school, the *Cours de Chant*, at Rue de la Victoire; at the same time she went to see Marie and Léon Escudier who opened their musical and social doors to her.

Another article recounted that in Italy Signora Strepponi was considered not just a great singer but a woman of class. And, it continued, wallowing in that snobbery that was congenial to the comfortable classes: 'She has always been much sought after by the nobility who, after applauding her on stage, loved to acclaim and admire her in the course of her brilliant gatherings.' This was an inducement to get her invited to the splendid Parisian salons. Everybody in Paris read the musical publications: *L'Artiste*, *La Gazette musicale de Paris*, *La Revue musicale*, *Le Ménestrel*, *La Revue de Paris* and *La France musicale* which belonged to the Escudiers. In order to attract pupils into her apartment, Giuseppina got her name more widely known with two concerts at the Salle Henri Herz, which was announced in *La France musicale*. Several new theatres opened in Paris and the first public concerts were given. Public concerts were a natural progression from the private ones held in the great salons and at court, a necessary development for a class that was both rich and bored. In this way, the middle class could see and hear Lizst playing variations on the operas of the moment, like those by Meyerbeer. Other famous virtuosos were Sigismond Thalberg and François Habeneck who conducted in the old fashion, with his violin bow. The salons showed their superiority to the *salles publiques* by giving private concerts with virtuosos of the calibre of Chopin. In such settings one could expect to see such eminent figures as Hugo, Lamartine, Delacroix, Auber, René de Chateaubriand, Théophile Gautier, Charles Sainte-Beuve, Ingres, Dumas père, George Sand and Alfred de Musset.

Berlioz spoke of an 'avalanche of concerts that has swept over Paris. Never before it seems to me has Paris been taken with so much music.' He wrote in *Le Journal des débats*, a daily newspaper which employed him; he would never have been able to get on in music alone. His cry of passion in the *Symphonie fantastique* had left as deep a mark on the Romantic age as Delacroix in painting and

Hernani in literature, nonetheless Berlioz found it difficult to make ends meet. Criticising the voice of a Mlle Clary, Berlioz went on to say: 'Mme Strepponi, who followed her performance in concert, is a splendid primadonna, singing generously and nobly, with a very powerful voice, a good style and a stirring warmth. This is the great Italian school in all its elaborate luxury.' Thus, if one can believe Berlioz who was not easily pleased as a critic, Giuseppina was singing as she had in the past.

Giuseppina's successes, the position she had found in musical life, were reported by the Italian musical journals, both those controlled by Ricordi and by Lucca. In *Moda* there was an account (in French) of her concert given in Paris on 15 November 1846: '*Mme Strepponi, voilà une artiste consommée* . . .' She was one of those superior singers, it specified. The soprano had sung the cavatina from *Ernani* and a new work of Maestro Verdi's 'The Chimney Sweep', one of six songs published by Lucca in 1845. Unlike many foreign stars who were arriving in Paris to a great fanfare of acclaim but then flopped, the account went on, Strepponi was a model of taste 'formed in the new Italian school'. And Verdi's song, like the very voice which had interpreted it, was the messenger of that school and of that style. For another concert given that same month in the rooms of M. Orila, Giuseppina 'only performed music by Verdi, the Maestro of the day . . . Halévy who was present, gave Madame his warmest congratulations, and complimented her on her choice of pieces, which were of rare beauty.' Berlioz also attended: '. . . two very interesting concerts, one offered by *La France musicale* to its subscribers, the other given by Michel Lévy and the company he directs.' Just over a month later, Peppina wrote a letter to Giovannina Lucca (5 January 1847) from which we learn a few details about her new life: she had been at the Opéra to see Rossini's *Robert Bruce* performed by Rosina Stoltz – who was the mistress of M. Pillet, the director of the Opéra. She missed a note on the first night and was ill treated but, since the servant who was supposed to deliver Giuseppina's ticket had mislaid her address, she had been able to go to the opera on the second night. The performance passed peacefully, 'and nobody stirred apart from the formidable army of claqueurs controlled by a supreme commander whose place is directly under the chandelier . . . and people talk of Italian intrigue!' Giuseppina went on to write about Rossini. Some of his operas, like *La donna del lago* (*The Lady of the Lake*) were new to her. 'It is still music by the best of all composers . . .' she commented. 'The costumes and decorations are superior to anything you can imagine: in Italy we do not have such splendour and such beauty. As for the singers, you will have heard of them: Madame Stoltz is a good actress.' She mentions Cirelli, referring to him as an intimate friend, the only person with whom Giovannina could discuss her letter. She adds a piece of advice that sounds as if it came from Verdi himself; she suggests impassively:

> You would do well to sell all the operas that Verdi is to give to you to the Escudiers. I think it would be to your mutual advantage, write and tell me what you think. The Escudiers are happy with the songs you sent them. If you wish to make me a mediator in handling Verdi's operas with the Escudiers, I will see to it and I hope that you will be mutually happy. . . . I am pleased to hear of the success of *Attila* which is confirmed by all the letters I have received. Is Verdi in Milan? Tell me if he has had any health problems this year and if he is cheerful because gaiety is a sign of his good health. I need not remind you to think of Camillino but thank you for the solicitude you have shown towards him. Your friend, G. Strepponi.

Her son Camillino was nine and Giuseppa Faustina (Sinforosa), her abandoned daughter, was almost eight years old – she lived in Via Toscanella, near Palazzo Pitti, in Florence. Probably not even Giovannina Lucca knew about her existence. Camillino was the only 'official' child and travelled between Florence and Milan where he would stay with the Luccas or with Rosa Strepponi. Since Giuseppina asked news of Verdi in her letter, she was underlining that she was not in regular contact with him. In a second letter to Giovannina Lucca written a month and a half later, Giuseppina played the agent's role and made fun of her friend, not being able to reprove her directly:

> The Escudiers are still gazing open-mouthed with their glasses on their noses, not sure whether they have read correctly the amount you have asked for *I Masnadieri* (ten thousand francs!). They are all the more amazed at such a demand since none of Verdi's operas bought from Ricordi exceeds the sum of three thousand francs, not excepting *Macbet* [sic] which shows every promise of succeeding in Italy and is one of the most suitable subjects for the French stage. Today they have received a letter from your husband who urges them to answer *sans le moindre retard* either yes or no.

Giuseppina added that she had read the letter by chance, although it is obvious that the Escudiers asked her to act as intermediary. It would be a pity to break up Verdi's musical output, she wrote, which had all been handled by these French brothers with the exception of *Nabucco*. It was not fair 'to make them pay through the nose' for an opera like *I masnadieri* which had two drawbacks for Paris,

> the subject and the fact that it has been composed for London. I advise you to deal with the Escudiers for many reasons, also because I am persuaded that Verdi will prefer these publishers to any other in Paris. I would like to see an agreement that benefits both sides, with no hostility, no selfishness and no enmity . . . I thank you for the care you have shown to my son, and send hasty greetings, because the post is about to leave. Love from your friend G. Strepponi.

How happy was Giuseppina in Paris? She may have felt rather lonely, somewhat isolated, but she was earning well and she felt that she was surrounded by excitement. Nobody poked their noses in her private affairs, she felt free, far from her shameful past, from her children, from the impresarios and tenors.

The country Giuseppina had arrived in was far more advanced than Italy. However, although politically united, the process of urbanisation and unification was creating a brutalised proletariat much worse than the one in Italy – which still did not have a working class: its poor were farmers. Paris was a metropolis, crowded, exciting, but after the 1830 revolution which had installed Louis Philippe, the country had sunk into a sea of tedium that was suddenly alleviated – if not actually swept away – by the impetus of Romanticism. The bourgeoisie might be deficient in martial arts and heroism, but they made up for it with imagination. Romanticism had spread from England with Shelley and Byron; and from Germany with Goethe and Schiller – *I masnadieri* was based on a text by Schiller, *Il corsaro* on a text by Byron, and *Lucia* from Walter Scott; and with Victor Hugo (*Hernani, Rigoletto*) Romanticism found expression through a taste for history, for an exacerbated nationalism. France had produced the greatest literature of the century; the novels of Balzac, the great narrator of the bourgeoisie, and Victor Hugo, the Verdi of literature, were read by everybody and they fired the nationalistic imagination. Music was the popular voice of Romanticism: there were three opera houses: the Opéra-Comique, the Théâtre des Italiens and the Académie Royale de Musique et de Ballet, generally known simply as the Opéra: this last vied with La Scala for the title of world-supremacy. If it was not foremost in terms of music, the Opéra won for the opulence of its scenery and the grandiose scale of its ballets.

Paris had already affirmed itself as the European centre of creativity; wisely the city opened its arms to artistic exiles of all kinds, people such as Liszt, Chopin, Cherubini and Rossini; the political exiles went to London. But Paris was growing out of all proportion. Masses of people, clustered around the factories, had flocked to the city from the countryside only to find far worse living conditions. They were the new enemy and the victorious bourgeoisie defended their rights as the aristocracy had done before them.

In 1833 the metropolis had 714,000 inhabitants; by 1848 this had increased to 1,300,000. Carriages were everywhere, there were 160,000 vehicles in the gaslit streets. In the course of the year before Giuseppina's arrival, a serious economic crisis had hit the continent, bringing hunger in its wake. There was anger in the whole of Europe, in Paris as well as in Italy.

Politics were discussed in the salons. But now the decline of the aristocracy was expressed in the bony face of Madame Récamier, whose enormous eyes added to her spectral appearance; she would reveal herself to visitors in her salon of Rue de Sèvres dropping listlessly on a silk *causeuse*, beside a crackling hearth. Tall, thin, with a white lace bonnet on her grey hair, she was still one éminence grise of Parisian society, although she was shortly to die of cholera in 1849 at the age of seventy-one. George Sand, Chopin's mistress, a famous writer who dressed as a man, had another famous salon at Rue Neuve where writers like Lamartine, the great Romantic who rewrote history, would read his poetry.

'I noticed that the salons that were most widely talked about were the salons of four foreign ladies; that of Mesdames Swetvchine, that of Princess Belgiojoso and that of Madame de Circourt: three Russian ladies and an Italian,' wrote Countess d'Agoult, whom we have already met in Milan in the company of Liszt. Having become Alfred de Vigny's lover, the Countess had just opened a literary salon. The salon that most irritated her was Princess Belgiojoso's, with all its neo-gothic and Romantic fripperies. The Princess had befriended Barberina and Rosa Strepponi who, for a certain time, had lived in an apartment at the Belgiojoso's Milan palace; Giuseppina knew her and it is likely that she went on seeing her at Rue d'Anjou when she was in Paris; those who visited Cristina Belgiojoso, an eccentric and colourful aristocrat, would find the Princess kneeling in her private oratory, a skull at her feet, in the glow of orange light that filtered through a pseudo-medieval mullioned window. The fashionable preacher, whether bishop or curé, would discreetly withdraw, leaving her free to exchange some worldly pleasantries with her Parisian visitors, who – and we can hardly blame them – might burst into laughter at the sight of her bedchamber, all in white apart from the silver bed 'like the catafalque of a virgin', remarked Madame d'Agoult. In the antechamber stood a turbaned negro in picturesque contrast with the virginal candour within: more operatic than opera itself. 'Nobody could exorcise the art of effect quite like La Belgiojoso,' concluded Lamartine who belonged to the original Romantic school.

Giuseppina, who was no romantic, was profoundly irritated by this mystical Gothic scenario; but, generally speaking, performers were not allowed full entry into high society. The aristocratic salons entertained with private concerts; at times Giuseppina performed in private houses but she preferred the new public halls. The French aristocracy looked down on such vulgar affairs. Marie d'Agoult went on: 'Wanting to give a good concert, one would turn to Rossini who, for a very reasonable fixed fee – 1,500 francs if I remember rightly – would take charge of the programme and its performance, thus sparing the hosts the trouble of choosing and rehearsing.' The great Maestro would sit at the piano all evening accompanying the singers. Before and after 1848 the musical geniuses continued to converge on Paris. In the concert halls and the salons there moved George Sand, Heine and Stendhal, de Musset, Vigny, Sophie Gray, Benjamin Constant and Lamartine whose writings overturned the French political order. Politics, literature and music were discussed and analysed, created and destroyed. Giuseppina, converted to politics by Verdi, had moved towards the Centre-Left; but she did not talk of such matters with the Italian exiles, whom she did not much like – apart from Rossini. With Madame Rossini, however, she waged the usual singer's war.

Earlier, in February 1847, Verdi had gone to Florence for his new opera *Macbeth*, which he had written for Lanari. In Florence he found interesting people like the sculptor Lorenzo Bartolini and the poet Giusti, friends of Manzoni's. Bartolini kept links with the Bonapartists, the painter Piatti and his brother used a printing press for clandestine propaganda. In these homes there was open talk of revolt and of Austrian tyranny; people rejoiced in Italian culture, organising tours to get to know the masterpieces of the Renaissance and Verdi became an ardent admirer of Michelangelo. For the first night of *Macbeth* (14 March 1847), an opera that Verdi had dedicated to Barezzi, the composer was joined by his father-in-law and by Andrea Maffei who was finishing the libretto for the London opera. According to some writers, Giuseppina was in Florence secretly; a hotel porter had surprised the Maestro in his room 'with his wife'. But it is unlikely that this lady and Peppina were the same person. She could not have abandoned her classes and her pupils so easily and it would have been uncharacteristic of Verdi to summon her to his side when he was in the company of his father-in-law. The woman who was spotted in Verdi's room must have been one of the many who were happy to spend time with Giuseppe Verdi, altogether likely considering he was such a desirable single man. Just as it is not hard to understand that the friendship between him and Countess Maffei arose out of a love-affair, and it is probable that there were various other ladies in his life up until the time his relationship with Peppina became more binding. One can easily sympathise with them: Verdi was a wonderful man, extremely good-looking, brooding and interesting.

Verdi was dedicating time and care to his father-in-law: he should leave behind his provincial shell, Verdi told him, breathe the air of great cities like Milan and Florence, dress elegantly; the roles of father and son-in-law were reversed. Verdi returned to Milan in late March 1847, he was overworked, weak and he fell ill; he was sickly in those years, with a nervous stomach and severe headaches. In Milan, where he spent a whole month recovering, the atmosphere was incandescent and the Austrians knew it. The theatres, where popular sentiments could only be expressed by veiled metaphors, were kept under observation by the police and swarmed with spies; skirmishes would break out during the performances.

Verdi's *Giovanna d'Arco* (*Joan of Arc*) and Federico Ricci's *Michelangelo and Rolla*, not to mention *Nabucco*, provoked political demonstrations, during which the librettist and poet Ghislanzoni was arrested. Angelo Mariani, a young conductor, was threatened by the Austrians. But so much was happening which stimulated the people; in Rome a new Pope had been elected: Pius IX was less reactionary than his predecessor and, with wishful thinking, people saw him as a symbol of liberalism. In Piedmont, Count Cavour made England his model but looked at France as a potential ally against Austria. He did not believe in the republican ideas although he disliked his own king – and one can hardly blame him for this. Like all the Savoys, Carlo Alberto was inept and most unattractive. Being a monarchist, Cavour hoped that the French King Louis Philippe would not fail to support a war led by another monarch.

Italy was a long way away from democracy: the reforms that were conceded here and there by the various principalities to conciliate the people counted for nothing 'if not backed up by a profound change in the State. What is needed is a Constitution that envisages the existence of a Parliament which is the only organ capable of overseeing the work of the government,' Cavour wrote, pointing out that, as things stood, the sovereigns could withdraw the reforms they had conceded as and when they wished. He thus put pressure on Carlo Alberto to grant a constitution so as to draw the moderate forces to his side.

At last recovered, Verdi left Milan for London with Muzio, his loyal pupil and secretary. He was amazed to be stopped by the customs only once; how different from travel in Italy, where the luggage was inspected at every border, at every suspicious customs-post. They went to pay homage to Beethoven's tomb and stopped at Waterloo which, according to Muzio, was in France. This simple companion had become indispensable to Verdi and, as Massimo Mila has observed, above all he was unable 'to do without his services as a copyist, secretary, and go-between with the printers, and also a valid theatrical substitute in the harpsichord rehearsals.'

'This morning at seven we arrived in Paris,' wrote Muzio. It was June 1846. Muzio proceeded to London almost immediately while Verdi remained in Paris for a week and saw the Escudiers. And he saw Peppina who had been in Paris for seven months waiting for him. 'She leads a very secluded life,' Muzio wrote in a letter, 'she lives alone and she hates – so she told me – the theatre and the stage; she says she is unhappy and will feel content and pleased when she no longer has anything to do with theatrical people and with the stage itself.'

Verdi and Peppina had a lot to tell to each other; they went to concerts together, and to see plays. Sitting on a sofa at Rue de la Victoire, Verdi attended some of the lessons she gave. Clearly he was staying with her; we can only use our imagination, but those few Parisian days must have been wonderful for both of them; Verdi was relaxing, seeing beautiful things, hearing his notes being taught properly; Giuseppina had been longing to see him throughout those long months as she propagated his music and looked after his French affairs. She expressed her overwhelming joy in a letter to Giovanni Ricordi: 'My health has recovered completely, I have regained my appetite and the ability to sleep which I had lost. I hope I will have an opportunity to repay the kindness which you have shown me; and if the Metternich of publishers is not too proud to accept the friendship of a former artist, please accept that of your friend G Strepponi.'

While Muzio was shipped to London – which he described as 'a Babylon, the noisiest and most expensive city in the world', Verdi enjoyed Paris and Parisian discretion. But then he was forced to leave Giuseppina to move on to London.

Between March and April 1847, Peppina performed in two public concerts. In the first she sang an aria from *Ernani* and another from *Attila*, Verdi's latest operas. The score of *Macbeth* was too new to have arrived in Paris as yet. 'A unique honour in this matinée!' *La France musicale* commented. 'Strepponi was called back by the unanimous applause of the most intelligent and perceptive part of the auditorium.' In *Teatro, arte e letteratura*, which was published in Bologna (15th April 1847) we read that: 'Madame Strepponi is the most fashionable singer in Paris today; she is to be found at all the splendid soirées and at the festivities of high society. Recently she sang for Signor Cavaliere P . . ., where all the foreign ambassadors were gathered; Madame Strepponi achieved a definite triumph.' In September of that year we find that she is writing to Lanari asking him to pay two gold Napoleons to the maidservant who was in charge of Camillino. She was beginning to earn quite well in Paris and to erase the bad memories she had left behind. In June she gave a highly successful concert at Versailles where she sang an all-Verdi programme. *La Moda* (20 October 1847) commented:

Giuseppina Strepponi has made herself one of the most ardent propagators of the new school, one of the most valiant performers of dramatic singing: Verdi wrote *Nabucco* for her. The music of the new school is not as easy as some would have us believe: the style is bold and powerful, and demands great intelligence above all. This music is full of gradations and unexpected effects. With poor performers the passionate and graceful melodies would pass unobserved; but if sung as the composer imagined them, then they change physiognomy and arouse enthusiasm.

The article continued: 'Strepponi will have the merit of having taken the first steps in Paris towards a revolution in singing, a revolution that will not be long in bearing fruits.' It would have been better not to talk about revolutions, in the musical field or any other: this was hazardous territory. *Il Pirata*, 22 December 1847, too wrote that: 'Strepponi's lessons are in fashion among high society; she has already trained highly distinguished pupils.'

On the other side of the Channel, barricaded in three rooms, Verdi worked on orchestrating *I masnadieri* which he had written for the impresario of Her Majesty's Theatre, Benjamin Lumley, while Muzio was busy transcribing the score of *Macbeth* for Covent Garden. Lumley, who had achieved an unprecedented success with *I Lombardi*, was in fierce competition with Covent Garden. The latter opera house was managed by the composer Persiani, husband of the soprano Tacchinardi and the bitter war between the two theatres broke out when Covent Garden 'stole' the main conductor from Lumley. Her Majesty's Theatre was therefore relying on *I masnadieri* to get its own back.

In their rooms Verdi and Muzio were waited on by servants who knew only cockney English although the composer had been assured of the contrary – a fairly forlorn hope to find English waiters who spoke foreign languages. The food was appalling and the smog unbreathable. In addition Verdi was working under terrible pressure, waking up every morning at five and orchestrating for twelve hours a day. And he missed Paris and Peppina. However after delivering *I masnadieri* and rehearsing it with orchestra and singers, he allowed himself some relaxation.

Certainly it is difficult to classify as relaxation the visit Verdi paid to Mazzini in the modest house where the latter had lived for the past ten years. We cannot be sure how this meeting went; the popular iconographic versions are deceptive. Bearded and whiskered in spite of the London fashion, Mazzini had played havoc among the women and gave new life to the humiliated spirit of the Italian exiles.

The famous politician asked the famous composer to write a national anthem; were Mazzini to have had greater sensibility, he would have realised that the chorus from *Nabucco* had shaken the Austrian eagle far more profoundly than any of his own writings. It is unlikely that the two men took to each other, although they could hardly say so. Verdi was curt, caustic, a moderate in politics and a real celebrity – Queen Victoria sought in vain to meet him. Mazzini, on the other hand, was frustrated, verbose and authoritarian. But they had many mutual friends, such as Carlo Tenca and the sculptor Bartolini. In the following year, Verdi did send Mazzini a hymn which spurred men to march; it was not one of his greatest pieces, to put it mildly, but Verdi hated to compose under moral obligation or on commission. Verdi also met Prince Louis Bonaparte at a dinner that Lumley gave in the composer's honour; the future emperor of the French was living in London as a political exile, but not for long.

Although Paris was way ahead of Italy in many ways, London outstripped them both. It was the richest capital in the world, England was the most powerful, most adventurous and, in scientific and industrial terms, the most advanced nation in the world. At the head of a vast colonial empire, London protected its interests with an agile Navy, a more or less stable monarchy – with two Germans at its head – a well-organised State and a pragmatic Parliament. Verdi found the capital extremely stimulating; he often went to the theatre to see the tragedies of Shakespeare, the playwright he felt closest to, although he never made a romantic fetish of him, as Berlioz did. Like all fashionable cities, London – we learn from Muzio – was extremely expensive and extended for miles pulsing with frenetic activity, with intense traffic. The effects of progress were on display everywhere, the illuminated streets were crowded with people on their way to the City, where the business affairs of vast colonies were decided, trains linked up all main towns, new communications systems had paved the way for England's intense entrepreneurial activities. The gentlemen, with their black top-hats and malacca canes, clearly belonged to a different world from the workers: they dressed and spoke differently. They lived in huge country-houses and pretended to love opera. For this reason wages in London for theatre-people were the highest in the world.

Verdi had changed his mind about London: it was not a city, but an entire world, its streets were beautiful and the houses were clean. On the other hand he wrote to Countess Maffei: 'If I get away whole from London this time, it is unlikely that I will ever return . . . London is a marvellous city, the countryside around it is stupendous, but the climate is horrible.' When he arrived in London, he wrote to his various countesses: 'The chaos of London, the confusion! Paris is nothing in comparison! People shouting, paupers crying, steam flying in the air, men on horseback, in carriages, walking . . .' and also 'What a magnificent city! but this climate paralyses all beauty . . .' It was a climate that did not allow one to work, he observed. 'Long live the sun!'

I masnadieri was moderately successful, on account of the famous soprano Jenny Lind and the mighty bass Luigi Lablache, Cirelli's brother-in-law. Verdi conducted the first two performances; at the first, Queen Victoria was present and she noted in her diary that she had seen 'a new opera by Signor Verdi "inspired by Schiller's *Die Rauber*" the music (was) very noisy and trivial'. Muzio recounted that 'countless lords and dukes attended' as well as the Prince Consort and the Duke of Cambridge; Lumley offered Verdi a contract to compose and direct at Her Majesty's Theatre: eventually he turned it down. Five days after the première, on 27 July 1847, Verdi joined Giuseppina in Paris and sent Muzio back to Milan.

Sharing his life with a woman after so many years put him in a strange mood, like a character from Byron or an anti-hero of Kleist's, as he made it clear in a letter to Luigi Toccagni sent from Paris:

> What can I say to you? That I am still the same, still dissatisfied with everything; when fortune is propitious to me, I desire it against me, when it is against me, I desire it propitious; when I am in Milan, I would like to be in Paris. Now that I am in Paris, I would like to be . . . where? . . . I don't know . . . on the moon. After all, here I enjoy the individual freedom that I have always desired and never been able to attain. I visit no-one, no-one knows me and I do not have the inconvenience of being pointed out, as in so many cities in Italy. I enjoy good health, I write a great deal, affairs are going well, apart from my head which I always hope will change and never does change . . .

He was tired and hoped to have done with his work, he was 'much better than in London. A month's rest has done wonders for me. Oh, if I only could not work! Do you know this short word? NOT . . .' He wrote to Piave, in October 1847. Although he missed his games of bowls and cards with Muzio, life with an intelligent, highly organised woman such as Giuseppina suited him. This was the perfect opportunity for her to gain a permanent place in Verdi's life, slipping into that space that Muzio had been obliged to leave temporarily vacant; she had the added attraction of a good culture, of housewifely care and good taste in both literature and music. The elegance with which Giuseppina had decorated the apartment, with which she dressed and spoke, her spirit and sense of humour, became an ideal remedy for Verdi's periods of irrational grudges.

In January 1848, Antonio Barezzi came on a visit: he had to consult

Verdi with regard to some question of land in Busseto and thus he met the Signora Peppina. He saw Giuseppina in her role as the lady of the house, mingling with the guests, hosting dinner-parties, introducing him to her friends. He admired her as she gave lessons to her pupils and as she discreetly managed the life of successful Maestro Verdi. But he would never have dreamt that this much discussed lady who had redeemed herself from her well-known past, could become the official companion of his son-in-law, the man he had always believed to be the best of all. They had been so cordial and kind towards him, Verdi and La Signora Peppina, they had included him in their dinners, in their life which despite their two slightly different addresses, had become the same. Meanwhile in Milan gossip was rife and letters flew in all directions; everybody now knew: Verdi was living in Strepponi's house.

Peppina surrounded Verdi with interesting people who could be useful to him: 'I greatly desire that M. Castel-Blaze should come and eat with us on Sunday; but I am not familiar enough with him to take the liberty of inviting him directly. Would you be so good as to drop him a line and persuade him to join us on Sunday? It would please Verdi as well. Of course it will be an informal affair, and Castel-Blaze shall come in his wide boots, and hunting-hat etc etc. So he can have no excuse for refusing.' This suggests that in Rue de la Victoire, they entertained a lot. 'I would have liked to ask the same favour of Albert Le Clerc and his daughter, but I think he is still in the country. If by any chance he should have returned, ask him on my behalf to honour us with his company. I think you like these people, as I and Verdi do. You will not forget, then, that I asked you to invite them. I value your friendship . . .' It is not unlikely that this letter was addressed to Rossini.

Even when Verdi was composing, Peppina stayed by his side. Indeed in the score of *Jérusalem*, the opera Verdi was writing for Paris, his companion's hand-writing appears for the first time: a love-duet in two hands reveals the strength of their bond: *Jérusalem* was dedicated to Giuseppina. Verdi was expected back in Milan; but he continued to change his mind as much as he had done when he had been with Peppina in Parma. At the beginning of February 1848, Verdi wrote to Muzio to expect him in Milan soon but the latter then said to Barezzi: 'My hopes of seeing the Maestro were disappointed. This morning instead of Verdi, I find a letter of the 12th, saying that on the eve of his departure he had a slight temperature and a cold, and he did not want to set forth on a journey for fear that he might get worse.' Apart from this cold, true or false as it might be, there was a matter of politics. On 24 February King Louis-Philippe was deposed: Giuseppina and Verdi witnessed the birth of the new French Republic. For the whole of the previous day the alleys of Paris had been blocked by hundreds of barricades, made with beams, stones and bricks; liberals and students, socialists and stolid burghers, democrats and workers fired from behind them at the soldiers of the king. The following day the revolution had spread to the rest of France and the Second Republic was proclaimed. Contemplating the events, Giuseppina complained that the 'quavers and semi-quavers cannot have any effect against gunfire and cannons, because of the old truth that the stronger prevails! But let all notes go to the devil, if there are too many crowned heads still oppressing it.'

Writing to Pietro Romani she confided: 'So many things I thought impossible have happened, that I find myself doubting everything and everyone!' She was not only amazed by what was happening in politics, but also to find herself loved by Verdi, the man every woman would have liked to conquer. His attachment was a wonder to her: the way they could talk, discuss things, but also the way they could read their books enjoying the silent presence of the other: these were all new experiences. And to be appreciated for her intellectual qualities was a novelty too; she liked to be by his side as he composed, sharing his work which – she was fully aware – was truly great. As the notes flew on the piano, she would tell him: 'This is wonderful, this is new! This is fine!' She was also acting as a musical agent; in a letter to Giovanni Ricordi (15 March 1848) she said that 'The brothers Escudier have decided for personal reasons to retire from business.' They had asked Giuseppina to inquire whether Ricordi was interested in buying their stock of musical plates. 'I believe it's a good deal.' She enclosed the list of all the works in their possession and details about money and contracts. And they talked about politics as everyone did.

Extraordinary things were happening: a month before the French events, the spark had been ignited in Palermo, which had risen up against the Bourbons; in March the revolt exploded in Vienna, the capital of the Austro-Hungarian Empire, and it was taken up in Bavaria and Berlin. Hungary too proclaimed itself an independent kingdom. The news of the Viennese insurrection hit Milan like a bomb: Venice and Lombardy rose up as well. It was like a chain reaction; discontent had been seething throughout Europe, and now it exploded. Every nation, apart from England and Russia (for opposite reasons) felt the shock and produced their own flame which they passed on to their neighbour, like a Mediterranean forest-fire.

But in the case of France, the blaze had been sparked off by the class-hatreds between the middle class and the proletariat. It was 'a conflict between the workers and the bourgeoisie, that was the character of the 1848 revolution,' wrote Lamartine. Or, as André Maurois put it aptly, 'the smock against the frock-coat, the casquette against the hat.'

The classes were divided by language as well as by clothes; the workers and the middle class did not understand one another. The social nature of the French conflict was underlined by the fact that the Préfecture and the Town-Hall were occupied by armed workers. Lamartine wrote with pride that the revolution 'took the world by surprise'. He thought it was his revolution, shaped by him, he thought he could handle it. It took Giuseppina and Verdi by surprise too: Verdi was thus prevented from leaving Paris; the delay did not bother him in the least, nor her.

In France, the new republican government voted an electoral reform that increased the number of electors from 250,000 to a dizzy nine millions. But the demands of the Socialist party scared the moderate forces which, in April, excluded them from government.

In June the Parisian proletariat rose up again. They were alone this time and the repression was fierce. About three thousand rebels were shot without trial, many others were deported; the red peril had been quashed. That same year a book stirred up a good deal of fear, *The Manifesto of the Communist Party*: 'A spectre is stalking through Europe,' wrote Karl Marx in his introduction, 'the spectre of Communism.'

Europe was infected by the fear that the workers of the indus-trialised countries might force their claims upon the middle class, that they might take possession of politics, thus halting the rise of industrialism. These events spurred Verdi into action. 'Now it is our turn,' he wrote to a friend on 11 February 1848. And 'our turn' came about. In a well-organised revolt, Milan rose up against the Austrians and in five days of barricades, drove them out of the city. The Five Days of Milan had been violent but it was not a question of class conflict as it had been in France, since the Italian working class was not yet a proletariat. The revolt had broken out in a picturesque way: protesting against an Austrian tax on tobacco, the whole city had refused to smoke. When a group of soldiers walked past a café smoking with an air of challenge, the

Milanese booed them. The Austrians lost their nerve and started to sweep their sabres and shoot: thus started the most splendid page of the Italian Risorgimento: students, aristocrats and intellectuals fought the army of General Radetzky, an eighty-year-old general whose name had become anathema. Barricades were erected as in Paris and a hastily improvised Lombard army proved itself heroic.

Giuseppina's friend Princess Belgiojoso left her Paris salon and burst onto the scene in splendid attire, appearing in the thick of the fray with a plumed hat Ernani-style. She rode into the embattled city by the ramparts of Porta Romana on her white horse, brandishing the tricolor. The crowd watched her from the barricades and the piazzas with the stupefaction of an audience at La Scala. One would not be surprised to learn that they applauded her. She was at the head of her own private army, one hundred and sixty soldiers, but her valiant men disbanded. Some joined the people at the barricades, others made their way to Venice to defend the besieged city, which lay under the scourge of cholera, hunger and Austrian gunfire. Casa Maffei, just like other palazzi, had been transformed into an infirmary: Clara looked after the wounded. The Milanese had succeeded in driving 'the Germans out of their city', wrote Peppina from Paris. She was enthusiastic although she went on: 'But now things are getting worse and the Italians are unable to renounce their political coterie, there is always too much talk and discussion and not enough action.' Verdi had left Paris but did not reach Milan until after the battle was over. Awaiting re-inforcements from Vienna, Radetzky retreated to the impregnable Quadrilateral, four cities distributed on a defensive line. Happy to find himself in a free Milan, Verdi returned to his apartment: the city wanted him as a tribune.

In Paris Peppina found herself short of work: theatres were closing, singers had little opportunity, and wages were reduced. That winter she had worked well until the February Revolution came along with its far-reaching consequences: in the evenings nobody left their houses. Peppina had decided not to return to Italy, though. Were she to leave her Parisian house she would lose out 'selling furniture at a time when money is scarce, and I would waste money on travel . . . and anyway where would I go to do good business?' Certainly not to Italy . . . 'You ask me about my voice . . .' she answered her friend Romani, 'my voice has suffered and it is now as it was in those final days with Lanari.' She no longer enjoyed Paris, especially without Verdi. 'Society, festivities, dinners etc, when I am obliged to sing in some house, I stay there just as long as is necessary and then rush home. I do not enjoy dancing, I do not enjoy dinners, and supposing I had enough to get by without working, I might stay in Paris for the freedom one finds here but they would never see me again in any place where society is.'

Verdi was enjoying life in Milan, life continued in the cafés and the clubs, but he did not stay long because he had to return to France not only to write two more operas but also to collect some money. Besides, Giuseppina was waiting for him. He delivered the score of *Il corsaro* (The Corsair) which he owed the Luccas and left on 31 May 1848. *Il corsaro* was premièred in Trieste where he had no desire to go, not only on account of the Luccas but also because Trieste was Austrian. After such a hectic period, Verdi returned to the peace of domestic life. In fact Giuseppina urged him to move to the country, the fresh air would have done him good. 'Many years ago, loving the country very much,' Giuseppina recalled, 'I asked Verdi insistently to leave Paris, to live beneath the pavilion of the open sky and enjoy the healthy air and light that give as much vigour to the body as they do calm and serenity to the mind. Verdi who, like Auber, practically had a horror of life in the country, after much pleading agreed to take a small house not far from Paris.'

They went to live in what was then open country, in Passy; it was a situation very similar to that described in the second act of *La traviata*. They settled in the shady avenues of the Ranelagh, for a whole month; it was then that Verdi conceived a love for the countryside that was never to leave him. The country meant freedom, the right to solitude, contact with nature. They went for long walks; she would struggle to keep pace with him, underneath the wide straw hat that protected her from the sun, and with her gloves to maintain the whiteness of her hands. In an open-necked shirt and a hat with a drooping brim, he would stride along in silence. At the end of the month, Verdi had no wish to go back to live in the city: why not stay there? For Peppina that would be fatal, who would ever come all the way to Passy for singing lessons? It was a two-hour carriage-drive at least. But even so, Giuseppina, tired of the social whirl and the endless stream of visitors, had revealed to him the pleasure of seclusion.

It was in Passy, in the solitude of the country, that Giuseppina achieved her real aim: she became Verdi's indispensable companion, his mistress, his secretary and his friend; she proved an excellent substitute for Muzio who, for all his docility and kindness, was not a stimulating companion for a person of Verdi's intelligence. During their solitary walks, their long conversations, Peppina and Verdi managed to conceive of a life together; for Giuseppina, as I have said, this had been a dominant thought, even if it could not have been easy for her, as a primadonna and a lady of fashion, to suppress·her own personality and reduce her role to that of a mere shadow. She would become the shadow of a man she loved; perhaps no longer with passion, but with a feeling that contained something of gratitude. There was also an element of maternal affection; she acted as a substitute for that mother who had been absent from Verdi's life. Also Giuseppina had taught him to get over his provincial awkwardness. She smoothed the sharp edges of his touchy character, which had been so deeply marked by his terrible losses. When they arrived back in Paris at the end of 1848, they found that new elections gave the presidency of the republic to the Prince Bonaparte whom Verdi had met in London. The two classes at first allied against the aristocracy, finding themselves at opposite poles; the middle class used the money accumulated by the new industrial economy, investing in factories and commerce but they required a constitution, a guarantee of a united, independent nation. This is the key to the hasty restorations of 1848, in particular that of France.

While Verdi, inspired by the events in Milan, was thinking once again of Risorgimento subjects, he witnessed from afar the victory of the Austrians, first against the Piedmontese who abandoned Milan to Radetzky, then of Venice. In fact Carlo Alberto of Savoy had waited so long to march against the Austrians that Radetzky had all the time to reorganise his forces. On the night of the defeat (23 March 1849) the unpopular king abdicated in favour of his son, Victor Emanuel, who signed his surrender to the Austrians. On 5 August the sky above Milan flickered with the lurid light of houses set ablaze by the Austrians. Princess Belgiojoso and other Lombard patricians were punished with a severe tax of 800,000 svanziche each. The patriots Carcano, Tenca, Clarina Maffei and Princess Belgiojoso chose exile. 'I will tell you nothing about our country. It is simply pitiful,' wrote Verdi to Léon Escudier. He was writing *The Battle of Legnano* which was to be staged in Rome. Verdi continued to shuttle back and forth between Italy and France, while tongues wagged about the Maestro's strange choice of lover. Moderate France had re-opened the doors of the Opéra whose pillars were still Auber, Halévy and Meyerbeer – not yet Verdi.

At least the events in Rome filled Verdi and Giuseppina with enthusiasm: on 8 February 1849, the Roman Republic had been proclaimed. The Pope had fled and the democrats had proclaimed a republic governed by a triumvirate consisting of Mazzini, Aurelio Saffi and Carlo Armellini; the Roman army was led by Garibaldi at the head of his colourful troops. Flanked by Aguilar, a South American Indian, the blond general was acclaimed by the Romans. The army of the Roman Republic beat the French who had come in aid of the Pope, as well as the troops sent by the Bourbons. Garibaldi was a general of genius, but Mazzini was not equally skilful as a politician: he gave the enemy time to bring their cannons up to Rome. A furious siege, against which the city put up a desperate resistance, ended the Roman Republic. Aguilar was one of the many soldiers who died on the Roman barricades. Garibaldi, hunted by all the armies of Europe, made his way towards Venice: his wife Anita died in his arms. The following month, in August, Venice surrendered, the last revolutionary government to fall. Verdi and Giuseppina decided to leave Paris, together.

They decided to settle in the palazzetto that Verdi had bought the previous year in Busseto, the town near Le Roncole where he was born, in the province of Parma. While Verdi made his way directly there, Giuseppina made a necessary journey to Florence; she would join him later. She had to find someone to look after Camillino since he was now growing up. For some reason Cirelli was no longer looking after his illegitimate son; maybe he had moved to Milan with his family; by this stage he was old and ill. On 10 March 1849 Rosa Strepponi wrote to Ricordi from Pavia. She stated, in a dignified way and writing in a fine hand, that her daughter was sending her money for her to collect.

Arriving in the Grand Duchy of Tuscany after a long journey followed by her luggage, part of which had been sent directly to Busseto, Giuseppina brought with her many letters of introduction: through Verdi she became acquainted with the whole group of intellectuals linked with Manzoni.

From Florence Giuseppina wrote Verdi the first love-letter that we know of, full of jokes and fond expressions, using a private vocabulary that had developed during months of life together. It was 3 September 1848 and the couple had not seen each other for about a month:

I will have finished my business on Wednesday, and maybe on Wednesday evening itself I will set out for Parma. But don't come to fetch me until Friday evening or Saturday morning, because I would be sorry if you had to wait at Parma in vain. When I tell you who has taken charge of Camillino's artistic education, you will be amazed! . . . Be content with the knowledge that I kissed the hands of the great man who said to me: 'Will you trust him to me?'

This was Bartolini, the sculptor who offered to attend to the question of Camillino's upbringing: poor Giuseppina, the man was to prove the source of great trouble.

Giuseppina was taking a major step; she was now in her thirties and, if it would turn out to be a step along the wrong road or if the road should prove a dead-end, there would be no turning back for her. She was staking everything on Verdi: she was leaving her singing courses, the pupils she had so painstakingly acquired, her Parisian apartment, her new friends, the world of the theatre; she was burning her only bridge. Giuseppina was at an impasse, as is clear from the way she expresses herself: keep Verdi waiting at Parma? Keep him waiting in a hotel, for her? How the tongues would wag! In Florence she had seen very few people, she adds ('No aristocrat, it goes without saying . . .') knowing that Verdi would be pleased to hear that her time had not been spent in the social whirl – but everyone had tried to help her.

Addio my joy! Now that I have nearly finished my business, business that is too serious to neglect, I would like to be able to fly to your side. You talk to me about the ugly countryside, the bad service, and then you say, 'If you don't like it, I will have you accompanied – I will have you! – wherever you want to go.' What the devil! In Busseto do people forget how to love one another and how to write with a little affection . . . ?

Certainly in comparison with Passy, with the undulating countryside around Paris and with the French maidservants that Peppina had trained so well, Busseto could scarcely have seemed a paradise. But Peppina reassured him – what did she care about the country? and the service? It was him she cared about. 'The country, the service and all the rest will suit me fine as long as you are there, you ugly, unworthy monster. *Addio, addio*. I have just time to say I detest you and I embrace you.' And in a postscript she added a plea, that was clearly tormenting her: 'Don't send anyone but come to

Parma yourself to fetch me, because I would be very embarrassed to be introduced to your house by anyone other than you.'

Verdi, however, was fairly confident about the way things would go: he did not care much about his father Carlo, his mother would be on his side in accepting Giuseppina. He had no doubt about Antonio Barezzi who had been charmed by her. He had even written: 'You make me hope for a letter from Signora Peppina and I must tell you I look forward to it eagerly ...' Demalde, Barezzi's dear friend and relative, had been conquered by Peppina's grace as well, when he met her in Parma, before going to Paris: 'How is Peppina's health ...? Tell her that I remember her because I have good reason to appreciate her gifts, her fine spirit and her virtues. How happy I would be to see her again.'

She was an exceptional woman, fully worthy of making her entrance on Verdi's arm into one of the most beautiful houses in Busseto. It was still early to talk about marriage, and besides there was that child who, one day, might claim part of the inheritance, of that money Verdi had earned with passion and hard work over the last years – the 'prison years' which, thanks to Giuseppina, were about to end.

But Giuseppina's prison years were about to begin.

7
A GENIUS OBSERVED

From Florence to Busseto. The months of solitude and
musical apotheosis of a genius: *Rigoletto, Il trovatore* and *La
traviata*. Death of Camillino's guardian. Peppina on her
own at Busseto. Giuseppina – no longer the Generalina
– alone again in Leghorn. Ever alone, Verdi's secret
companion at Sant'Agata.

———————— • ————————

Ed or contenta in questi ameni luoghi
tutto scorda per me
Qui presso a lei io rinascer mi sento . . .
And happy now in this pleasant place
she forgets everything for my sake
Here by her side I feel myself return to life . . .

LA TRAVIATA, ACT II

The stifling heat of Florence in August is almost proverbial:
people escape to the hills, to Fiesole or Settignano, from
where they watch the heat-haze thicken over the Arno. Giuseppina
contacted Lanari, who had not left the city. But she only did so in
order to obtain an address from him; she had no desire to pick up
the threads of the past.

Florence, 31 August 1849

Dear Lanari,
    I am in Florence for a few days, staying at the Albergo della
Luna, Via Condotti. If it is not too much trouble, come and
see me and tell Tonino [Lanari's son] that I am here and give
him my best wishes. Also do me the favour of asking Stefano for
Livia's address which I have lost; better still, please send it to me
immediately, immediately.
    A cordial handshake.

Lanari retraced Livia Zanobini who was in charge of Camillino and also of Giuseppina's business affairs in Florence; Peppina even had an outstanding debt with Livia's brother-in-law, Filippo Pagliai, which she took care to settle during her visit. The Pagliai family had another lodger of the same age as Camillino – one of Lanari's illegitimate children, the 'mistake' of a female colleague – later Camillino was to study medicine with him. And now that Giuseppina had earned good money in France by leading a quiet life, she could decide what to do with her savings; the shortage of money that had dogged her from 1842 onwards was no longer a problem. At the height of her stage career, with major contracts always on offer, she had given no thought to the future. Like all young people, like all grasshoppers, she imagined that her voice, her beauty – and her youth! – would last for ever. And so, when times got hard, she found herself forced to play the role of the ant. With help from Lanari but above all from Monier, her new Florentine agent, the ex-Generalina decided how to portion out the money she had brought from Paris, in investments that would guarantee Camillino an annual income. She put money in groceries and textiles; the latter was an industry with centuries of tradition in Prato. As soon as she had arranged things, she set out to join Verdi.

She was accompanied on the journey by Livia; a lady could not travel alone, and Livia was going to look after her during her stay in Busseto, a stay that might be short or – as Peppina hoped – definitive. But a letter that she received in Florence from Verdi did not bode well; there were sentences that bore all the signs of his black moods, as if he regretted having invited her to Busseto. We must use our imagination to picture the journey along the Futa in a dusty coach carrying passengers from Florence to Parma, passing the customs-houses of the Grand Duchy of Tuscany, of the Papal States, of the Duchy of Modena and finally the Duchy of Parma. There were probably a dozen or so people in the coach, including at least a couple of spies and agents provocateurs. Her fellow-travellers can hardly have failed to note this elegant lady, with her lady companion and twenty or so trunks, a check, knitted shawl to protect her indigo silk dress from the dust. Every time the coachman stopped at a staging post, to change the exhausted horses and to allow the travellers to refresh themselves, this somewhat haughty lady would step out, and then walk up and down on her own. She had left the summer heat behind her, and up here in the Apennines the air was cooler. The spies knew all about her while the others wondered. Her mind was heavy as she travelled; she was worried about the son she was leaving behind. Her daughter weighed less on her; she had sent Giuseppa into a kind of limbo, from which there was to be no redemption; Giuseppina was now thirty-four years old, she had slipped into maturity without noticing. It seemed to her that she had completely missed out on her youth. Thirty-four as an age was not the same then as it is today; peasant women were considered old then, middle-class women past it, no longer able to procreate. And yet she had the good fortune to find someone to settle with, even if only temporarily, while on the threshold of old age.

After Fiesole, they passed Pratolino on the right; there stood one of the Grand Duke's favourite villas where she had sung a couple of times. They then began the ascent of the Mugello and the air got fresher. They reached Covigliano, a disreputable coaching inn, a pair of oxen were attached since the road was too rocky for the horses. Travellers recounted the tale of how coaches used to arrive at Covigliano and set off again empty; there was talk of bandits and cannibalism – but these were typical mountain stories. Her black hair, which was still glossy and tied at the nape of the neck with a tortoise-shell clasp, was protected from the dust with a silk turban; it gave extra prominence to that nose of hers, which she saw protruding whenever her eyes focused on the landscape on that wearing journey. At Scaricalasino they changed the two horses again; the soldiers of the Grand Duchy inspected all the luggage and studied their passes; they were finally let through, only to be subjected to an even more tedious inspection on the part of the papal army. They spent the night near Pietra-Mala and some of the travellers went to admire the nocturnal flame and the spring of Acqua Buja. The following morning they descended to Pianora, where the landscape was totally different, the Tuscan olive trees and cypresses were replaced by Emilian corn and then by the red bricks of beautiful Bologna. In the distance, San Luca stood out sharply on the hills to announce to the travellers that they had arrived in the great Paduan plane.

When she reached the Hotel Corona in Parma, she found Verdi waiting for her. They strolled together through the Piazza Grande, returned to the Ducale, the theatre that had seen them together in *Nabucco* all those years ago, when they could never have imagined a future together. They visited San Giovanni, the church frescoed by the great Correggio, then wandered through the fifteenth-century courtyard and got someone to open up the ancient chemist's with its oak shelves and ancient pottery. The pink marble Cathedral, the

Baptistry, with its magnificent statues by Antelami which seemed to describe Vivaldi's seasons, closed the piazza with the Archbishop's Palace, where Stendhal's protagonist of *La Chartreuse de Parme* were described as living. The hem of Giuseppina's dress swept the paving-stones, as she walked along bedside that man whom everybody turned to stare at in admiration. Verdi had become instantly recognisable from the many prints of his face, with his wide-brimmed hat above his irritated eyes, his hair hanging over his eyes in the fashion that was now known as '*alla Verdi*'. He had been in Busseto for over a month, having arrived there on 10 August; three days later he received from Salvatore Cammarano the complete libretto of *Luisa Miller*, a story he had very much at heart. He finished work on it quickly before Giuseppina's arrival: Muzio was by his side to transcribe the notes.

The change from Paris to Busseto was not an easy one; there was great joy at this return of the prodigal son, and everybody had tried to take possession of him; Verdi stood firm and only saw his brothers-in-law, Antonio Barezzi his beloved father-in-law and a few friends. He felt a certain irritation towards Barezzi's sons; Giovannino, for example, had been left in charge of matters while Verdi was in Paris but had done nothing. The young Barezzis were spoilt and it was only natural that they felt a degreee of jealousy towards Verdi, who had practically been adopted by their father and was certainly better loved by him than they were. When he arrived in Busseto, the composer had paid a visit to an old flame of his, the Baroness Eroteide Soldati, the wife of a minister of the Duchess; she had helped – and loved – him in his youth. But he found her more or less in the arms of a new lover, the Marchese Malaspina. He determined to forget all about her; but this visit does show that the Maestro's attentions were not focused exclusively on Peppina.

Verdi and Peppina did a little sightseeing in Parma before setting off towards Piacenza; when they arrived in Borgo San Donnino, the Maestro's new carriage came to meet them. They made their way across the plain, past brick farmhouses, large stables and brimming granaries, along country-roads bordered with plane-trees, with the blue Apennines hanging hazily to their left; the carriage took them straight to Busseto. It was 14 September. Muzio was awaiting them at the crossroads; he had walked in the sun to meet them, but as the coachdriver stopped the horses, Giuseppina turned to Verdi and said: 'Emanuele can come along on foot.' Thus the Generalina 'made her famous triumphal entrance' into Busseto, an entrance that she did not want to share with her most dangerous rival; Peppina knew that the only way to anchor herself to Verdi was to agree with him, act as his musical assistant, his silent lover, compliant friend and discreet adviser – without any interference from Emanuele Muzio.

The arrival of the Maestro, who was now the town's most keenly admired, envied, respected and discussed citizen, attracted the attention of hundreds of pairs of eyes blinking behind shutters, behind the pillars of the elegant arcades along the *palazzetti*. The woman who sat next to Verdi, with her glossy hair and lively eyes, was spotted at once, disappointing a good many mothers of marriageable daughters, and offending the respectable: Verdi was taking a woman into his house, in his own town! There was no knowing where she came from, some gambling-den perhaps, maybe she didn't even speak Italian, certainly not their dialect. The mysterious silhouette slipped into the entrance-hall of Palazzo Dordoni leaving a good deal of rancour behind her. Palazzo Dordoni, which Giuseppina was seeing for the first time, was elegantly built around an internal courtyard and an open gallery. The carriage drew up in the entrance and one climbed the stairs to the *piano nobile*, with its salons decorated with timid ninenteeth-century frescoes in graceful colours. It was a beautiful place in which to live, more spacious and elegant than her apartment in Rue de la Victoire, but there was no garden. Its façade gave on to the main street in Busseto, where all the carriages and fine *bussetani* paraded, where people saw each other, saluted each other, commented on one another – in short where Busseto's life took place.

Verdi and Peppina did not reappear, except furtively to do some shopping. At first, invitations poured in, all for the Maestro: not one bore the name of Peppina or even hinted at her presence. Verdi ignored them. On the few occasions Giuseppina did decide to go for a walk under her parasol, with her embroidered gloves, nobody acknowledged her greetings as she stopped at the meagerly stocked little shops. After a few days, the whole of Busseto knew that Verdi had brought along a woman 'with a past'. The couple were known to have lived together openly in Paris; Giuseppina's arrival alongside the most prominent man in Busseto was considered an affront by his parents – and even by Antonio Barezzi who had met and admired her in Paris.

They led an almost monastic life; they ate alone, they worked and every so often the coachman harnessed two horses to the carriage and took them for a drive in that melancholy, mosquito-ridden countryside. But at night, the arcades of Busseto echoed with the insults directed at Giuseppina; all the town's malice was devoted to mocking and ostracising her, with the thought of getting rid of her. However, if there was one way to bind Giuseppina more closely to Verdi's heart, it lay in that cruel rejection.

Verdi's parents, Carlo and Luigia, had only recently moved from Palazzo Dordoni to live on a farm which the composer had bought near the river Ongina in the Sant'Agata area. They hoped that their son would join them and Verdi's mother had transferred his bed there, putting it in a room which she thought would suit him nicely; after all, how could he possibly manage by himself, with all the cleaning and cooking to do? And with that awful woman?

It is important to remember that since the death of his sister, who was probably insane, Giuseppe had been brought up as an only child. If we accept the idea that genius and madness are two sides of the same coin – or rather that both states are in some way anomalous or abnormal – we can perhaps guess at some genetic quirk in Verdi's make-up which might help to explain what is otherwise unaccountable. Giuseppe Verdi was the son of normal parents, he had grown up in a normal household and studied under normal people; without some freak gene, how could he have broken so confidently through the barriers of his epoch and invented another? Giuseppina had grasped the fact of his brilliance, his genius, this chance combination of characteristics which is granted to so few people and which can only bear fruit if it is inherited by an individual imbued with tenacity, good health and ambition. Without just one of these ingredients, we would no longer have had a Michelangelo Buonarroti working for months clinging to the roof of the Sistine Chapel or we would be without our Mozart, thus depriving our times of the men who contributed so vitally to their transformation.

Quite simply if Verdi, the son of modest people, had not been a genius, his music would lie buried together with that of Mercadante or Luigi Ricci and many others; he would never have succeeded in transcending his own period. Giuseppina venerated this capacity in him, this instant connection between his mind and his hands, this fierce tenacity of purpose.

Once settled in Busseto, without further distractions, the perpetual festivities, the lengthy political discussions, Verdi changed his life-style. This was probably premeditated and clearly he must have discussed it with Giuseppina. She was to write to him one day: 'How often do I fear that the love of money will re-awaken in you, condemning you to many more years of work!' But the period which Verdi referred to as his 'prison years' was over; he had saved money and he had his acres at Sant'Agata, now he had earned time to concentrate his thoughts, to reflect. Furthermore, with the deterioration of the political and economic scene, the opera world had changed, many houses had closed, attendances were down and operas that were considered politically inflammatory were not even staged. A compliment to Verdi who had turned opera into a political weapon which could threaten a regime on the retreat. At this point Verdi resolved to ignore music that was directly provocative; not only would the censors reject it, but his two latest operas which were in that vein, had flopped (*Il corsaro* in Trieste, director Luigi Ricci; and *The Battle of Legnano* in Rome).

The political climate had undergone fundamental change and the subject of independence was not even discussed any longer. Most of Europe was returning to absolute monarchies with the exception of France and Piedmont where Vittorio Emanuele had maintained a Constitutional Parliament. After bombarding Vienna and crushing the revolt there, the Austrian emperor had recalled Metternich and it was as if 1848 had never happened. Lombardy-Veneto remained in Austrian hands with Naples under the Bourbons and Rome suffocated by the Papacy. It was a cruel disappointment to the Liberals; their defeat was mainly due to disagreements amongst individuals and petty ambition. All this left its mark on a man like Verdi. He no longer wanted to talk politics in the salons which had once nourished his dreams. A united Italy had not been achieved and the Italians had only themselves to blame. But a Piedmontese aristocrat, Camillo Count of Cavour who in 1847 founded a magazine called *Il Risorgimento*, wrote that the political resurgence – *risorgimento* – of a nation could not be separated from its economic well-being. As things stood it was necessary to put pressure on the king of Savoy and unite all moderate Italian forces, both liberal and Catholic, behind the Savoy cause. Verdi began to see that this was the only way, that the path to unification could only come from moderation.

The political field being a minefield, Verdi decided to devote himself to more intimate subjects, to use his music to penetrate the emotions of the individual rather than of groups. To reveal the contemporary world through such themes as an evangelical pastor – Stiffelio – with an unfaithful wife or a prostitute – Violetta – who discovers true love and then dies of consumption. He wanted to plumb human emotions using concepts like Lear, the king who only learns to see after he has been stripped of all his possessions or the hunchback with the dual personality who is servile in public but privately noble and deeply affectionate; the gipsy woman who is above all a mother. To this end he asked his publisher to send him an Italian-Spanish dictionary so that he could understand *El Trobadur*, a drama by Antonio Garcia Gutierrez which had proved enormously popular in theatres all over Europe. It was Giuseppina herself who translated it from Spanish for him.

At this extraordinary time of his creative fertility Verdi, humiliated and ostracised by his parents and his own people – he had expected quite a different reception – found a major source of inspiration in the bond between father and daughter. In *Luisa Miller*, a daughter lies to the man she loves in order to protect her father; in *Rigoletto* the buffoon lives only for his daughter Gilda; in *Il trovatore*, Azucena destroys herself by burning her own son in error; if Verdi had composed *King Lear*, he would have given us a striking Cordelia. Even in *La traviata* there is a father who wrecks the lives of the protagonists thinking only to save his son's reputation and his daughter's marriage. Then there is *Stiffelio*, which portrays the narrow world of bigoted minds, people who merely wish to condemn a repentant adulteress, a woman who has fallen but sees the errors of her ways in time for her husband, a pastor, a man of peace to forgive but too late to receive forgiveness in the eyes of the cruel society in which she lives. It is easy to recognise in this summary the portrait of a hostile Busseto, of the repentant Giuseppina and of a man who is bigger than his contemporaries – Verdi himself – who is capable of forgiveness but whose mind is distracted by his personal dialogue if not with God with Art.

By now Verdi was composing operas that described his own world, operas which featured his private feelings, emotions which he himself was experiencing. When he touched people's hearts by setting great choral sentiments, of Babylonians and Lombards and maidens, corsairs and countesses, he had done it by applying his inventive genius and not by drawing on personal experience. *Macbeth* is the only opera composed before he retired to Busseto in which it is possible to hear a cry of suffering that is rooted in experience. From now on, the sentiment that Verdi was to express better than any other was that of sorrow. The sobs of the cellos, the lament of the double bass, the passion of Rigoletto's angry grief, the anguish of Violetta, the tears that flow in the Lacrimosa of the *Requiem*, all are based on real life, on his own and Giuseppina's.

It is clear that, when there is a genius in the house, he takes precedence, and he remains a genius with or without the women who tend to him. It is thus natural that, in this chapter of their lives, Giuseppina takes second place. Her awareness that she was living in the shadow of a great man, gave her pleasure, peace of mind: not to be the protagonist on the stage meant tranquillity. But in this chapter she goes into the background; however she is my subject and I am her biographer and even if I have no desire to support the fashionable theory that behind every great man there lies an even greater woman, I do wish to point out that Giuseppina was necessary to the composer – and to explain why. She was not a Cosima, partly because Giuseppe Verdi was a more engaging person than Richard Wagner, even if no less complex. Like Cosima she kept a diary in the hundreds of letters she wrote. Unlike Cosima she had no children from her man, and with the children she did have, she behaved badly from fear of her own reputation and later, from fear of harming the precarious equilibrium she had created between herself and Verdi.

That the now middle-aged couple could not have any more children together is made clear in the writings of Giuseppina. We can but imagine the effect on her body of those births and of those forbidden abortions in her youth. But Verdi's preoccupation with filial love, with the bond between father and daughter, is something that arouses suspicion. Why did he wait until he was living with Giuseppina to lament his lost fatherhood? His little Virginia had died many years ago and more than ten years had passed since his small son's death. Could it be that one of those abortions or miscarrages of Giuseppina's had represented the last chance of becoming a father with this woman? A chance that would have been unacceptable at the time, both because of Margherita Barezzi, and because of the life that the Generalina had been leading. Now that Giuseppina was by his side, his domesticity reminded him of that lost joy. This could well have represented a bond between them, a reason why Verdi felt almost under obligation to her.

There is a suspicious birth recorded in April 1851 which Mary Jane Phillips-Matz, Verdi's latest biographer, discovered in Cremona; a foundling by the name of Santa Streppini abandoned in the turnstile may have been brought up with the name of Santa Stropellini in a farm of the Verdi estate. But this find contains too many buts, including Giuseppina's own words in a love letter which, I hope, does not deceive intentionally in order to confuse posterity. As we shall see, their life together was a difficult one, with Giuseppina often pushed to the sideline, but when it was Busseto that chose to ostracise the former *traviata*, Verdi became the staunch champion of his lady.

During the day, Verdi worked with Francesco Maria Piave who was now both his librettist and a dear friend; ever since his enlistment in the revolutionary army that had liberated Venice, he had grown in Verdi's esteem. He was not entirely popular with Giuseppina, since word reached her of how he dragged Verdi along with him in his woman-chasing, practically playing the pimp for him. It was around that time that an anonymous publication appeared, recounting the story of Peppina's various chidren; it was on sale in the Duchy of Parma. Almost every night vulgar songs resounded in the bars, stones were flung at their windows, together with wounding insults. Busseto was an inferno. Apart from Muzio and occasionally Piave, they saw no-one, not even Verdi's parents: Carlo Verdi who had been hostile towards Peppina, was considered a leader of the 'enemy' faction. Anyway Verdi's parents felt sure that in the long run their son would return to the bosom of his family; the fascination of those ignoble petticoats would soon wear off.

Remaining ostentatiously aloof to all this, Giuseppina and Verdi made a list of subjects that could serve as the basis for an opera: a story of contemporary values, not heroic ones. The characters would represent a condemnation of the moralistic censure they both resented so deeply. They were subjects based on novels, on fashionable or well-known dramas, texts that they ordered from abroad and which they studied behind the lowered lace curtains, in the secrecy of Palazzo Dordoni. Giuseppina read and translated books like *Le Roi s'amuse* by Victor Hugo, a drama that had scandalised Paris and had led to the closure of the theatre where it had been staged, *Kean* by Dumas Père, *Hamlet* and *The Tempest* (as well as *King Lear*, which was still under consideration), Byron's *Cain* besides two other works by Victor Hugo, *Marion Delorme* and *Ruy Blas*; they were interested in *Die Ahnfrau* by Grillparzer, Racine's *Phèdre*, *Gusman el bueno* by Moratin and a text that Verdi did not know, with the title of *Filippo II*, which Piave had rendered in a libretto as *Elisabetta di Valois* and which was to re-emerge as Schiller's *Don Carlos*. Verdi had always been fascinated by Charles V, the great emperor.

In Busseto Piave had talked about another text, *Stiffelius* by Emile Souvestre and Eugène Bourgeois which would suit Verdi's creativity. They discussed it at Palazzo Dordoni, Piave and this team of recluses, Verdi, Giuseppina and, at times, Muzio. Those three men with such different characters got on well and spent their days quite cheerfully between the piano and the desk, so long as they gave no thought to the intrigues of the town. Three stories were finally chosen, one with a hunchback protagonist, one about a troubadour and a gipsy, and one concerning the affairs of a Parisian prostitute: the choice was revolutionary – not in a musical sense, but in terms of the literary context. The three operas bring the bourgeois world into the melodrama, a world that Verdi had only just conquered, had not known long and had only recently abandoned. The after-dinner conversation between those three men and Giuseppina, around the crackling fire after a good meal (Verdi was fond of the local cooking, *culatelli*, *tortelli* with marrow and ricotta cheese, the salamis of the Po plane, parmesan cheese) were stimulating and creative. But during the day she was left to herself.

In the evening they would discuss politics, sadly and without a gleam of hope. They had no contact with Milan; there were rumours that on 8 September in London there had been founded a National Liberation Committee with Mazzini, Aurelio Saffi and Aurelio Saliceti; Garibaldi, however, had been arrested and exiled to New York. But if there was no liberty, progress was in the air; and inevitably it would bring with it the necessity of choice, hence of liberty. Verdi himself had been on a train! There were stamps! The new postal system invented in England had been introduced into Lombardy-Veneto by Austria; the Duchy of Parma was hastening to adopt it as well, reforming the postal network. The telegraph, once restricted to the army, had been opened to the public. But businesses were failing, people were going to the opera less and less, partly because they had no desire to show off their idle luxury, opulent clothes and jewels. This reluctance to indulge in display, this sense of shame, were new as well. Singers' fees had been halved, but the popular message of opera remained an inflammatory one. Donizetti had died in 1848; in Italy therefore there was only Verdi now – at this point the theatres that wanted him had to accept his conditions. Despite the political and economic crisis, the opera theatres could not call themselves such if they did not stage at least one 'Verdi'.

When the composer set out for Naples in the company of Antonio Barezzi, Giuseppina was left on her own and she went to see her mother in Pavia; Rosa had moved to this small and attractive city near Milan but was soon to move again to the north of the Lombard capital. Giuseppina could not have possibly stayed on in Busseto by herself. But relations between her and her family had worsened; Giuseppina was no longer a precious source of svanziche. However, she still felt a close link with Barberina, who was now twenty-one and not only was she still unmarried but she had given birth to an illegitimate child, whom she had abandoned in Lodi. For Peppina this younger sister, a pale, plain girl, was like a daughter. She felt guilty about her. She felt angry with her mother who had not helped Barberina to avoid what she herself was now paying for in Busseto with tears; and had paid for in Paris with the sweat of her brow. Where would Barberina find the money to look after her child? Naturally everyone looked towards Peppina's purse, which had been stripped of everything in paying for her own bastards. Luckily there was her brother Davide, now the municipal doctor in Locate Triulzi, who was to influence Camillino in his choice of profession.

Verdi and Barezzi had had to stay a while in Genoa because of an outbreak of cholera in Naples, but when the emergency was over they set sail and spent some time sightseeing, visiting the baroque and Angevin churches, the islands in the bay. They took the train that linked Naples with Portici, and went on to Herculaneum and Pompei as well. *Luisa Miller* was staged at the San Carlo in Naples on 8 December, ruined by the poor quality of the singing. The Bourbon regime was on its last legs, as was the San Carlo, which tried to get out of paying Verdi as agreed; there were quarrels and all sorts of unpleasantness. But Verdi continued to love Naples and to put up with treatment that he would never have tolerated from any other city.

On 28 December he returned to Busseto where Giuseppina was awaiting him and he set to work on a new opera for the Fenice. Busseto's rancour had not changed nor had his brother-in-law softened towards him. On 3 June Giuseppina and Verdi travelled to Cremona by stagecoach and Verdi continued on to Padua, then to Venice. 'I might have another subject which, if the police were to allow it, would be one of the greatest creations of modern theatre,' he wrote to Piave. 'Try! The subject is grand, immense, and there is a character that is one of the greatest creations that the theatre can boast of in all lands and all ages.' In a postscript he added: 'As soon as you receive this letter, put on four legs: run throughout the city and find an influential person who can get permission to stage *Le Roi s'amuse*. Don't sleep on it, stir yourself. Hurry!' These words have all the enthusiasm of one who feels the hot breath of the Muse down his neck.

In the same letter Verdi asks about *Stiffelius*, but it is the other subject that has truly stirred his imagination. In fact Verdi later replied to Piave: '*Stiffelius* is good and interesting.' But he passed immediately onto what really interested him: 'Oh, *Le Roi s'amuse* is the greatest subject . . . Tribolet is a creation worthy of Shakespeare . . . Now, as I was looking over several subjects, when *Le Roi s'amuse* crossed my mind it was like a flash of lightning, an inspiration . . .' Piave returned to Busseto in August; in the meantime *Le Roi s'amuse* had become *La maledizione* (The Curse). But the Austrian censors in Venice still refused the story of a king who was a villain and of a girl who dies inside a sack.

Writing to Antonio Somma, future librettist of *The Masked Ball*, Verdi expressed what he wanted to dramatise now: 'today I would refuse to write subjects of the kind of *Nabucco*, *Foscari*, etc, etc. They present very interesting theatrical points but without variety. It is all one chord, elevated if you like, but always the same nonetheless. To explain what I mean: Tasso's poetry may be better, but I prefer Ariosto a thousand times. For the same reason, I place Shakespeare above all dramatists, not even excepting the Greeks.'

On 30 December 1850, Verdi, Piave and the secretary of the Fenice reached a compromise: the duke (not a king any more) was allowed to be a libertine; the buffoon was allowed to be deformed and Gilda 'with respect due to the stage' could die in a sack. After long maturation *Rigoletto* – this was the definitive title – was composed in forty days: when it was staged at the Fenice on 11 March 1851, it was a huge success and caused a stir in the musical world. Angelo Mariani, a great conductor, described it as a masterpiece. In this story Verdi found metaphors, probably he *felt* them rather than found them, for his own situation; a protagonist who was different from other people, who was isolated in his world and pointed out as strange, a man who had two faces, a public one for the salons, a silent, suffering one in private. The drama of *Rigoletto* consists in penetrating the heart of the hunchback, recognising the normal man in the monster, the paternal feelings in the babble of the hired buffoon. Rigoletto and Violetta are both redeemed whores: both prostitute themselves for money, and are saved through sacrifice. Beneath the hunchback lies the father, beneath the whore lies love.

Giuseppina's musical awareness was profound and she had followed the genesis of *Rigoletto* with emotion: if Verdi knew he had produced a masterpiece, so did she and she may even have considered it partly hers. Verdi spent long periods in Venice now, he loved the city. The Fenice was dear to him, he enjoyed the rhythm and beauty of the lagoon and liked to linger in the cafés with Piave and his friends, drink a glass in an osteria, talk over a *granseola* and a *saor*; besides, in Venice, since 1841 he kept a lover. The friends would meet in the music shop of Antonio Gallo, a composer and violin teacher; there, under the Procuratie Vecchie, they would join Cesare Vigna, a learned doctor, and the lawyer and librettist Antonio Somma. On a shelf of the shop, there was Verdi's portrait with a dedication to Gallo which testified to the friendship between them. In correspondence Verdi's mistress was referred to as *Sior Toni* or 'that Angel'. At a certain point the Angel threatened to come and see him in Busseto. Peppina would have flayed her alive! In terror Verdi appealed to Piave: he must try to stop *Sior Toni* – and the kind librettist succeeded, thus depriving Busseto of yet another scandal to talk about. What would his father have said had he known that, besides Peppina, there was another 'bad' woman.

Relations between Carlo, Luigia and their son were at a new low now in the spring of 1851 when the composer and Giuseppina moved themselves to the croft at Sant'Agata, asking Verdi's parents to settle at the nearby hamlet of Vidalenzo. Giuseppe and Giuseppina felt they wished to be in the countryside and wanted to avoid Busseto altogether; under Giuseppina's guidance a small squad of decorators, bricklayers and carpenters moved to Sant'Agata which was then but a modest croft. From the simple farmhouse that it originally was, Sant'Agata was to become a rather grand villa which Verdi and Giuseppina built, little by little, adding wings and floors as money became available. It was to house the fine paintings, including a Salvator Rosa, that they bought, an exceptional library, good antique furniture and a billiard room, since both Verdi and Giuseppina loved to play.

It was to become the house of his dreams – rather than hers – a refuge where he could work. It stood in the centre of just a few acres which, as his finances flourished, expanded into a very large estate. They planted trees to shelter the house from both the sun and the curiosity of others. They created an attractive garden to which Giuseppina dedicated time and care (she kept several gardening books next to her bed). Sant'Agata, still inhabited by the Verdi heirs, has preserved a nineteenth-century gloom; it glows with beautifully kept materials, objects and rooms. It is indeed a very fine place in which to live.

Luigia Verdi was broken-hearted: the humiliation of being cast out by her only son who had made her so proud threw her into despair and that summer she died. Verdi was seized by a feeling of guilt. 'I cannot tell you his grief . . . Peppina suffers to see him cry and I am left with the sad business of arranging the mortuary, the priest,' wrote Muzio.

That May, Giuseppina had to pay another visit to Florence: something had happened. Bartolini had died leaving a very confused situation. It is likely that the sculptor had tried to blackmail her over the identity of her daughter. But despite all her difficulties, the tone of the letter that Giuseppina wrote to Verdi is more confident. She was eager to rejoin him and Verdi wanted her back at once; he felt desperately alone.

Florence, 18 May 1851

My dearest,

I delayed writing to you, to no purpose as it turns out, since I have not yet succeeded in my intent and cannot tell the day of my arrival in Parma. In any case you can count on having me at home by the end of the month.

Unfortunately various things had gone wrong; Livia Zanobini, her son's guardian, had not consulted her and 'in business there is nothing worse than slow-witted people, especially when they are directed by a malign influence'. The malign influence that had intimidated Livia Zanobini was Bartolini who had cheated her financially. 'From now on, I assure you, I feel sure that things will go differently. The trouble all came from there; and not only for me, but for the other. Fortunately I have got out of the mess unscathed, but there is someone who will not, to her own detriment. Livia has become terribly thin. Poor women, how stupid we can be!!!' Maybe Livia Zanobini had fallen in love with the sculptor who had died only five months after taking Camillino in his tutorial charge; she may have lent him some money or revealed certain secrets relating to Giuseppina's illegitimate children. Peppina then went on giving Verdi the details of her investments:

Tomorrow I must have an answer from Dini, a trader in colonial goods who has promised to talk to Smith, who deals in cloth. The customs league that is about to come into operation has led to a notable reduction in business for the big firms, and as you will understand this affects me badly at the moment. I hear that Piave has written to me with a great display of Latin grace and wit. It is like walking triumphantly over corpses; when I wrote to him I didn't give the least thought to pretences but just dashed off an intimate, modest letter, quite unlike those ornate texts full of big words that he receives from some primadonnas who write in the pale moolight, or under a weeping willow.

Ah! Piave with all those women! Peppina had no doubt about the Venetian evenings those two men spent together. 'Besides, I will not be able to avenge myself by making a similar display of knowledge and wit, but I shall display friendship because, to tell the truth, Piave is an excellent meddler and I am very fond of him both for his own goodness and because you love him.' Then, knowing she had no formal right, whether Sant'Agata was to be considered her home or not, she added: 'If you desire me to return, I am yearning to be back. I repeat, I count on being home by Ascension Day.' She concluded her letter with a heartfelt plea in a tone that Verdi recognised:

> I beg you with both hands clasped not to force me into any intimacy with your heirs, and it is not out of malice that I ask this, I swear, but because it would be impossible for me to endure further worries of the kind that I had to bear for almost two years. Human nature appeared so foul in recent events that it is better for us to take every precaution that the veil which you managed to drape over it shall not be lifted again. *Addio*, my Magician. I will not waste words trying to express myself, waiting to do so with kisses on my return. Farewell! Farewell!

The heirs she refers to were Verdi's two brothers-in-law, the Barezzis.

Verdi went to meet her in Parma and they spent a couple of days in the city. But on their return they were greeted by an unpleasant surprise; burglars had climbed a ladder to the first floor of Sant'Agata and, breaking the windows, had even stolen the gold Napoleons that Verdi kept in a secret drawer of his desk. Giuseppina recounted the story to Mauro Corticelli, a theatrical agent in Bologna, an old acquaintance with whom she now began to correspond regularly. It was the start of a long friendship.

> I arrived quite happily until a mile from Busseto I met a man who gave me bad news. There had been a night raid; the house in the country had been broken into. The thieves had seized the opportunity of Verdi's momentary absence to get into the vacant

building by the window of my room and they went straight to the money drawer in Verdi's room. But, as they forced the secretaire in which the money was kept, the wood broke with such a loud noise that the manservant woke up and started to call the women and a villager who, by pure chance, had spent the night in the house. They all got up in a fright and their fear increased when they saw the light in the room through the key-hole. The women, more courageous than the men, tried to open the door but panic and some impediment within prevented them from turning the key. So they went down to the kitchen and armed themselves; one with a knife, one with a hatchet and one with some pieces of iron, and they went back up and again tried to force their way into the room. This time they succeeded but the thieves (who were perhaps afraid of being recognised) had taken the opportunity to flee; when the villager and the servant entered all they saw was the wide-open window of my room, a light in Verdi's room and the secretaire open and empty.

The police later discovered that the thieves were actually members of the domestic staff. 'A doctor was called at once to bleed them.' After this somewhat dubious treatment, the police experts arrived, delighted to have an official reason for interfering and wasting time. Verdi reacted to the whole affair with a certain detachment.

'When the bricks are covered and the rooms in a decent state at least, I hope you will come and eat a nice stew and polenta with us,' wrote Peppina to Piave just after she had settled at Sant'Agata. She was trying to gain his friendship in order to break the male exclusiveness of his bond with Verdi, and thus dispel that sense of juvenile intrigue. It was her method of self-defence; she would try to suborn Verdi's friends who might otherwise threaten her. However in the spiteful eyes of the outside world and especially Busseto, the Verdi household was becoming a den of sin: amongst others Ricordi stayed at Sant'Agata with his mistress Marietta. A great deal of building work was being done which was gradually transforming an old farmhouse to a villa. Giuseppina was consulted for her Parisian taste but, when it came to choice of materials, Verdi did everything himself. They had decided to buy the materials and the trimmings in Paris. In Parma there was very little available, and Busseto was beneath consideration.

It was probably in order to avoid another long winter on the Po valley that the two decided to return to Paris. Verdi wanted to escape from a region that filled him with a sense of guilt towards his dead mother, and also with anger, because he did not feel adequately recognised; Busseto had treated him badly in his early days of want and it was mistreating him now.

The works that were being undertaken at Sant'Agata were proving expensive; during a brief visit to Milan; Giuseppina negotiated a loan of 10,000 francs from the Ricordi publishing house, an operation that recalls the team-work of Cosima and Richard Wagner. It was always she who was sent to handle the less agreeable transactions. Their accounts were always kept separately, right until the end of Giuseppina's life. Verdi valued money highly, too highly. Although often charitable, he was mean to those near him who might have expected a certain degree of generosity from him.

In Paris they took an apartment at Rue de la Fontaine St Georges. They often went to the theatre and in February 1852 they saw *La Dame aux camélias* by Alexandre Dumas fils at the Vaudeville Theatre: they already knew the book which was based on a real life story that had set all Paris talking. The model for that story, Marie Alphonsine Duplessis, had just received a glorious burial in the Montmartre cemetery, she was celebrated more for her death than for her love-affair with the younger Dumas. When Giuseppina read the novel and then saw the play together with Verdi, she must have been struck by a curious sensation of déjà vu.

Just as they were getting over the hostility of Busseto, Verdi received a letter from Antonio Barezzi who had taken on the yet-to-be-written role of Germont Père, Alfredo's father in *La traviata*. Verdi replied to his father-in-law in a truly memorable letter:

Paris, January 1852

Dearest Father-in-law,

After waiting so long I did not expect to receive such a cold letter from you, containing, unless I am mistaken, some stinging phrases. If this letter were not signed by Antonio Barezzi who is my benefactor, I would have replied sharply or not at all; but as it bears his name which I will always make it my duty to respect, I will try as best I can to persuade him that I do not deserve any reproach. In order to do this I must of necessity go back over things, talk about other people, about our town, and thus this letter will become a little verbose and boring, but I will try to be as brief as possible.

I do not believe that on your own account you would have written a letter knowing that it could only hurt me; but you live in a town that has the nasty habit of meddling in other people's business and of disapproving of anything that does not conform to its own standards; it is my habit not to involve myself, if I am not invited, in other people's business, precisely because I require that no one else should interfere in mine. This is the cause of the gossip, the complaints, the disapproval. This freedom of action that is respected even in less civilised countries, I have every right to demand from my own town as well. What harm is there in my living in isolation, if I consider it right not to pay visits on titled people, if I do not participate in festivities, or in other people's celebrations, if I administer my estate as I like and as I please? I repeat, what harm is there?

And since we are now revealing things, I have no difficulty in raising the curtain that veils the mysteries hidden within the four walls of my house, and of telling you about my life there. I have nothing to hide. In my house there lives a free, independent lady, a lover – like me – of the solitary life, with means that satisfy her every need. Neither she nor I have to account to anyone at all for our actions, but besides, who knows what relations exist between us? What business matter? what ties? what rights have I over her or she over me? Who knows whether she is or she is not my wife? and if she were, who knows what particular reason, what motives we might have for not publicising that fact? Who knows whether that is a good or bad thing? Why should it not be good? and if it were bad, who has the right to denounce us? Indeed, I will say that in my house she is owed equal or greater respect than I am, and that no one is allowed to fall short in that for any reason whatsoever; and that finally she has every right to it, on account of her behaviour, her spirit and the special regard which she never fails to show towards other people. By this long harangue all I intend to say is that I demand my freedom of action, because all men have a right to it, and because my nature rebels against doing as others do; and that you, who are fundamentally so good, so just and so kind-hearted, should not allow yourself to be influenced and should not absorb the ideas of a town which as far as I am concerned – I must say so – in the past did not even deign to have me as an organist, and now complains wrongly about my behaviour and my business. This cannot continue, but if it should, I am man enough to stand up for myself. The world is large, and the loss of twenty or thirty thousand francs will never be such as to prevent me from finding another home elsewhere. In this letter there can be nothing to offend you but if you have been displeased by anything because it has been misunderstood, then I swear on my honour that I have no intention to cause you any kind of displeasure. I have always and still consider you to be my benefactor, and I am proud of that and boast of it. Farewell, farewell.

We can only admire his terse, mordant style and the respect with which Verdi speaks of the lady living in his house; he has left no other description of her but these words are enough. It did not take long for the affectionate bond of mutual esteem between Barezzi and Verdi to re-assert itself. Giuseppina later wrote to him signing herself 'Your most affectionate almost-daughter', and addressed him in the Lombard dialect as *Nonnon* (grandfather).

In France Peppina and Verdi witnessed events that were almost bizarre; the *carbonaro* who had lived in exile in London had himself elected emperor under the name of Napoleon III. His wife was a Spaniard; Eugénie del Castillo was a beautiful ballerina who prided herself on her virginity; the British ambassador commented admiringly on the skill with which Eugénie had played her cards so as to be crowned empress. In 1856, after the birth of the hereditary prince which almost cost her her life, she broke off conjugal relations.

Things were improving in Piedmont, at least as far as political passions were concerned. Count Cavour who had introduced a more liberal climate, despite the hostility of the king, had become Prime Minister. Following the example of England, Cavour launched a fiscal reform, opening a central bank and submitting a budget to Parliament for the first time in the history of Piedmont.

In 1852 Verdi followed Giuseppina's advice and signed no contract that forced him to write any works within a deadline, for a particular publisher or a particular theatre. He chose to be free and to follow his own inspiration. 'In your place I would not tie myself for the moment. I would look for a book that I liked and I would set it to music without any commitments and in my own time.' This was the end of an age: Verdi marked the turning-point between the oldstyle composer, the puppet of the courts or the impresarios, and the modern composer. To return to the example of the cinema, it resembled the moment when Orson Welles sent the producers to the devil and made *Citizen Kane*. Or Abel Gance, with *Napoleon* and

Kubrick with *Dr Strangelove*, felt they could only express themselves properly if they freed themselves from the control of the 'impresarios'. And they created masterpieces.

Ricordi had sent a recommendation on behalf of Davide Strepponi who had therefore been appointed doctor at Locate's hospital. 'You cannot imagine with what feeling of gratitude I read your last letter,' she wrote from Sant'Agata on 20 July 1852. 'Verdi also tells me that Locate is a beautifully situated place . . . And in any case, as you correctly write, one has to pursue one's career and even more so when there is a real necessity for gold coins which are also liked by Verdi, as you well know, my very dear Croesus of Publishers past present and maybe future.'

Her passport had to be renewed and, once again, she asked for help from Giovanni Ricordi: 'Winter advances and the countryside is not only sad but barren.' She wrote from Busseto on 12 October 1852, 'so, as in past years, I would like to go to Paris or to other cities where I could use to advantage my scarce artistic talent . . . I told Marietta that the baby peacocks are lovely and that I would send them before I leave my hovel. I fear that they are both males but, since they are not to "be married" until they are three, we shall have time to find some females.'

Verdi and Giuseppina made a pleasant twelve-day journey from Paris to Italy; he then plunged into work: he still owed an opera to Jacovacci, the Roman impresario with whom Giuseppina had worked often. It was *Il trovatore* (*The Troubadour*), a subject that Verdi had picked himself without an impresario choosing the subject; he had even commissioned the libretto which he had paid for out of his own pocket.

He had hardly spent a month at Sant'Agata when Léon Escudier arrived bringing with him the Cavalier's Cross of the Legion of Honour: France was paying homage to Verdi by awarding him its very highest honour. The little ceremony took place in the dining-room of Sant'Agata and Barezzi came to dinner: relations between the two men were good once again. When the award was made amidst champagne toasts and speeches – Barezzi was moved more than Verdi himself and threw his arms around his son-in-law – the latter asked permission to show the Cross around to everybody in Busseto.

Then they left for Leghorn; Verdi set sail for Civitavecchia, leaving Peppina on her own. He did not want her with him in Rome for *Il trovatore*, her presence embarrassed him. Besides, Peppina had to visit

Florence for family reasons, matters in which Verdi had no wish to get involved. Sad, alone, abandoned . . . she wrote to him from a hotel bedroom. She had even spent New Year's Eve without a toast or a hug:

2 January 1853

Tomorrow I expect news from you and pray God that it will not fail to arrive, as I need it greatly! I hope you will have had a better New Year's Day than I did . . . I fear that when you return I will have lost the use of my tongue, as I have practically observed the silence of a trappist monk since Tuesday! I go out very little because it bores me to drag my way through the streets and besides Leghorn is not large enough for me to go out freely without receiving excessive attention . . .

I cannot tell you how impatiently I look forward to your return! . . . I have taken up reading, and I read, read, read until my eyes are red; but I fear that sadness and boredom will assail me violently during these days in which you have condemned me to a cell-like existence. You will say: spend money and enjoy yourself. But firstly I do not like you to say 'Enjoy yourself' and then, I do not know what to do for enjoyment! If I could see you for a quarter of an hour of every twenty-four, I would be in high spirits, I would work read and write and time would go past even too quickly. As it is . . . but let's leave this topic, because it makes me cry.

She had begged him to take her with him, saying that she would keep out of sight. She felt insecure, a silent spectator of his genius; he wanted her to remain a mere shadow. Although various sources affirm that it was Giuseppina herself who did not want to get married because she felt unworthy, there is no evidence to support such claims and everything suggests the contrary. Peppina's letter had not yet been posted when Verdi's arrived. She therefore continued:

3 January

My dear Pasticcio,
I have just this moment received your letter and I cannot express my joy . . . I am greatly pleased that you feel lost without me, and I hope you will be so bored as to give up the barbarous idea of leaving me all alone, like a saint from the Thebaid! . . . I ask you, by way of conversation, is it true or not true that all the meddlers and nosey-parkers believe blindly that I am with

you in Rome? You will answer: of course, let them believe it. I continue (still by way of conversation): what difference would it make to you if, next to your bedroom, there were your poor Pasticcio's bedroom? Instead I am in this monk's cell, with just a little mouse for company. (I have forgotten to tell you that I have got over my dislike for mice ever since I became acquainted with this night-time companion, who comes to eat the breadcrumbs I drop at mealtime.) Now as I am able to stay all alone, alone, without anything to entertain me in the room, instead of being unhappy, I would be alone and happy were I to know that at night, when you come back from the theatre or from a chat, before going to bed, you would come as you do at home, and say: Good night, Pasticcio! and in the morning, before opening your room to visitors: Good morning, Pasticcio! It seems to me that no orator has ever found more persuasive argument than mine. Since people believe that I am with you and since you say: let them believe it; and since I do not show myself either to confirm or to disprove that I am there or not, it seems to me you could be kinder and give up playing the part of Diogenes, tyrant of Syracuse, because you are certainly too generous to go on signing sentences of exile! The day after tomorrow I am going to Florence and if it is possible I will also go to Pisa to hear Piccolomini. Were there any letters for me in Rome? I won't make any remarks about my family's silence! When I inherit 500,000 francs, they'll start writing most amiable letters again! That's the way of the world! . . . *Addio*, write me a nice letter and stage our *Trovatore* quickly . . . a kiss on your heart, Peppina.

From this letter there emanates a sense of solitude; she is afraid of being abandoned, not only by the only support she has clung to but also by her family; just then Giuseppina could not send any money to Rosa, and so her family neglected her.

It is interesting to note the possessive 'our' applied to *Il trovatore*, the text Peppina had translated for Verdi and which they discussed together. In Rome things were going very well: the Apollo Theatre resounded with triumphant applause on the evening of 19 January 1853. From then on, *Il trovatore* was Verdi's most popular opera until overtaken by *Aida*. When another letter reached her in Leghorn, Peppina replied immediately, using the same envelope:

3 January 1853

My dearest,

I've received your second letter and I thank you for thinking of me on the first day of the New Year and the eleventh year of our acquaintance! If I didn't send you holiday greetings it was because I know such things do not matter to you . . . but you can imagine how much I desire you and I will desire you on the first and every day of every year of the rest of your life! (May God grant it that you close my eyes!)

Is your arm hurting? I hope it will be but a fleeting pain, but in any case protect yourself as far as possible from the night air and use oil of camphor. My dear Verdi, I confess my weakness to you, but this separation has been more painful to me than many others. Without you, I am a body without a soul. I am (and so I think are you) different from many other people who need frequent separations to revive their affections. I would stay with you for years and years without feeling either bored or satiated; indeed after such a long time together, without being separated for a moment, I feel this separation even more keenly, even though you promised me that it will be short.

She was about to set off for Florence where she hoped not to find any more trouble. But she would not get to Pisa.

It seems unsuitable that I should stay the night there just to go to the theatre! You will understand that when I was an artist too, it was different: my name kept me company, in a certain sense, or I could ask for letters of introduction, etc etc. Now that I have – thank God – disappeared from society and after all these years of solitary, almost primitive life together, my identity feels as though it is floundering when I have to go to one place or another in the inhabited and civilised world . . .

Do you see? we have lived out most of our lives, and you would be mad if, instead of enjoying the fruits of your labour in peace, you were to sweat to accumulate money and to humour those who in dreaded Death, see the moment when their infamous wishes come true in the wicked word inheritance!

We did not have children (since God is perhaps punishing me for my sins, in preventing me from enjoying any legitimate joy before I die).

Let us pause for a moment to consider this sentence, since it has been suggested that another daughter was born around this time, the fruit of Verdi's love for Giuseppina, so she would have been their own daughter, albeit illegitimate. Why should the couple not have recognised this child then? Verdi's latest biographer has dug up the name of a girl who, born in these months, would seem to have been entrusted to share-croppers on a farm near Sant'Agata. But Peppina expresses herself using the remote past ('*Non avemmo figli*'): she can no longer have children. At thirty-six, she was relatively old, menopause arrived at around thirty-five to forty years of age. This is why her tone is so heartfelt: 'I cannot and I would have so much liked to have your children, you can, but not with me.'

So why did she not suggest that her children should move in at Sant'Agata? By law she would have been bound to declare the truth about them, Camillino then fourteen and living in Florence; Giuseppa Faustina thirteen, probably unknown to Verdi. Adelina had been left behind in Trieste while Giuseppina and Cirelli boarded a steamer rushing towards Venice.

Were Verdi to marry Giuseppina, under the law he would have become Giuseppina's children's stepfather, responsibilities that at this stage of his career and of his relationship with Giuseppina, he would have refused. Moreover Giuseppina would not have married him in order to avoid embarrassing declarations about her past that she had no intention of revealing, especially to Verdi. Once it was decided to leave the baby on the turnstile, there was no turning back: the general public hated unmarried mothers who, in their eyes, created a social problem by leaving foundlings and adding a financial burden to what was already a poor society. I am convinced that Peppina had not revealed to Verdi the existence of her two daughters, maybe because she would have had to admit her cruelty towards her children. But we should not judge Peppina according to the standards of our century: foundlings and orphans were a common phenomenon and parents who abandoned their children were liable to legal and social punishment if they were discovered; the number of foundlings was a serious social problem. 'Well, not having children from me, I hope you will not hurt me by having any from another woman; now without children, you have a fortune which is more than enough to satisfy your needs and which can also provide you with a little luxury.'

They now find a common joy in the countryside, she reminds him; animals bring them satisfaction, not human beings. 'If only you knew what a sad life I lead these days! . . . and have you written anything yet?' She is clearly asking about *La traviata*, the opera that they had planned together.

Don't you see? You don't have your nagging Bore [Giuseppina's nickname for herself, *Livello*, means something tedious or boring in the dialect of Lodi] in a corner of the room curled up in an arm-chair, telling you 'this is good, my Magician, this isn't, stop. Play that again, this is original, stop.' Now without your old Bore, God is punishing you, slowing you down and making you rack your brain, before opening up the compartments of your mind to release your magnificent musical ideas.

In Rome, Verdi had in fact already begun composing *La traviata*. He had a piano installed in his hotel room, but obviously he too was longing to see his lover again, his safety net, his moral support with whom he had shared so many battles, but the success of *Il trovatore* was such that Verdi decided to put off his departure for a day and to conduct a fourth performance.

Florence, 12 January

Dearest,

I have received here in Florence your few lines which, if I may say so, without insulting your hand-writing, I had all the trouble in the world in reading . . . Listen, my dear Magician, I have nothing in the world that consoles me save you! I (and maybe this is wrong) love you above anything else and above all others! no matter how great, how many and how unremitting my sorrows may be, your love is so good for me, that it is enough to give me the courage I need to put up with all the bitter things that afflict me. So, if some action, word or oversight on my part should cause you any unhappiness, forgive me and think of all the sadness and misfortune which attends me!

She stayed in Florence for longer than she had intended because she was tired and the calls she had to make had cost her time and money. She had decided not to hire a carriage because travelling expenses always mounted up, what with a passport between Leghorn and Florence, the inn, and other incidentals.

> Even Signor Ronzi, thinking to do me (of course *you*) a favour, brought me the key to a box and I had, to my great chagrin, to go to *The Prophet* which Frezzolini will not even sing at Carnival, and I had to spend twelve paoli! Don't ask me anything about *The Prophet* nor about the performers. I will save my criticism and philosophical remarks for your return.

She recounted other stories and teased him with a few references that may well have aroused his curiosity – and certainly arouse mine. Not long after this time Verdi decided to take Giuseppina with him on his travels, which shows that he was no longer ashamed of her in public. These letters therefore give a rare insight into their lives together.

> Leghorn, 17 January 1853
>
> Dearest,
>   I am truly desolate over what you tell me about the opera destined for Venice! But I hope that the devil is not as ugly as you paint him and that, when you arrive in Leghorn, you will have several finished pieces in your trunk.

They had obviously made plans for a trip together on his return but Verdi's letter makes a different request as is shown by her reply:

> I would be very unhappy if you were seeking some kind of pretence by means of which you could take me back to Sant'Agata and then set off again without me. If this is your aim all you had to say was . . . Peppina, this is a sacrifice I beg of you! I have made so many sacrifices for others who have and continue to repay me with immense ingratitude that I am very happy to agree with anything you like since you are the only person in the world who has never caused me sorrow! So let it be as you wish: let us return to Sant'Agata and thy will be done, so long as my eyes stay open and I still have the strength to say that I love you with all my heart! . . .

The theme of sacrifice, of unjust – but justified – moral condemnation, was of course central to *La Dame aux camélias*. Seeing the play in the theatre had been like reliving her own life: Giuseppina's past and Marguerite Gautier's had a great deal in common. Verdi had wanted a libretto dealing with contemporary issues which would impress his public and confront them with their own hypocrisy. Not surprisingly it was blocked by the censors and the drama had to be presented as having happened in an earlier age.

Verdi's inspiration was fired by the frailty of Peppina who, abandoned by all, had helped him with her devotion and love. She had saved him from the oppression of others, she had taken him to the countryside where she had offered him a different style of life. She had made him appreciate the importance of contemplation.

Since she had started keeping a watch over him, the composer had produced his best work: she played the part of little Bore; it was she who persuaded him to eliminate clichés and to drop weaker passages. From her letters, we can see how a relationship of true mutual esteem had grown up between them.

> I will not talk about myself! . . . I'm incredibly sad and heaven help me if I should go on like this! In Florence I had things to do, I had problems, not distractions; but the steam clouds from your boat on the 24th will announce the return of my Magician and he will bring with him moments of good-humour and fun. Oh! if only Sant'Agata were in France, in England, in America! . . . who, apart from you, my joy, would ever see me again on this earth? Believe me that the aversion I show towards society in general is much less than that which I feel within myself!

She felt terror at the idea of returning to the Po valley.

> I love Sant'Agata because it is in my nature to grow fond of places I live in for a long time; nonetheless for eight or ten years at least, there are many reasons, many passions (good and bad) that will prevent us from enjoying there that total peace which I think would restore our youth and make us both live wholly fulfilled lives.

She was probably spending Verdi's money since at that moment she had none of her own after the havoc that the sculptor and Zanobini had wrought on her finances; she had to prepare her account.

> My dear Pasticcio,
> I spent a huge amount of money . . . and I haven't even bought anything beautiful or important. It is true that the journey to Florence has rocked my accounts (all the more so because I hardly ever eat alone); as you will see from the records I was

very careful but money just flows away. Oh yes, it never even crosses my mind to taste claret or champagne, as I do when I am with you; indeed, in Leghorn I do not even know what a black coffee tastes like! So, if you do not come until the 24th, I certainly won't have any treasures of Croesus left – and I am sorry, so I won't write to you again and I will expect you on the 24th. For the love of God, do all you can not to be late. A kiss on your heart. Addio, addio.

Finally, as in the last act of *La traviata*, the long-awaited lover returned; Verdi rejoined Peppina, whose health was deteriorating. He finished *La traviata* at Sant'Agata with Peppina singing the motifs as they flowed from the piano – and she saw herself re-interpreted by Dumas, Piave and Verdi.

Piave was staying with them complaining about the bad weather: 'I can assure you that when it rains here, one spends one's time gazing into the mirror to see if one is still human or has turned into a toad or a frog.' It was the very tedium of the countryside that helped Verdi to compose. He was not well and Peppina was also ill; she did not trust the local doctor, a certain Dr Frignani from Busseto whom she considered sly and wicked.

Before leaving for Venice with Piave but without Giuseppina, Verdi, who did not trust the company of singers, knew that *La traviata* would be a fiasco. He had barely left before Peppina wrote to him:

23 February 1853

Dear Magician,

I promised, I am writing to tell you that I am neither better nor worse than on Sunday: but Frignani assures me that with the powders he gave me today I will improve noticeably and quickly ... You cannot imagine how much I suffered over the last few days, seeing you, my poor Magician, slaving away like a black and moreover having to put up with my ill health! Because I will get better and I will try with my good-humour to make you forget the trouble you have been through. You are so good to your poor old Bore ...

Emotion had robbed her of the means with which to express her gratitude to him, she wrote. Maybe Verdi had written off the debt she owed him for her stay in Tuscany.

> ... And to think that somebody like you should have sprung from such a ghastly place as Busseto! You would need the faith of St Thomas to believe it. Write to me if you can: speed up the rehearsals and return to your home. Our youth has passed, but we still mean the whole world to each other and we can observe all the human puppets with utmost compassion as they get excited, they run, climb, crawl, fight, hide, reappear – all so that they can dress up and be seen in the first rank of the social masquerade.

She did not miss the opportunity to draw a damning picture of his 'heirs'. Demetrio Barezzi had called on her early in the morning unannounced, which displayed a lack of respect. He had kicked up a row in the kitchen recounting his nocturnal conquests. Fortunately she had her animals to keep her company: Loulou, a white terrier, followed Peppina around the garden and slept in her bed. On the lawn – to the gardener's dismay – there were eight peacocks which Peppina tried to induce to sleep in a little shed, but they insisted on staying out in the pouring rain and there were caged nightingales in her bedroom by the bust that Tenerani had made of her in 1842, at the height of her career.

On 2 March, a restless Giuseppina wrote. 'If, as you hope, the opera is to open on Saturday the 5th, there is no point in my writing another letter to you in Venice.' The winter cold affected her health. Her spirits were low on account of the news she had heard from Florence. 'I desire you like God. A kiss on your heart.'

She thanked Piave:

> thank the great Devil for the few lines he has written to me and tell him not to prove his friendship to you by pimping for you. I know that he has great talent and inclination for the job (he has proved it to you), but do exhort him on my behalf to give vent to his erotic zeal only with friends that resemble him. Joking aside, send him my best wishes and tell him that if poor Peppina is here in the snow (which has fallen again since you left) it is because such is the wish of the only person in the world who can command her.

She knew that Verdi's heart belonged to her, but she was not so sure of other parts of his body.

She continued to send money to Barberina, seventeen gold francs as 'pension' – just what sort of pension could that have been? – 3490 francs and sometimes 400; 160 for Christmas Day and to carry out some works at the house in Locate Triulzi where Barberina lived now together with her brother and mother.

When he returned from Venice, 'the great Bear' brought her a present from 'the great Devil', a little bag. But this was the last long separation; the tyrant of Syracuse no longer passed sentences of exile. In September, Verdi wrote to Cesare De Sanctis asking if he could find an apartment in Naples and whether the Bourbon police would create trouble for a lady who was to accompany him with a valid passport. 'Are you able to keep a secret?' he asked.

But in the end Peppina and Verdi decided to go to Paris where they were to stay for two more years. Sant' Agata, Busseto, and the fog of the Po valley, the insults shouted from the arcades in the middle of the night, were all part of a past nightmare.

They were never to return under the same conditions.

8

A RESPECTABLE
LADY

In Paris again for two years, from 1853 to 1855. Venice
and *Simon Boccanegra*. To Rimini with a young, enthusiastic
conductor, Angelo Mariani. *A Masked Ball* in Naples and
then in Rome. The siege of Piacenza and the war against
Austria. The Regent of Parma has to flee. Violetta –
Peppina – the Generalina becomes Signora Verdi: the
marriage is celebrated in Piedmontese Savoy.

━━━━━━━━ • ━━━━━━━━

Oh gioia ch'io non conobbi
essere amata amando . . .
Oh a joy I never knew
to be loved loving . . .

LA TRAVIATA, ACT I

The letter in which Verdi mentions the possibility of his visiting
Naples in the company of a 'signora' marks a turning point in
Giuseppina's life. For the first time ever her cantankerous companion
had decided to be seen with her in public, not to be ashamed of her
– and in Naples at that! Verdi's letter to his friend De Sanctis was
written on 9 September:

If I were to decide to come and spend the winter in Naples, tell
me: 1) Whether I could find a pleasant, comfortable apartment,
in a beautiful position by the sea, if it should be inconvenient for
me to stay in a hotel. It would have to be furnished, and for two
people, plus one or two servants. 2) Whether I could find one or
two servants. 3) If I were to come to Naples for purely leisure
purposes, would I be subjected to any bother from the police.
They are said to be so strict . . . 4) If a lady companion with a
regular passport would have to endure the same trouble. Reply at
once to all these questions. I repeat: it must be a secret. I will make

up my mind on the basis of your answers. If I do come, in Naples I shall be Signor Giuseppe Verdi and not Maestro Verdi, which is as much as to say I do not want to hear operas, nor propositions for operas, etc. *addio* and silence!

But their winter sojourn in the bay was postponed; there was an outbreak of cholera in Naples and Verdi's latest operas had not been successful. Consequently he had to go to Paris to make money. Also, the conversion of Sant'Agata from a farmhouse into a villa, a house where he could work, entertain friends and above all enjoy solitude, was proving expensive. So Peppina and Verdi made their way to France for an opera that Verdi unenthusiastically had agreed to compose. Not only did he dislike writing for the incompetent management at the Opéra, but he considered Scribe, who had been forced on him, to be a careless, second-rate librettist. Scribe, born in 1791, was thought by many to be the most important librettist in Europe; he was the poet of 400 operas, ranging from *Robert le Diable* to *La Juive* and *Les Huguenots*. But Verdi knew that Scribe had a workshop to whom he assigned most if not all the work, reserving for himself the trouble of collecting almost the entire fee.

Paris in October 1853 was very different from the city they had known in their younger days. The little neighbourhoods were disappearing, swept away by Georges Haussmann, the architect and Prefect of police for the Department of the Seine. The task to which Haussmann had been assigned by the Emperor and which would take seventeen years to complete, was that of restructuring the entire city. Napoleon III had grasped the advantages of open spaces where barricades could not be erected and which would provide roads wide enough for an army to advance and deploy artillery against any popular uprising. Haussmann's new urban system installed the bourgeoisie into the heart of the town, separated from the proletariat who were displaced into the suburbs. The '*Misérables*' (soon to be immortalised by Victor Hugo) were evicted from the centre where the old houses and narrow alleys were demolished. Haussmann laid out the tree-lined avenues that the Parisians called 'boulevards' which all converged in the star-pattern that we know today. The public crowded the Boulevard des Temples in which the first *cafés chantants* had appeared, rather in the tradition of the old taverns but also poor copies of the salons. In these cafés excerpts from operas were performed, which were thus appropriated by the general public since, although often discussed, the system of copyright did not yet exist. On either side of the boulevards rose tall houses containing apartments designed for a wealthy bourgeoisie. Haussmann's city became a model for other European capitals, destroying the fabric of cities and dividing social classes.

In Paris preparations were under way for the First Universal Exhibition. The new streets were to bear the names of battles that the new Emperor considered to be victories. Verdi's new opera, *Les Vêpres siciliennes* (*The Sicilian Vespers*) with its libretto by Eugène Scribe and Charles Duveyrier, was to be featured in the celebrations. Science revolutionised Giuseppina's life, she now travelled by train, she used the telegraph and, while in Paris, she had given orders to install central heating at Sant'Agata, one of the first houses in Italy to have it.

For Peppina, living in an apartment near the Opéra, life was very different from what she had known a few years previously. Then she had to earn her living, make a name for herself in the city, find pupils and mollify the critics. By now she had become a lady, she went on shopping expeditions escorted by her maid, who was English. She wore a walking-out dress; the ladies of France exaggerated their fashions and with their swelling skirts when they went to the opera or to Court, they looked like air-ships! Giuseppina's beige shoes peeped out from under her silk skirt, and over her shoulders she wore a cashmere shawl in blue, matching her hat. She bought crimson velvet curtains, divans and chairs for Sant'Agata. She arranged occasional dinners for close friends, received people and paid social calls. She looked after Verdi's correspondence and tried to solve some of his problems at work. She was happy and all that she lacked was the comfort of legality. However, nobody knew this because Verdi referred to her as 'my wife', and she began to sign herself Giuseppina or Josephine Verdi. Indeed, when Giuseppina Appiani addressed her in a letter as Giuseppina Strepponi, Verdi himself replied crisply, thereby destroying an old friendship. But this friendship had developed from an earlier affair and the sharp rebuke was certainly written in Peppina's unmistakable style.

They received an invitation to Court at Les Tuileries, they dressed in full ceremonial finery with all the required accoutrements and then, putting on their best smiles, they paid their visit. Giuseppe and Peppina with impeccable manners, as if they had spent all their lives in Court circles, looked at the magnificently dressed women who wore impressive jewellery; the Empress shone with beauty if not with charm in a Court where Spanish was spoken more than French. It was almost impossible to believe that the Emperor, with his waxed moustaches, elegant in tight white garters and epaulettes dominated by a magnificent array of medals and decorations, was the nephew of Napoleon Bonaparte.

At Court, they found an old acquaintance, that ageing beauty who had been removed from people's visiting lists in Milan because of her marriage to a baritone: Countess Giulia Samoyloff was on her third husband, the Marquess de Mornay from whom she separated shortly afterwards. Despite her thick make-up, she was still beautiful and men continued to admire her. After the first formal invitation, others followed. Napoleon III's Master of Ceremonies was Count Baciocchi whose grandmother, Elisa, was Napoleon's sister; we have already met Count Baciocchi's father, in Peppina's early life. Verdi and Peppina found such receptions desperately boring and, in any case, he could only eat a few dishes because of chronic indigestion while she felt ill at ease in the company of so many tall people. (Actually, the Emperor was as short as herself, but he always stood on a step!) Verdi excused himself sending word to Count Baciocchi that he was *obsédé* by work. But it was not true; he simply preferred to avoid the social world. In any case, Napoleon III was no longer the carbonaro that Verdi had met in London, no longer the elected President of a Republic.

They were both disappointed by Paris. The atmosphere of intense creativity had been swamped in the industrial boom, the only French composers they saw were Berlioz, who had expressed his admiration for Verdi, and the Rossinis whom they visited. They maintained a suspicious friendship with Rossini based on mutual admiration although, in private, Peppina often ridiculed his black wig balanced on a bald head. Even the newspapers described the receptions in Rossini's house: 'The famous composer's salon is filled with friends both mornings and evenings,' wrote *La France musicale*. 'He talks to everybody and appears generally happy to meet his admirers. The other evening, whilst embracing Maestro Verdi, he said: "Look what a Carnival you've got yourself into!"'

Elsewhere we read how Peppina protested at Rossini's flattery when they were sitting together on a sofa. Verdi's head appeared round the door of the next room where he was playing billiards, to enquire what all the fuss was about. '"Your wife is scolding me!" Rossini explained. "But why?" replied Verdi. "I was praising her beauty and her skill as an artist of our times." "And I really can't take that . . ." said Giuseppina.' In the presence of such intellects, she felt a strong desire to fade from the scene. Perhaps she also wanted to reject the advances of an old gentleman. It is in any case clear from this that Peppina was still a beautiful woman.

During another visit to Rossini's house, the aria 'Il balen del tuo sorriso' from *Il trovatore* was performed by a baritone rarely heard in public: King Louis of Portugal. When Verdi went to the piano, Rossini said: 'Leave it to me, this is music I understand.' And he himself accompanied the illustrious singer.

The socialising was eventually interrupted because Peppina had to nurse Verdi who was suffering, probably from colitis, which was always the case when he started work on a new opera that he had no desire to compose. He did not like Scribe, he disagreed with the management of the Opéra, and the French on their side were sceptical of him, treating him like a poor cantankerous cousin. This irritated him profoundly, wounding his pride which was his most vulnerable point.

They rented a villa at Mandres in the Pyrenees during the summer of 1854 because it was unbearably hot in Paris. But in August, Peppina returned alone to Italy where her brother Davide had died at the age of only thirty-seven. They had not spent much time together, they did not know each other well, but Peppina loved this only brother who had taken Feliciano's place so early and had tried to be in charge of an unruly family of poor females. She arrived in time for his funeral, the few remaining relatives were there and Rosa, of course, crying like a fountain. On the death of Davide there was no longer a head of the family to take care of Camillino, Barberina and her child. There were now only the two sisters surviving, Barberina and Peppina, as well as their mother Rosa. Giuseppina went into mourning, ordering a shawl in black velvet which fortunately Verdi paid for, since it was extremely expensive. She was now no longer working and had only her Florentine investments to live on. For the remainder of her wardrobe, Peppina managed by removing the coloured ribbons and putting on one side the crinolines in champagne-silk. She was careful with her purchases, resisting the temptation to acquire elegant clothes that would never be available in Busseto let alone appropriate to wear.

She probably heard of Cirelli's death through a letter: somebody must have informed her, maybe even Giovannina Lucca. But no trace of her reaction to the death of somebody who had been a companion for many years exists; she would have hidden her sadness from Verdi, and from others. Camillo Cirelli had fathered her son and had agreed to give something of a name to her second child; he had behaved well to her and of course he had not been able to marry Giuseppina. He was already a husband and a father when they had met, so many years before, in Milan, when her father Feliciano was still alive and when her life looked so full of promise.

She made herself heard at rehearsals – she was not somebody who followed quietly from the wings – giving advice to Verdi, listening to voices for the new opera, criticising the sound of an orchestra, of some instruments. The rehearsals of *Les Vêpres siciliennes* were long and excruciating for both of them, contributing to Verdi's bad humour. The problems were compounded when the soprano Sofia Cruvelli on whose voice Verdi relied, suddenly disappeared. 'Cruvelli has fled! Where? The Devil only knows! At first this news was like a kick in the crutch, but now I am laughing up my sleeve,' he wrote disarmingly. The disappearance, which became an international scandal (a farce was staged in London entitled *Where's Cruvelli?*) gave him the chance to break his contract with the management of the Opéra. In the meantime, almost as though to snub them, Verdi had agreed to produce and conduct *Il trovatore* for the Théâtre des Italiens. He declared that he wanted to show the French what his operas were really like when performed properly. It is hard not to sympathise with him because his operas had often been badly mangled in France and, in fact, this version of *Il trovatore* was a resounding success.

Cruvelli's disappearence caused such an uproar that the Minister for Home Affairs himself intervened. The soprano's property was confiscated and the world press took the matter up. This gives an impression of just how important nineteenth-century primadonnas were considered to be but, as suddenly as she had vanished, Cruvelli reappeared in time for the final performances of Meyerbeer's *Les Huguenots*. The golden voiced beauty had absconded to the French Riviera with a Baron Vigier whose wife she was to become a few months later. On 20 November the splendid Cruvelli appeared on the stage of the even more splendid Opéra and, as she came on stage, the Queen (in *Les Huguenots* not in real life) reproached her: '*Dis-moi le résultat de ton hardi voyage?*' Naturally, the theatre echoed with laughter.

The Universal Exhibition in Paris was inaugurated with *Les Vêpres siciliennes*. *La Revue des deux mondes* wrote:

The main event of the Season is an opera in five acts, *Les Vêpres siciliennes* which Verdi has composed expressly for Paris and which had its opening performance on 13 June. The work was greeted with great curiosity as it could mark a new development in dramatic music. Thus the auditorium of the Opéra presented a curious spectacle: supporters of the Italian composer had come en masse and it is no exaggeration to say that almost all the wealthy opera lovers of Milan, Turin and the other large cities of Lombardy, attended this solemn occasion which for them took on all the importance of a public ceremony. Indeed for Italians today artistic questions are not simply matters of taste, which are raised and discussed in the serene areas of the spirit, they involve the passions and interests of everyday life, and in the success of a virtuoso, of an artist, or an opera, no matter what, the Italians recognise a national success as one further qualification to earn the esteem of civilised Europe.

Berlioz himself was enthusiastic and compared *Les Vêpres siciliennes* favourably with *Il trovatore*, but for once he was wrong.

Verdi went to London twice during this period in order to prevent clandestine performances of his music; Peppina, who accompanied him, was overwhelmed by her first impressions of the city. Its size and wealth were phenomenal. It was possible to buy ready-made clothes, one could find Indian textiles, coloured cottons and expensive wools. There were trams, people took photographs! The men were extremely elegant with grey top hats and silk waistcoats which protruded below their tight jackets. Indeed, they were more elegant than the women who wore bonnets and chequered dresses. London had already staged its own Great Exhibition at the Crystal Palace in 1851 where there had been 14,000 exhibitors. Peppina, like Verdi, found the climate dreadful, the food depressing and the smog excessive: 'I study English,' she was to write some years later, 'and so far I have the consolation of not understanding a thing, not a single spoken word. These English wretches swallow half of what they say and the remainder they keep between their teeth; one would have to stay for a long time amid this jarring concert to comprehend even a few sentences.'

The spoken language was very different from the one she had learnt and which she wrote in 'her' kind of English, using some code words. Her correspondent, Mauro Corticelli, was thinking of working as a secretary for an actress. Corticelli was one of the few friends from the past with whom Peppina had maintained contact. Here, she is writing in English to him:

Dear Friend.
   Well! Very well! You have some good aptitude for commercial style and I should employ you as a secretary when I shall be able to open a cheesemonger shop. But you must submit yourself, before I put you in possession with such a noble charge at an experiment with closed door. You are right in giving all your mind and time to your important things. I am not so silly to pretend that a future cheesemonger's secretary might to occupy himself with trifles, but I am very glad to know it, because things being so, I should buy some trifle in London myself. I beg your pardon for every error that, I am sure, you shall find in this letter. Be indulgent and think, Mr Secretary, that I am all alone without hope today to see some English person able to correct it. I send thee the requested autograph and beg you to remember:
   Josephine Verdi.

The 'cheesemonger' and 'the secretary' were part of a code that had developed over the years between Peppina and Mauro Corticelli. Their refererences were to Ristori, an actress whom Verdi had praised after seeing her perform in Paris. She was one of those primadonnas who performed the classics travelling to both the New World and the snows of Russia; who was universally acclaimed and advertised, but pretended to be a tender Ophelia even at an advanced age.
   Verdi and Peppina had seen Ristori act, anyway they often went to the theatre to keep in touch because successful dramas were regularly turned into librettos. At the theatre Giuseppina, with her shoulders barely concealed by a shawl and with flowers in her hair, could still turn the men's heads. They also went to see operas and listen to concerts. One evening the famous couple were discovered by a friend not in the foyer but in a dark corridor of the Théâtre des Italiens, where Verdi who had just seen Rossini's *Otello* and started to talk about Shakespeare rather than Rossini, even though he greatly admired the latter. In October they were Napoleon III's guests in Compiègne, from where they returned to Paris and stayed in a sumptous apartment in Rue Neuve des Maturins. They would have preferred to leave almost immediately but Verdi found himself contesting various stolen editions of his operas.

The Verdis spent part of the summer 1855 at Enghien, near Paris taking the waters because it was considered to be good for Peppina who had respiratory problems. After spending the remaining months in Paris, they returned to Italy in December, by train, via Alessandria, where Muzio was conducting *La traviata*. He then accompanied them to Sant'Agata where the couple remained for several months.

Verdi resumed farming the land and Peppina reverted to her role in his shadow. She felt that Verdi's love of the countryside had become a mania, something of an obsession, even an illness. They would both wake up at dawn when Verdi would immediately rise but she preferred to observe the sunrise from 'a supine position'. She would read almost anything that she thought might become a subject for an opera; dictionaries arrived at Sant'Agata at Peppina's request. At this stage she played an important part in choosing the subjects for Verdi's operas.

Peppina was bored in the lonely world of Sant'Agata. Verdi, by six a.m., was already in the stables with his cattle and horses; he would then return hungry at about eight-thirty and have breakfast with Peppina. The meal was served by a trimly dressed maidservant, in bowls that bore the monogram G.V. and white china cups on a silver tray. In May, breakfast was consumed on a little table outside Peppina's bedroom where she would appear in elegant *déshabillé*, but in winter or in the high summer, when the sun was too hot, it was served in the dining-room. Verdi ate very little and as a result, he remained thin, but he wanted the best quality. Not so with Peppina who, although she had once been perhaps too slender, now took little exercise and she was often confined to her bed by illness which meant that she had no means of working off the large helpings she often consumed out of boredom.

The lack of diversions and social life at Sant'Agata encouraged routine (friends were imported and the only local to be admitted was Antonio Barezzi). Thus it was the perfect place for composing and for contemplation. In this, in fact with everything, Peppina humoured Verdi. She understood how vital it was for him to 'ruminate' even when he was not writing. She understood how he needed to think of music in the abstract and also to discuss future projects with her in the evening.

She was busy at her desk during the day when she not only dealt with her own correspondence but also Verdi's; she had begun to make copies by hand because of course at that time neither typewriter nor carbon paper existed. She would dash off the original version of his letters in a large book entitled the Letterbook ('*Copialettere*'), then she would correct them for the final version of which a fair copy would be made and signed either by Verdi or herself. Although he had been absent from Italy and its politics, Verdi remained in the eyes of the Italians a symbol of the unified state and one of its few heroes. Cavour, to whom Verdi was drawn on account of his anticlerical policy, procured him an important decoration. Verdi accepted the decoration because he approved of Cavour's progressive policies. When Piave came to stay, they had political discussions in the evenings at Sant'Agata. Piave, who had problems with his health and his finances, no longer lived in Venice; having fought the Austrians he had been forced to leave the city. He was working at La Scala with Merelli who, having returned to Milan, had suffered financial losses in the revolution of 1848. The latter was ever more strongly suspected of Austrian sympathies as indeed were most people in opera management. Merelli's fortunes were declining and he was scorned by the Verdis, partly because he had spent 300,000 francs, a large sum, on buying an Austrian title which was then refused him on account of the old suspicion of theft.

Verdi, Peppina and Piave went out for drives in the carriage. The three of them would go and dine with Antonio Barezzi in his fine town-house which was not far from Palazzetto Dordoni where Peppina had endured the scorn of the town's people. There had been a significant change in her father-in-law's life. After a few months as a widower – his poor deceased wife must have been a woman of little character since her name was never mentioned – Barezzi had married his young maid, Maddalena, much to the scandal of Busseto and the ire of his sons who saw their inheritance at risk. Thus Barezzi joined the 'sinners of Busseto' and became an object of criticism and condemnation. In some ways this shared experience united the father-in-law to the clandestine younger couple.

Piave had brought with him a contract from the Fenice. The subject and the libretto for a new opera were for Verdi to choose. Peppina, who at that time had devoted herself to a certain area of Spanish literature, told Verdi about a play by Antonio Garcia Gutiérrez which described the tragedy of the Genoese Doge Simon Boccanegra. It struck Verdi as a suitable subject because it had all the ingredients he liked, including class struggle, forbidden love, an abducted daughter and her reunion with her father. A Genoese

Doge was not ideal for Venice, just as, later, it would seem somewhat tactless to sing of the victims of Egyptian oppression in Cairo, and as it had been to feature *Les Vêpres siciliennes* in Paris since that famous event was the only occasion on which the Sicilians had risen successfully against their many oppressors, in that instance the Angevins.

Verdi continued to dream of *King Lear*, but he also wanted to rehash *Stiffelio*, the opera written for Trieste. He realised that the libretto was not suited to the Italian public, so it was the story rather than the score that required radical alteration. The need to do that was the main reason for Piave's long stay at Sant'Agata. The librettist had never liked the place, but he now had to admit that the villa was much more comfortable with all its new accessories from Paris and as a result of the building work which had now been completed. Verdi described the house to Clarina Maffei as follows: 'It is impossible to find an area which is uglier than this, but on the other hand, it is impossible that I could ever find anywhere where I could live in greater freedom; and this silence that allows one time to think is a good thing as is the fact that one never sees uniforms of any colour whatsoever.'

He did not disclose to Clarina and his elegant friends Peppina's existence although everybody in Milan knew about her. Peppina was one of the reasons why neither of them had set foot in the Lombard capital for years. They avoided it again by going to Bassano del Grappa for a brief holiday; the mountain air might be good for Peppina's health. The idea that he, Verdi, should worry about her well-being, filled her with pride at the same time as surprising her. It could only mean one thing: that she was loved. It seemed impossible that she might be the object of so much attention from such an extraordinary man, someone who was respected and appreciated not just by her, but throughout the entire world. They had an appointment with Peppina's doctor in Bassano following which he accompanied them to the Venice Lido.

The doctor recommended sea bathing and this became a real holiday which they spent walking along the sands, strewn with shells and starfish. This was not the Venice of the debaucheries, of his former lover *Sior Toni* and jokes with Piave; on this occasion, Verdi was recognised in the alleyways and he had to sign autographs. He was continually invited out by the patrician families. One day, whilst travelling by gondola, Peppina dropped an elegant lace handkerchief with the initials GV; it was picked up by the gondolier who noticed the initials. Although the gondolier in question was no Iago, Giuseppina-Desdemona thus achieved her aim because she let it be known that she had become the Great Man's wife, which although not entirely true then, would become so later.

Verdi was at that time, according to Peppina, tired and bad-tempered; he was trying to preserve what we would now call his copyrights because he was aware of a new phenomenon in the European musical scene. Whereas in the past an opera might be expected to last for one season, now it might become part of a repertoire. Opera motifs, such as the great tunes from *Rigoletto*, *La traviata*, etc, were then made known amongst an even wider public via the pianos in the drawing-rooms of Europe, reaching those who were unable to see the original production; opera was thus popularised in this way. Not only Verdi, but the other composers of the day, spent much of their time in litigation against pirated editions of their works. Verdi found it impossible to keep pace with all the illegal editions of his operas which were plagiarised not only in the Italian provinces but also in London, Paris, Geneva, Brussels, and even in the major cities of the New World. For this reason, he was surrounded by people who made it their business to prevent his work from falling into the hands of opportunists and unscrupulous impresarios. These people included Muzio who conducted Verdi's work as well as composing his own, and the increasingly famous Angelo Mariani, whom Verdi had known since his Milan days although he had seen little of him recently.

The day of the première of *Simon Boccanegra* at last arrived between strolls along the Lido and gondola rides. The libretto was a mess, half written by Piave and half by Montanelli, a Tuscan exile who lived in Paris and who had written the libretto in prose, a scandalous novelty. In his completed *Simon Boccanegra* it is easy to recognise a 'foreign' and more sophisticated vein in the score which indicated a step towards the path of the later Verdi. *Simon Boccanegra*, performed on 12 March 1857, was a flop and it never received the recognition it deserved. The confused and dark plot was an extremely difficult one to interpret. Despite endless gossip and differing opinions, defying the natural outcome of a failure, Piave, Verdi and Peppina remained friends, for the moment.

From Venice they made their way by train along the Via Romana. When they arrived in Rimini, they found that the librettist Piave and the conductor, Mariani, were already there and had been working for days. Peppina wrote: 'Happily we have arrived in Rimini but found the city an inferno of heat, insects and many other inconveniences that we have to put up with.' Like Piave they had been invited to stay with Count Bandini, but Verdi valued his independence so they stayed at the Albergo della Posta which was far from comfortable. *Aroldo* would be conducted by Angelo Mariani. At that time, in 1857, Mariani was thirty-five years old, having being born in Ravenna in 1821. He was younger than Verdi and his attitude was that of an admiring adolescent towards a star; like so many people, Mariani was awe-struck by the sublime Maestro. He was an extremely handsome man with black curly hair and large dark eyes, to which Rossini, whose pupil Mariani had been, alluded with admiration. He was a sentimental, talkative man of humble origins, bursting with enthusiasm and passion. In short, he could not have been more different from Verdi and, for this reason, they liked each other. Peppina, on the other hand, did not approve of Angelo's verbal diarrhoea. Furthermore, Verdi's relationship with Mariani began to recall his friendship with Piave before she intervened, so she felt pushed on one side. Peppina was witty and possessed a fine sense of humour but when it came to defending her territory, she was ice-cold and fiercely possessive.

In addition, Mariani was a womaniser; he wore his beard and hat *alla Verdi*, favoured wide lapels and big silk cravats. In Denmark, where he had spent years as a political exile after 1848, Mariani had composed a Requiem for the king. He had also spent months conducting Italian operas in Constantinople, where he had become the centre of sentimental and social attraction. Ministers and beautiful women received him, giving him every kind of attention but, since 1852, he had been the permanent conductor at the Carlo Felice in Genoa which was Savoy territory. He was thus an employee of Piedmont, the state to which modern Italians looked with hope in their hearts. His romantic air had also conquered aristocratic hearts, indeed in Genoa, Angelo had an affair with Marchesa Sauli.

The meeting in Rimini between Verdi, Peppina and Mariani is of great significance because it would change the lives of all three of them. Although Rimini, a town of some 16,000 inhabitants, declared itself enthusiastic about its distinguished guest, not everyone was happy with Verdi. He had been a little difficult; the fee he had demanded for *Aroldo* was considered excessive, especially since the opera was a reworking of an early piece. It was therefore important that he had the support of the very important Mariani. Despite the stifling heat, Mariani worked hard and Verdi attended all the rehearsals. He went for long walks with Peppina on the endless beach. The city was full of historical remains that interested them both, they went to visit the Rubicon: *Hinc Italiae finis quondam Rubicon* was written on a rock near the little stream that Gaius Julius Caesar had crossed at the head of his legions, thus passing from Gaul into Italy.

Amongst the sights were the great triumphal arch of Augustus and a basilica by Leon Battista Alberti, but Verdi and Peppina were not particularly interested in the earlier Renaissance. They moved to the Hotel dell'Aquila, which was rather more comfortable but the mosquitoes in their suite showed the same appetite as those in the Albergo della Posta. They enjoyed their meals with Mariani and Piave, dining on grilled seabass and stuffed cuttlefish. But Mariani's endless chatter was intolerable for Peppina to stomach. However Verdi was pleased to think that his music enjoyed the passionate support of this young and widely respected conductor: for the first time he felt like an Old Maestro.

The sensational success of *Aroldo* was in fact greatly due to Mariani who had taken meticulous care over every detail of this production. Verdi received twenty-seven curtain calls, each number was applauded and even Piave was acclaimed. The composer and his librettist were escorted in a boisterous torch-light procession back to the hotel where Peppina waited for them. Afterwards Mariani, who had not only conducted but also joined in the celebrations, with indefatigable energy, wrote an account of the proceedings for Ricordi, telling him about the enthusiastic reception that the opera had received. After Rimini, Mariani took on the role of the favoured conductor for Verdi's operas; they used the informal 'tu' when addressing one another and they began to correspond regularly.

When Verdi returned home, he had not yet chosen the subject of his next opera which would be for the San Carlo in Naples. He tried to convince the theatre to make do with some recycled work as he had at Rimini, but the Neapolitan management, understandably enough, rejected this proposal. Verdi was once again tempted by *King Lear* for which Somma's libretto was ready. But there were no singers available. However he finally decided on a story by that old fox Scribe, who was unbeatable when dramatic situations were needed. He asked Somma to compose a libretto based on *Gustavus III of Sweden*, a drama by Scribe.

In December Verdi wrote that on this occasion he would come to

Naples 'with my wife and perhaps a maidservant'. They stayed in Naples for almost four months: Verdi had a terrible time, he had to face all kinds of problems including double-dealing and it was the end of his idyll with that city. However for Peppina, Naples was a revelation: the climate was marvellous and the city fascinating. Peppina was happy, this was her first visit to Naples, the capital of a kingdom where one could buy anything from mozzarellas to leather gloves or fashionable veils or hats. All of them cheap. She arranged for her purchases to be sent by order to her hotel.

She would take the carriage and with a veil over her face and Loulou under her cape, go for drives along the sea front to Mergellina. It is easy to understand why Verdi wished to spend the winter in Naples with Peppina. Naples was extremely beautiful: the Angevin fortress and the Castel dell'Ovo stood out against a sea of purest blue, and vine-clad hills enclosed the town; in the distance stood Vesuvius crowned by a tuft of feathery smoke. It was easy to fall in love with the place and indeed, when Neapolitan songs celebrated beauty, it was nearly always that of the city rather than a lover. They were taken by friends to see the wonders of the past, Pompei and Herculaneum, the collection of mosaics and statues from Attica, the Royal Factory of Capodimonte and the summit of smouldering Vesuvius. The Neapolitan composer Mercadante put an end to his ten years' feud with Verdi, sending a mellifluously worded dinner invitation to Peppina. We do not know whether the Verdis and the Mercadantes actually ate that meal together. Athough there was no lack of social life in Naples, it is unlikely that Verdi and Peppina paid a visit to Court because the Bourbons did not like this hero of Italian unity who had been awarded the order of San Michele, nor did they appreciate avant-garde music. Equally Verdi did not like the Bourbons. Their stay in Naples was immortalised by a series of caricatures made by a friend, Melchiorre Delfico, who gave them to Piave. In his turn Piave gave them to Giuseppina, and thus we are able to see her short and plump with Loulou under her arm, standing beside the tall figure of Verdi. All their friends are there including Cesare De Sanctis and his family, Baron Giovanni Genovese, Vincenzo Torelli of the San Carlo Theatre, Nicola Sole, a fairly well-known poet, and two fashionable painters, Domenico Morelli and Filippo Palizzi. There was also the librarian of the conservatoire called Francesco Florio but nicknamed Lord Palmerston.

Verdi was irritated despite the cheerful atmosphere and wonderful climate. He was enjoying a moment of special success, with his operas performed all over the world and even his barber selling locks of his hair for huge sums of money. Nevertheless the establishment of Naples boycotted him. *A Masked Ball*, which was the final title of the opera that had started as *Gustavus III* after various versions had been tried, was not staged at the San Carlo: the idea of featuring the murder of a monarch was already shocking enough, when at that time an Italian anarchist called Orsini tried to assassinate Napoleon III in Paris. (Strangely enough, this particular assassination attempt had fortunate consequences because the French Emperor, having read a letter from Orsini sent prior to his execution, became convinced that it was necessary to solve 'the Italian problem'.) While *A Masked Ball* was at a standstill in Naples, Verdi re-established contact with the impresario Jacovacci. The Apollo Theatre was very happy to stage the new opera and all the more so since Scribe's play had already been seen in Rome, staged regicide being considered less dangerous there than it was in the Kingdom of the Two Sicilies. The opera's acceptance in Rome was a clear humiliation for the San Carlo and further proof, as if any were needed, that its reputation as a great opera house was no longer deserved. Verdi reached agreement with the San Carlo that, in order to replace the censored opera, he would take charge of a production of *Simon Boccanegra* in Naples the following winter. Peppina was greatly pleased because she would do anything to avoid spending the cold months at Sant'Agata. Their Neapolitan friends accompanied them to the ship and 'after the turmoil of Naples', Verdi and Peppina set sail for Civitavecchia enduring a terrible voyage during which everybody, except Verdi, was terribly seasick. All of them, including Loulou, arrived exhausted after nineteen hours at sea.

Things were not happy at Sant'Agata. Antonio Barezzi had had a stroke and one of his grandchildren had died. But he had been so well looked after, Giuseppina recounted to Léon Escudier, that Barezzi had recovered and was immediately down to the shop to count his money. She had been to Locate Triulzi, south of Milan, where her mother and sister were living after Davide's death. Giuseppina contributed to their living costs and kept in touch with them, especially with Barberina. On this occasion, Verdi wrote to Ricordi to ask him to help her in any way he could whilst she was in Milan.

On 12 September 1857, Peppina wrote to Vincenzo Torelli who

was editor of the magazine *Omnibus*. He was a Neapolitan whom Peppina liked. Writing to him gave her the opportunity to make fun of Busseto and its so-called services.

Here in Busseto, there is no post office and twice a week a man turns up on foot because he has no horse, just his walking stick, and he collects or distributes the few letters to and from these illustrious townspeople who, although they may spend much of their time thinking, hardly ever put pen to paper and if they do, it is just a few business letters about stuffed pigs. You know that the salamis are exquisite in this progressive town!

And she continued:

As for Verdi, he is as strong as an ox (fingers crossed) and, judging by his colour, he would look well in the colonies planting sugar cane. I swear that in these last few months he has not written one note! As for letters, he has written a thousand or so, less than the last two noughts. He has also carefully supervised the construction of a bridge opposite the house, and not a single tree has been planted or uprooted without his presence, body and soul. Now he is beginning to cast an occasional reluctant eye over the new score, which will almost certainly be performed in Rome. I hope for bad weather, making it impossible to go out, so that he will be free to take up his pen again.

Later they both went to Tabiano, a spa near Parma which was less luxurious than Salsomaggiore although probably more beneficial and, in its homely way, far more charming. 'At the moment we are at the baths of Tabiano, a few miles from Busseto, but we shall return shortly,' she wrote to De Sanctis on 12 July 1858. 'Verdi is very busy ... doing nothing. His biggest project at the moment is dressing, eating and sleeping, so that his belly, much to his satisfaction, is becoming larger. I have not been very well, at one point I feared that I was threatened by a terrible and painful illness; but now, thank God, I am better and my fears are vanished.' Her health, always poor, troubled both of them. Mariani wrote from London and then came to stay at Sant'Agata the following summer, a sign that he had become a close family friend.

But news arrived that the indolent Roman officialdom, which had previously agreed that Scribe's play could be staged, changed

its mind. The Pope's censors had decided that they could not
approve of a monarch being murdered on stage during a masked
ball. Another device must be found so King Gustavus of Sweden
became the English Governor of a North American colony. Once
again Verdi and Peppina set sail from Genoa. On the quay in Naples
they were greeted by some twenty friends including De Sanctis with
his wife and small child who was Giuseppina's godson.

The Neapolitan *Simon Boccanegra* was a great success, but it was
Rome and *A Masked Ball* that really interested Verdi. The voyage
from Naples to Civitavecchia was again extremely uncomfortable
with a choppy stomach-turning sea, nevertheless Verdi rushed to
the Apollo Theatre immediately on arrival, eager to commence
rehearsals: he was confident that the music he had composed was
beautiful.

They rented what Peppina declared was an utterly ugly apartment
in Campo Marzio. In January she wrote to Mauro Corticelli whom
she referred to as *Don Cappellari* because he was constantly taking
offence, i.e. 'always taking up his hat (*cappello*) to leave' as the
Lombard expression had it. He had written to her to say that he
intended giving up his career as a theatrical agent in order to devote
himself totally to the actress Adelaide Ristori. She replied:

> Rome, 15 January, 1859
> You are leaving that stale atmosphere, which your honest nature
> could not endure without suffering. I told you from the very first
> moment you plunged into that stinking sea, 'Corticelli, this is not
> the place for you, nor is it the trade for you.' You could have gone
> earlier; but at last you are leaving it in time. *Bravo, benissimo*, my
> good Cappellari! I am extremely glad you have accepted Ristori's
> proposal and are placing your intelligence and probity at her
> service. I do not know Ristori personally but I follow her artistic
> triumphs with interest and her actions even more so, as they are
> truly noble and merit the same respect as her talents . . . Verdi is
> so tired and disgusted by the theatre that it is very likely he will
> say what Rabelais said about the stage at the very end of his life.
> 'Bring down the curtain, the farce is over.' Undoubtedly nobody
> can boast that they are more honest than he, or that they have
> earned their living and the right to lead an independent life with
> greater dignity.

The première in Rome of *A Masked Ball* on 17 February 1859 was a triumph, despite the poor quality of the singing and despite Peppina's usually accurate forecast of disaster.

Verdi was, by now, always successful, his music was sublime and his presence symbolised a self-confident future for a nation which was soon to be united. Cavour had, by diplomatic means, created the opportunity for a renewal of hostilities with Austria. On 10 January 1859 King Vittorio Emanuele II made an inflammatory declaration in Parliament stating that he was not unsympathetic to the cries of grief that reached him from so many parts of Italy. In the same month a defensive alliance was signed between France and Italy, which was why immediately after the performance of *A Masked Ball* the Roman crowd followed Verdi shouting 'Viva VERDI!' This phrase became a cryptic slogan which was written on walls all over the papal capital. The letters in the slogan stood for 'Viva Vittorio Emanuele Re D'Italia', but the Vatican police could not arrest anyone. Once more, therefore, Verdi found himself the symbol of Italian unity, the Risorgimento.

He was by now forty-six years old and the recipient of many honours and universal acclaim, he had composed twenty-three operas. He decided to stay in Rome for three more weeks; the city was splendid and the sharp turquoise light with the sunsets over the Tiber enchanted him. The Verdis gave a dinner on the eve of their departure to which they invited Vincenzo Luccardi the sculptor, Jacovacci, the impresario, and two other guests one of whom, a journalist, immortalised the occasion. With wit, he described how Verdi, in a particularly gloomy mood, responded to every remark his impresario made with the curt declaration that he had decided to give up music because he could no longer stand it.

They returned by sea, the port of Genoa was the most convenient for them and the city of alleyways, grand palazzi, taverns where fresh fish could be consumed and picturesque markets, was both fascinating and splendid. Above all, the Musical Director in Genoa was Mariani, by now Verdi's closest friend. They stayed at the Albergo Croce di Malta while Mariani was rehearsing *Aroldo*. Giuseppina followed the rehearsals and began to exploit Mariani, asking him to procure a dog licence for Loulou. It was far from being the last favour she would ask. In fact Peppina and Verdi were for ever asking their friends to go on errands, to obtain or deliver things for them, a common habit amongst the rich and famous. Admirers would always be found who would be prepared to do such things. From Locate a worried Barberina wrote to Tito Ricordi (25 February

1859), 'Since I have not received news from my sister Giuseppina I would be very grateful to you if you would forward her this letter. I know you are in regular correspondence with Signor Verdi. Therefore I beg you kindly to address this enveloppe for me.'

Passing through Piacenza, they were struck by the apparent state of siege that existed there. The entire Austrian army seemed to have occupied that beautiful city which, with its high walls, guarded the Po between Lombardy and Emilia. They spent one night in a hotel in the Piazza Grande with its gothic arches and magnificent bronze monuments to the Farnese Dukes, but there was no avoiding the smell of war, the turmoil of guns and troops. The atmosphere was taut with anticipation, the young men of Piacenza were absconding and secretly enrolling in the Piedmontese army. Austria had sent no less a personage than its Lieutenant of Police, Joannes Rohn, known as the 'assassin', to preside over what was considered to be one of the most impregnable fortress cities in Lombardy-Veneto.

When they were finally installed at Sant'Agata on 20 March 1859, they knew that the bond between them was by now indissoluble. Verdi felt an affinity with Giuseppina that he had not found with even his closest friends. She was the one person who could understand his moods and humour him. She felt an overwhelming gratitude towards this man who had accepted her for what she was, and had given her respectability and dignity which she had thought was lost to her forever. Respectability in the bourgeois nineteenth century was all-important, but Peppina had thrown hers away all too carelessly during her youth.

She now identified herself with him and idolised him. She would do anything for him and indeed did so. She suppressed her own personality and rights for his sake, indeed she had swallowed her own bile on the occasions when he deserted her obviously because he felt ashamed of her. She scrimped and saved severely in order to avoid asking him for financial assistance which, in any case, was only forthcoming if she did not request it. They decided to marry early in the spring of 1859, as Peppina informed De Sanctis confidentially in a letter of 21 May.

Despite censorship, letters and newspapers arrived regularly. Mariani sent frequent letters from Genoa written with great intensity and descriptive flair, keeping Verdi and Giuseppina informed of the political and military situation better than any newspaper. The couple in Sant'Agata were thus aware of everything that was happening within days. They knew that the Austrians had warned Piedmont not to arm and Cavour had agreed that his country would comply provided they gave up Piacenza. 'If the Italians want Piacenza, they must come and get it,' was the response. The bait was taken and, following an ultimatum on 30 April, the Austro-Hungarian army crossed the Ticino, thus entering Piedmontese territory. Cavour received the news whilst shaving, and promptly started to sing the great aria '*Di quella pira*' from *Il trovatore* in his tuneless voice. The die was cast.

There, in their province – Verdi and Peppina were informed almost immediately – the Regent of Parma fled and was immediately replaced by provisional Governors. On 6 May, the Austrian army, weakened by defections and by its great unpopularity (although there was no shortage of sympathisers and spies) began to raze the city of Piacenza – a custom with German armies. Mariani wrote to Sant'Agata saying that one hundred thousand well-equipped French troops had disembarked in Genoa in May and around the middle of the month, Napoleon III himself arrived: Verdi and Peppina were enthusiastic, although he was rather frightened. Their friends feared for their safety; Sant'Agata was on the front line of the most important war for Italian independence.

The Italians were fighting well, they heard. Garibaldi, the hero who seemed to have stepped out of an early Verdi opera, was leading his own army, in various operations designed to keep the Austrians engaged in Lombardy. He occupied Varese and Como while Napoleon III, using the railway, transported the rest of the French troops to the battlefield. In just a few days, the Piedmontese railway network managed to transport 200,000 soldiers to the front – this modern miracle was going to win the war. After a period of worrying Austrian victories, the Franco-Piedmontese army routed the enemy.

On 21 May Peppina wrote to De Sanctis – it is a real mystery how the letters went hither and thither amid the gunfire, particularly if one thinks that today's Italian post is unable to function with or without hostilities:

We are well, not afraid but worried about the serious events that are happening. This morning at eight the drawbridges were raised and the gates of Piacenza, which is about 18 miles from us, were closed. A section of the Franco-Piedmontese army is preparing to attack the fortress and tomorrow, or perhaps this evening, we shall hear the thunder of artillery. Everything is being prepared to make this a war of giants. Verdi is serious, grave, but calm and confident about the future. I am certainly more upset, more agitated but then I am a woman and have a more excitable temperament. Besides you will understand that the thought of such things can scarcely make one cheerful.

The next day, Verdi and Peppina were able to follow the Austrian columns from a distance as they retreated, dragging their artillery pieces along the banks of the Po. They were leaving!

Verdi and Peppina opened a generous subscription for the victims of the Austrian occupation. But the end was to prove a bitter one because in the final battle of Solferino, Napoleon lost 17,000 soldiers. The Emperor settled with Austria and signed the Treaty of Villafranca by which Lombardy went to Piedmont, the Veneto remained under Austrian rule, as did Mantua and Peschiera and the status quo was preserved in the Papal States. 'So where is the longed-for and promised independence of Italy?' wrote Verdi. In many people's eyes, Napoleon III had betrayed them. Having advised the king not to sign the Treaty, Cavour resigned as Prime Minister. In Parma resistance against the old order was strong. Luigi Carlo Farini took the situation in hand and, in August he received the Governor General who had been sent from Piedmont to organise a plebiscite: Parma voted for the first time asking to be annexed to Piedmont by 17,000 votes to 255.

Now that Italian independence was partly achieved, now that the war was over, Verdi and Giuseppina could marry. Not only decorated with medals and certificates, Verdi had achieved official status and the nation would require his services. Therefore Peppina could not continue at his side as an unofficial concubine, she had to be legally his wife. Even more important was the fact that Camillino had reached his twenty-first birthday which meant that Verdi, as a stepfather, would no longer be responsible for him. Giuseppina also knew that, for the same reason, she was not legally bound to declare the existence of Giuseppa, her second child.

So, when hostilities were over, in great secret Verdi and Peppina made their way to Geneva; they called on Abbot Mermillod, a distinguished prelate who had been the adviser on social questions to Leo XIII. Bishop *in partibus* of Hebron – he was to be Bishop of Lausanne and Freiburg whose university he founded, and became Cardinal in 1890 – this enlightened and distinguished man of the Church had prepared all necessary documents and, on 29 August, the three left

Geneva together and, by coach, reached Collange-sous-Salève in Savoy which still belonged to the Piedmontese crown. Without any pomp, Mermillod joined them in matrimony: he was forty-six and she forty-four.

The two witnesses who signed their names in somewhat uncertain hand, were the coachman and the church bellringer. There was no ceremony, of course; nobody was told and Verdi hurried back to Sant'Agata with his Peppina. There were many things to do and what Verdi considered a mere bureaucratic nuisance but Peppina regarded as the most important achievement of her life, was to be kept secret for many years.

9
ENTER STOLZ

The wife of a Member of Parliament. Garibaldi
returns to Caprera: problems for the new Kingdom.
Winter spent in Genoa, not Naples: looking for an
apartment. To St Petersburg for *La forza del destino* and
Paris for *Don Carlos*. Death of Camillino. Angelo Mariani,
Mauro Corticelli and Bologna. Little Fifao and Manzoni.
Mariani and Teresa Stolz get engaged. Peppina's life is
swept by the Stolz tornado.

———————— • ————————

Io sono franca, ingenua;
Altra cercar dovete;
Non arduo troverete
Dimenticarmi allor.
I am frank, ingenuous;
You must seek another woman;
You will not find it hard then
To forget all about me.

LA TRAVIATA, ACT I

Her life was now comfortable and tranquil. As the wife of the
leading Italian composer, the man who represented Busseto at
the Assembly, she herself had an official role to play. The delegation
chosen to take the petition for the annexation of Parma to Turin
included Verdi – by special request of Cavour himself. The meeting
with the King, reproduced in lithographs, was not as warm as
that between Verdi and Cavour. The ex-Prime Minister had all
the bearing and demeanour of an aristocrat (unlike the King, who
looked like a plebeian), and in Verdi he saw not only a man of
fine qualities but also a useful symbol for the cause. He received
him at his house in Leri, the appointment had been arranged by
Angelo Mariani, who had sought the help of Sir James Hudson,
an English minister at the Court of Piedmont. The conductor,
who knew just about everyone, had made Verdi his own cause: he
wanted people everywhere to meet and admire this man whom he

considered a composer of genius. It was now impossible for Peppina to keep him all to herself; this added to the rivalry between Verdi's wife-cum-guardian and 'Anzulett' ('Little Angel'), as Rossini used to call Angelo Mariani, who acted like a sort of younger brother or unruly son to the composer, entirely devoted to him. But Peppina had long ago carved out her own exclusive role and she had no wish to cede this role to Mariani. She was the saint whose intercession was required to work the miracle. Her influence over Verdi was enormous: the Barezzi brothers, once friends, never showed their faces now; Piave too had vanished from sight, as had all the elegant lady friends, apart from Clarina Maffei – and his bond with her was kept up by correspondence alone.

They spent the coldest months in a hotel in Genoa. They decided to buy an apartment in the town; Verdi wanted one on a grand scale and Mariani offered to find one: however, he was always too busy with his rehearsals and his women to procure anything; he may not have even looked. He was rather too quick to make promises. It was he who had dissuaded Verdi from going to Naples for the winter, praising the advantages of Genoa – much against the wishes of Peppina. It was quite likely that she knew Mariani from earlier days: she may well have met him in Sicily during her final disastrous tour. That winter Verdi had followed the example of Mariani, who was now his inseparable companion, and had taken up hunting: he was not very good at it, according to Peppina; when the two men headed for the fields, they would stay out the whole day, but if woodcocks were served at dinner that night, it was only because she had bought them at the market herself.

Mariani was a fervent admirer of Cavour and his policies, and was always ready to justify even his most controversial moves – such as his strict abiding by the terms of the agreement made with Napoleon III, and ceding Savoy and Nice to France, when he became prime minister again. In Palermo there was an aborted insurrection; Verdi and Mariani followed the events with immense interest. The insurrection was intended to supply the pretext for an expedition of volunteers led by Giuseppe Garibaldi. The idea was to liberate the Kingdom of the Two Sicilies and, in particular, the Papal State, in order to restore Rome to its ancient role as capital. The insurrection failed, but nonetheless dissent spread throughout Sicily; at the beginning of May, Garibaldi set sail for the island. 'Having decided to disembark at Marsala we made our way to that port, where we landed around noon. Entering the port we

found merchant vessels of various nations,' he recounted in his
Memoirs.

After disembarking at Marsala, with the tacit consent of the
English Navy, the Garibaldini, all volunteers, defeated the Bourbon
troops in three months, occupied Sicily and marched towards Naples.
Garibaldi continues:

> The victory of Calatafimi was indisputably decisive for the bril-
> liant campaign of 1860. It was essential to begin the expedition
> with a striking military success. It demoralised the enemy, who
> with their fervent southern imagination, recounted portents on
> the valour of the Thousand – there were some who had seen the
> bullets from their rifles bounce off the breasts of the soldiers of
> liberty, as if they had struck a sheet of bronze – and it encouraged
> the Sicilian heroes, who had been disheartened by the impressive
> array of armaments on the Bourbon side, and by the great number
> of their troops. At Palermo, Milazzo, and the Volturno many more
> men were wounded and killed. But, in my opinion, the decisive
> battle was Calatafimi.

From a social point of view, the Thousand – who were not in fact
a thousand, but almost double the number (and by the time they
reached Naples they had swelled to 25,000) – constituted a force that
would today be defined as left-wing. About half of them were from
the professional and intellectual classes and the other half consisted of
artisans and workers: the peasants were scarcely represented. Some
of them, veterans from the war of 1848 and the defence of the Roman
Republic and Venice, had fought with Garibaldi in the Cacciatori
delle Alpi and had experience of revolutionary soldiership. It was
thus a compact and united force. The Piedmontese government
tried to stop Garibaldi, but having failed, they decided to wrest the
initiative from him, blocking the march of the Thousand on Rome,
which risked sparking off a European conflict.

For this reason, Napoleon III consented to a Piedmontese advance
on the South. Annexation by Piedmont was one way of ensuring that
the social order, with all its privileges, would be preserved – and there
was no guarantee of this with Garibaldi. It was in this manner, and
with this motivation, that the Italian state was formed – to prevent
Rome from being taken; while in the north the enemy had been
Austria, in the south it was the landowners. Thus war was waged
against the foreigners in the north, against the rich in the south, and

against the priests in the centre. Three different enemies and three irreconcilable struggles. Even at the moment of unification, Italy remained divided. Or rather, it was the will of fate that unification should coincide with annexation.

The Piedmontese advanced on the Marches and Umbria, meeting the Red-Shirts at Teano. Despite the usual representation of this event, the encounter between the two armies was that of two enemies: the Garibaldini stood for Italian populism, while the Piedmontese army – all wearing magnificent uniforms – represented the conquest of one nation by another. Circumstances had allowed Piedmont to acquire territory that would not have fallen into its hands so easily otherwise. Victorious as a general, Garibaldi had thus been defeated politically. The Piedmontese accepted the handover of power. The disappointment of the peasants who had seen Garibaldi as a liberator, who had hoped for a new distribution of wealth, fomented the phenomenon of brigandage; it was the Mafia, a growing but never-mentioned force, that suppressed this nuisance in the name of the State, thus giving rise to that fatal alliance between the Mafia and the State, which was to survive until the present day. A plebiscite ratified the annexation of the former Kingdom of the Two Sicilies to Piedmont: Cavour's approach to Italian unification had borne the desired fruits. But at what price?

At the time it was difficult to grasp the reality of the situation; not even Verdi realised that Italy had not been liberated so that it might be founded, conceived and made anew, but rather had been annexed to Piedmont, one of the poorest regions, ruled over by a monarchy of mountain-dwellers. Busy with building-works at Sant'Agata, Verdi gave no thought to composing; he asked Tito Ricordi for 10,000 francs; he needed it to transform the house into a grand villa. This was what he had decided to do and this was what he stubbornly did. Verdi and Peppina had quarrelled and he slunk off to Genoa with Mariani, leaving her alone with the builders, and with her rheumatism and stomachache. His intention was to stay away for two months. 'As for us, we are surrounded by the gentle din of the builders, carpenters, etc.,' she wrote to De Amicis. 'I hope that one day or other you will find a moment to come and shake hands with us here at Sant'Agata. You should come here with the sentimental Mariani . . .'

Not expecting to see him again for some time, Peppina wrote to Verdi with affectionate melancholy. She felt less fragile than when she had been abandoned in Leghorn.

4 December 1860

My dearest,

This cursed town! You may not receive the letter I wrote this morning until Thursday. Here it has been pouring with rain uninterruptedly, and I fear that in Genoa it may be doing the same. Poor Verdi! What fun! My stomach has granted me a little peace today, but just to keep my patience in good practice my tooth has waged war on me; add the sadness of the weather and you will understand what sort of mood I am in! Today I had lunch in the dining-room, taking about ten minutes over it; this evening I dined in my room. The salon without you is too deserted and that empty place at the table makes me sad. Think of me as you go to sleep; think of your companion who lives with you and would like to live like that for centuries. Don't pull a face . . . I would seek in my heart and maybe find a way never to bore you, never to weigh on you, and in order not to do so now I will say addio and go to bed. I wish you a peaceful night, and a blue sky tomorrow morning!

She wrote to him again the next day: was he enjoying himself in Genoa? What was he doing?

Maybe when this letter arrives you will be in Turin if, as you intended, you are going to see Cavour and Sir James. What it means to be a genius! You visit Ministers of State and Ambassadors, just as I go and see Giovanna. And yet the thing that makes the world take its hat off is your quality of which I never think, or hardly ever. I swear to you, and you won't find it hard to believe, that often I am almost surprised that you know music! Although this art is divine, and although your genius is worthy of the art you profess, yet the talisman that fascinates me and which I adore in you is your character, your heart, your indulgence towards other people's mistakes, while you are so severe towards yourself. Your charitableness, full of modesty and mystery – your proud independence and your childlike simplicity, qualities inherent in your nature which has managed to preserve a primitive virginity of ideas and feelings amidst the cesspool of mankind.

   O my Verdi, I am not worthy of you and the love you bear me is an act of charity, balm for a heart that is sometimes very sad, under the semblance of cheerfulness. Continue to love me, love me even when I am dead so that I may present myself to Divine Justice rich in your love and prayers, my Redeemer!

Giuseppina's devotion is almost frightening; she continued: 'Forgive this despondency that has plagued me for some time and which is not the predominant defect in my character, although it is in yours. Oh, finally a defect, a failing that you have. Delighted that you have at least one or two.' She was not very well, she said, she had not had any further attacks of stomachache, but merely some threats: 'These minor ailments prevent me from laughing and it is peace of mind and good humour that I most need to shake them off, so as not to force on you, as I have done, the spectacle of these painful fits, which I would have liked to hide, but did not have the strength to do.'

This may have been why he had left. Active and impatient, Verdi got bored at home with an invalid. But before this letter arrived, he felt remorse at having left her and returned home. With a present: a magnificent velvet cloak. He loved her. Now that she was the wife of a rich and famous man, she was constantly pestered by Strepponi relatives – people whom she had never had anything to do with before; indeed, a cousin actually turned up at Palazzo Dordoni – while Sant'Agata was full of builders, they had taken refuge in the hated town – asking for money and assistance.

She wrote protestingly to her aunt: it was offensive to receive letters addressed to Giuseppina Strepponi and not Verdi; this was something, thank God, that could even now be checked at the Registry Office. Furthermore she had nothing but her own savings to rely on; she would open her purse for her aunt, but for nobody else. Their wedding had been kept so secret that many were still uncertain whether they were married or not. Verdi cared very little about it, but for Peppina it was a source of constant anxiety; as she grew older, she began to suffer from acute respectability.

She felt lonely and unhappy in her new role as a the wife of a '*fattore*' (farm manager), in that 'vale of tears and yawns'. If only Sant'Agata were by the sea, if only the climate were less humid . . . 'We will almost certainly spend the winter at Sant'Agata because Verdi (this is between ourselves) has found his purse-strings somewhat mortified, on acount of the building-works,' Peppina wrote to De Sanctis from Busseto on 14 December. 'What is curious, is that this year of all years, because it would hardly do to move, he has an immense desire to run around the world. The strange ways of the human heart!'

In 1861 the Italian State was born. The situation was disastrous. Out of 25 million inhabitants, 54% worked on the land and only 18% in industry. In Sicily the rate of illiteracy was 89%. But can the statistics be believed? According to an oft-quoted statistic only 2% spoke Italian, and not dialect. But that is hard to believe when we find a common language in the perfect Italian of opera librettos, which were sung by everyone from Neapolitan labourers to Venetian fishermen. As we have already said, Italy was a very backward country, compared with the northern nations of Europe; the areas of the Po Valley could just about manage, but not the South, which had fallen into the clutches of Piedmont, a gift from the Mafia, rather than Garibaldi. The Piedmontese really wanted very little to do with the Kingdom of the South; Vittorio Emanuele's mind had been set on Milan and Venice, not the South. Milan, a rich, cultured and sophisticated city – far more so than Turin – became the pride of the Kingdom. Venice, unfortunately, remained part of the Austro-Hungarian Empire. A few months earlier everyone had appeared deeply moved at La Scala when the Emperor Franz Josef honoured the theatre with a visit; now the same people displayed the same emotion when posters were put up announcing the arrival of King Vittorio Emanuele II. There were to be balls, festivities and illuminations, like those organised for Franz Josef's visit.

Verdi and Peppina were in Genoa, at the Hôtel Croix de Malte; Peppina had her belongings sent to her from Naples: '. . . my portrait, books, etc.' The goods finally arrived, and then they set off from Genoa for Sant'Agata: 'the portrait has arrived and aroused long 'ohs' and 'ahs' among all those who saw it,' Peppina wrote.

It is perfect, even too perfect, because it seems as if it is about to step from the canvas, and is almost frightening. As for Loulou, if we don't remove the picture, she will calmly sit down and lick it, believing it to be her aunt (for your information, Loulou's aunt is the undersigned, your most humble servant). St Dominic is a little grazed: he must have chosen to poke his nose into the books dancing all around him, so much the worse for him. The Madonna has remained virgin in every sense of the word: and the child and St Joseph are equally intact. The frame is a little scratched on one side, but what can one expect? Where have my white corsage and my beautiful blue and gold scarf got to?

In February she escaped to Locate; Rosa was on the point of death, but then recovered; she had aged, and was weak and embittered. After Davide's death the house at Locate had become too big for Giuseppina's mother and sister, and was too far from Sant'Agata. Peppina looked around for somewhere closer and indeed found a small villa in Cremona, then she returned to Sant'Agata as soon as she could; Verdi insisted that the building-work must be followed closely. The house was going to become their own little kingdom. It was to become a kind of ultra-bourgeois dream-house: the sort of house a man born into poverty must have always desired to own, the sort a woman would want for her old age. Some details would be altered over the years, some rooms would be added; after the huge financial success of *Aida*, other changes were made, such as the introduction of Egyptian-style divans in petit-point; but substantially Sant'Agata was to remain as it was originally conceived in 1860; the unification of Italy was matched by a newly unified house.

'Nature has given these places no attractions,' wrote Antonio Ghislanzoni, the librettist who spent long periods at Sant'Agata; he understood both sides of Verdi's nature, the poet and the businessman.

. . . Between the long lines of poplars, which we pass alongside, a ditch with hardly any water, suddenly your eye is surprised and almost saddened by the sight of two weeping willows that stand against a door . . . the person who planted those trees can have little or nothing in common with the character or habits of the people of the vast plain that you have traversed . . . To approach this door one has to cross a bridge, the only link that joins the artist's residence with those of other living people. Those who know the name of the person who dwells in this house, as they pass it at the hour of dusk, imagine they can see through the branches of these gloomy trees, they can hear the funeral dirge from *Il trovatore* or the last yearning cry of a dying Violetta. If a genius lives here, you must naturally understand that it is the genius of pain, the genius of strong and excited passions. A thick row of trees protects the house from profane eyes on the side that looks onto the main road, while on the opposite side, the garden opens up more smoothly and joyously, stretching towards the shore of a small artificial lake. But it is a fair prediction that when the recently installed plants have grown to their full size over the years, shadows and sadness will dominate the house entirely.

How true this description is, how accurately Ghislanzoni saw the dominating sadness of the shadows that are cast over the walls and the soul of Sant'Agata.

> Beyond the garden stretch the composer's vast terrains, with a long avenue where the eye loses its bearings; the land is dotted with peasants' cottages, with well-designed farmhouses . . . While the willows of the garden, the dense trees, the opaque shelters, and the tortuous and melancholy lake portray the passionate character of the artist, the cultivation of this wide area of countryside seems on the other hand to reflect the man's ordered mind.

The billiard-room became the heart of Sant'Agata; Verdi used to play after dinner and Peppina too tried her hand at it, with some success. But the ladies could follow the game from an elevated divan that ran around two sides of the room; above the billiard-table hung a splendid lamp. From this room one passed to a smaller one where cards were played: this too was a favourite pastime. As I have already mentioned, the Verdis dressed for dinner, and Signora Peppina chose her clothes with care. She wore dresses of dark muslin adorned with ribbons and she followed French fashion in her hair-style as well. In the hall she would study her appearance in the mirror, checking that all was neat and tidy; Verdi was a real tartar, complaining about every tiny thing; he was restless and worried and was often rude to her. The new hallway at Sant'Agata was furnished with a large coat-stand, which bore the initials GV; hats, sticks and cloaks were kept there. The cloaks were typical of the area and important as a defence against the fog of the plain; Verdi wore them when out in the fields.   Sant'Agata appeared solidly comfortable, protected by an intelligently planned garden – when it was begun, it was always referred to as Peppina's garden, she recalled. Later it became Verdi's garden and she was left with just a few square yards for her flowers and – a little later – for Loulou's grave. The reading-room, the 'central' library which in the 1860s was a salon, testified to the avidity with which they both read. It contained beautifully bound editions of Edgar Allan Poe in French, Sterne, Zola, George Sand, Jules Verne, Victor Hugo. Near the door there still stands the small armchair that Peppina embroidered. Verdi would sit at the table by the window and read poetry by Goethe, Foscolo, Carducci, Dante, Heine. Among the history books are biographies of Philip II and Charles V. In one of the beautiful bound editions of Shakespeare, various passages of *Cymbeline* have been marked in pencil, probably by Verdi himself, who had considered this play as a subject for an opera.

Verdi and Peppina worked mostly in their respective bedrooms. The Maestro's, on the ground floor, gave directly onto Peppina's garden; the room was furnished with several of the pictures that arrived from Naples. It was connected by a small wooden door to Peppina's room, where one's eyes were caught by the splendid counterpane in green damask and the velvet curtains from Paris. On a small table stood the bust that Pietro Tenerani had made of her oval face in Rome in 1841, at the height of her fame, when she was the 'primadonna assoluta' of the Italian stage. Two items of seventeenth-century furniture flanked the french window, adorned with heavy crimson curtains, such as Violetta Valéry might have had; on the wall hung portraits of Loulou and Loreto, her parrot. The bedside-table bore a reliquary that the Emperor of Austria had presented to Feliciano, her father who had died so prematurely. It was also where she kept the books she was presently reading, together with the relative dictionaries.

In the dressing-room stood Peppina's piano, which was almost always silent, unlike Verdi's; there was also another bookcase and scores. Soon space had to be found for photographs, the new form of portrait; friends would send the Verdis their pictures, usually with their elbows resting on tables, so as not to move while posing in front of the lens. She had one taken as well, but did not like it. Whereas Verdi – she used to say, laughing – grew more handsome as he got older. The various photographs included one of 'Fake-Head' which was Verdi's name for Angelo Mariani, who was also known occasionally as 'Good-Head'. Her husband treated him as a friend or a son – but also as a servant, a subordinate. However, the more Verdi asked of him, the more the duffer was prepared to do. Mariani, who could not survive without a woman, was at present living with Elena Massa; the Verdis drummed even Elena's mother, Signora Paolina, into their service, asking her to find laces, powders, and other things that were unavailable in Busseto. But Peppina doubted that Angelo would ever marry Elena; as a young man he had had a wife and daughter; he had got divorced and both had died; the marriage was a disaster. Peppina could not see Anzulett, vain and self-centred, in a domestic role.

In autumn 1860, Mariani conducted the first season at the Teatro Comunale in Bologna. Bologna wanted to secure him as their permanent conductor when his contract with Genoa expired; in the meantime, a proposal had come from Naples. Mariani always asked both Verdi and Peppina for advice about everything; his friendship was almost touching in its intrusiveness – he could do nothing without first consulting the couple; he appeared to be in love with them. Giuseppina, however, advised him against it. 'The present conductor is a father of a family and Neapolitan. He is thus doubly armed to wound anyone who might try to drive him from his post . . .' She also told him that Verdi was afraid of being elected to the Italian Parliament. 'Verdi is in a bad mood because he fears he might obtain a majority of votes, such as would make any other candidate happy.' And he was right: he became Member of Parliament for the constituency of Borgo San Donnino. Which meant going to Turin, changing his way of life . . . And she would become the wife of a Member of Parliament!

Verdi had been persuaded to stand by Cavour himself, but Count Minghelli-Vaini who aspired to the seat was not happy. The Count wrote to Peppina, asking if she could intervene. Showing a great sense of humour, Peppina replied on 13 February:

First of all, let us rectify a mistake. Our friendship does not go back 20 years but 14 or 15. I know that wine and friendship increase their value with age, but women lose it! Now, although I shall soon be taking on what is called a venerable appearance, I am still a woman, and consequently far from ready to accept, even from my best friends, the unwelcome gift of an extra half-dozen years. I already have quite enough. Having settled this first point, let us pass to the second.

In the second point, she explained that Verdi, now elected, was already preparing to leave for Turin, so things were already settled. 'I too will go to Turin and that will certainly make a great hole in my savings.'

The famous couple took rooms at the Albergo Trombetta in Turin; he was somewhat out of his element and she was far more interested in the architecture and the shops than in politics. However, she stayed in the hotel to see to his correspondence; she wrote a great many letters, both for herself and for Verdi – or rather his business-matters. Some time ago she had met Don Giovanni Avanzi, the canon from Vidalenzo, the village where Carlo Verdi had lived. The Canon was a broad-minded man and this was why the diocesan administration had relegated him to the Po Plain. They became friends and, what is even more important from our point of view, regular correspondents; their letters were occasionally a little rhetorical and lacked her usual flashes of humour, the jokes that Peppina liked to make at both her interlocutor's and her own expense – and even Verdi's. From Turin, Giuseppina enthusiastically described to the Canon the scenes she had witnessed:

Preg.mo Signor Canonico,
    The exordium, so to speak, is over and, with the opening of the first Italian Parliament, the new history of Italy begins. I witnessed this solemn and truly impressive occasion from a gallery, and I wish you could have witnessed it too. Among the many who repeatedly proclaim their love of the *motherland* and the few who sincerely love it, you, Signor Canon, are among the very few who love it, after God, above all other things in the world, without reserve, without designs of private interest, without party-spirit. Undoubtedly you, like me, would have wept with joy, when the King and Founder of Italian unity entered the Parliamentary Chamber and men and women rose to acclaim him with fervent cries 'King of Italy! King of Italy!' . . . so the dissensions of centuries are laid aside, they fall silent, and this wish, which Italians of little faith in their own destinies mockingly called a dream or even madness, is about to become an accomplished fact. It is true that the exultation could not be complete without the Members of Parliament from Venice and ancient Rome! . . . However, the Lion and the She-Wolf will tear off their funeral garbs and, thus redeemed, will wave the Italian flags along with the others! . . . I will point out to you, that here the people are merry without ever becoming plebeian in their cheerfulness; and it is in this calm and dignified spirit that the worthy Turinese of all classes have made the greatest sacrifices for the Italian cause . . . Some visits prevented me from finishing this letter and sending it off yesterday. Verdi is at the Chamber and as he set off he asked me to say a thousand things to you . . .

Barezzi wrote rather worriedly: friends in Busseto who had gone to

Turin had not seen Signora Peppina. Had she and Verdi perhaps quarrelled? Peppina set his mind at rest: 'I had an excellent position. Armed with my telescope I was able quite comfortably to study the physionomy of the King, the Ministers, the Ambassadors, the Generals . . .'

The first law to be promulgated on 17 March 1861 proclaimed Vittorio Emanuele II King of Italy; but the King was careful not to change his ordinal number from second to first, thus emphasising the concept of annexation. A week later the first Italian government was constituted. With the need to travel to Turin, Genoa became more convenient as a base than Busseto; besides, Sant'Agata was still an inferno of builders, most of whom were inefficient and dishonest.

Every day in Genoa they went and bought cakes and dined at the Restaurant Concordia, often with Mariani. One day, strolling along the seafront, they met an engineer. They fell into conversation, in the course of which Verdi, who had announced himself as a farmer, stated his admiration for the city. The engineer, whose name was Giuseppe De Amicis, thanked him for this; he declared his love of music, especially *Il trovatore*. Peppina intervened at this point, proud to be able to state that he was at that moment talking to the composer of the opera. Thus a new friendship was struck up: De Amicis, a cousin of the writer Edmondo De Amicis, offered the couple his help in finding a Genoese base. In addition, he went to all sorts of trouble for them, arranging consignments, finding mirrors and picture-frames.

On 6 June, they heard a devastating piece of news. Peppina wrote from Busseto that same day: 'Signor Canon, Cavour is dead!!!! It is impossible for me to add another word to this terrible news! . . . Calamity! . . . Immense calamity!'

Peppina was alone in Busseto in January 1861 and Verdi, who was in Turin, had authorised her to open his post; she received a highly interesting letter. Mauro Corticelli, on tour with Ristori in Russia, had been approached by Enrico Tamberlick, a famous tenor. The Russian public adored Verdi, the tenor wrote, and would like him to write an opera for the Imperial Theatre of St Petersburg; it was made clear that the fee would be considerable. Peppina answered at once, stating that Verdi 'would not be adverse to taking up his pen again'. And she continued – wittily! – that:

if I were not afraid to commit a forgery I would correct that imposing 22 degrees below zero which will make him stare wide-eyed in terror!! ... However feeble an advocate I may be, I will put together my best passages of eloquence in order to persuade him to expose his nose to the risk of frostbite in Russia ... If eloquence does not do the trick, I will put into operation a method which I am assured works even at the gates of Paradise with St Peter, that is to say, to pester until you get what you want. It is true that Verdi is less patient than St Peter, but if he packs me off to bed, never mind!

She had a great desire to travel, to explore such an exotic and mysterious land. Furthermore, Verdi was restless: it would do them both good to go on a journey together. As it turned out, Verdi was far from averse to the idea. His mind turned to Victor Hugo's *Ruy Blas* again, but the imperial censors did not approve. In the end, he changed his mind; he was inspired by a drama by Angel Perez de Saavedra, Duke de Rivas, *Don Alvaro o la fuerza del sino*, which came from Peppina's mine of Spanish treasures.

Piave returned to Sant'Agata, and to Verdi's piano, an instrument which was not restricted to its owner's private use. 'Around that piano I have heard some spicy anecdotes narrated about the Maestro's first compositions ...' Ghislanzoni recollected. And occasionally the Verdis would be found there, making music together, singing, improvising, and laughing.

The journey to Russia was altogether enjoyable and they stopped off in Paris and Berlin. When they reached St Petersburg Peppina wrote to Count Arrivabene: 'This terrible cold has not inconvenienced us at all, thanks to the apartments: the cold can be seen but not felt.' On 2 January 1862 she wrote to the Canon:

We have been in the heart of the Russian winter for several days now ... I was ill, but not because of the climate. I do not say so by way of praise for the climate: no, it is bitter, terrible ... but the rich have managed to invent and procure the means to protect themselves from it ... Not so the poor! alas! I will never stay long enough in Russia, even if I should remain here for twenty years, to get used to the sight of such suffering! Just think, Signor Canon that today, with the thermometer at 24 degrees below zero, the coach-drivers have to stay in their posts in the open air, as long as it pleases their masters ... and sometimes it pleases these masters to leave them there all day and much of the night! I will not mention the poor horses, on whose back they hardly ever throw a rag to

protect them from the ice that settles there and almost forms a
layer . . . The rich can say: long live the winter, the ice, the sledges
and the debauches! But the poor man! In this rawest of seasons
he has no joy! But yes, he has, alas, he has! But what joys? what
delights? The brandy that inebriates him to the point of delirium,
and the foul pleasures of the flesh, the only resources he believes
he has the right to procure by way of compensation for the cruel
sufferings that are forced on him by the laws and the whims of
the rich . . .

It is sad to see Peppina, who knew the world, yielding to this puritan
strain, to see her nose turning up now that her body had filled out
and her chin was no longer clear-cut but lay restfully on her breast.
Lately she had grown fat and was unable to work off a single ounce,
especially at Sant'Agata, where out of boredom she ate more than
she should. 'I am a Venus who gains by closing herself in her shell.'
And also: 'If there is anything irregular in my physique it is the
increase in the weight and circumference of my respectable person.'
The loss of her wasp-waist and youthful looks worried her. She was
small and slightly built, and thus every extra ounce emphasised that
lost sylph-like appearance. But she was still an attractive woman; her
strong features still shone with intelligence and determination.

Russia was a fascinating land and the couple led an unusually
lively social life. Peppina described this new life to the Canon. She
had been to a religious service:

The choristers (without an organ or instruments) strike up a hymn
to the Almighty with their voices and marvellous chords, then the
Priest withdraws, the gate and curtain are closed and thus the
altar and the priest are cut off from the sight of the faithful. And
yet, Signor Canon, this religious enthusiasm, in general, is nothing
but an external act, in which the heart plays no part. The Russians
are bigoted, superstitious and full of contradictions, like all those
who have no real religion.

In another letter, Peppina wrote: 'I saw the benediction of the Neva
by the Emperor and by all the Russian clergy, with bare heads! I
saw the sheds of the poor Lapps in the middle of the river and their
reindeer which I stroked and with which I hope to go for a ride on
the frozen waters, as I have already done on the sledge . . .'
But despite the supplies of macaroni and cold meats, bottles of

French wine and Chianti, that had preceded them, their stay in Russia was cut short: the primadonna fell ill, the understudy proved a disaster and Verdi insisted that the performance should be postponed till the following year when the Imperial Theatre would be able to guarantee good singers. 'We shall return to Russia next year,' Peppina announced. 'We shall stop off in Berlin on our way back; then, fully rested, after a short stay in Paris we shall set foot on the blessed soil of Italy.'

To find themselves in France after months of icy weather was like coming back home, even though their social engagements were now somewhat fatiguing:

At least for a month one must resign oneself to seeing men, women and horses running around and agitating themselves, to dressing two or three times a day – one must bow and talk seriously to people one is often tempted to laugh at – receive visits, pay them back and end up going to bed dead-tired, without having done anything at all – or at least anything worthwhile. This is called elegant life, fashionable life, which one is dragged into by particular occasions, and by the circumstances of such and such a position, especially when one is not settled in Paris, as, for example, we were some years ago . . .

She hoped that 'Verdi would quickly get some troublesome business out of the way so as to return to the prose of Sant'Agata which at times is transformed into the dearest of poems for us. Our little villages have remained practically immune from cholera and may God or chance be thanked for this partial or special favour,' she wrote to the Canon. 'Verdi wanted to make a trip to Germany, for both business and pleasure, but has given up the idea, hoping to be able to see to matters in Paris, all the more so because at the moment he is not disposed to indulge in trips. As for me, I understand perfectly well how the Jews must have grown weary of manna, being weary myself of this Paris which everyone else is so keen on!' She had started to study German, which would be very useful to her, in Russia as well. But just as she was settling into the city, news reached her of Camillino's death, which had come about on 26 June 1863 at the Hospital of Santa Maria delle Grazie in Siena.

He was twenty-five years old, a young doctor doing his apprenticeship; the death certificate gives only the Christian name of the father, and the mother's name appears as Giuseppa: her first child was allowed to die like a bastard without a history. In her notebook there is not a single line or word that testifies to a mother's grief. Giuseppina had managed to silence her conscience with terrifying thoroughness. She never betrays herself in any of the letters we possess. We do not know whether Giuseppina went to her son's funeral; it is improbable. Not only had she now become Signora Verdi, too well-known to allow herself to be recognised at her bastard's funeral, but Camillino had probably died of cholera and so his body was shovelled quickly underground. Camillino may have contracted the disease while aiding its victims; all that remains of him is a vague memory, several unanswered questions and a sense of suffering.

The obliteration of his existence, the cancellation of her three children, was one of the conditions for living with Verdi; there is no doubt that the complete absence of papers bearing any reference to Camillino's name at Sant'Agata means that a major clearing operation must have been carried out. With all the payments she had had to make, there must have been documents testifying to Camillino's upbringing, to Adelina's short life and to Giuseppa's vegetable-existence. And since all such evidence clearly went up in flames, we can feel authorised to exercise our imaginations: Camillino knew he was Giuseppina Verdi's son; he met her at Locate Triulzi, his grandmother's house, when Giuseppina visited it on the excuse of her mother's or Barberina's health. It is possible that the young man came to see her at Sant'Agata – during Verdi's absence – and that the relatives whom Peppina tried to keep at bay but who sent letters or called all the same, were trying to put pressure on her to give the poor student a name, and maybe a home. Without recognition, it would have been difficult for Camillino to get married, to find a good job, to be accepted by a fiercely hypocritical society. There may have been some indecorous scene, perhaps the result of a surprise visit to Sant'Agata: but Peppina never let anything show. However, it is a fact that later (though not much later) she felt the need of a friendly priest, a confessor and consoler: she knew she had sinned. This was the role of the Canon of Vidalenzo. Camillino's death left its mark on her; she began to grow old, her hair lost its colour. And for a while she withdrew into her shell. Perhaps Verdi's growing intolerance towards her left its mark as well.

From Paris, where they spent a month, Peppina was able to resume her correspondence; among her Neapolitan friends were some 'diehards' who remained faithful to the Bourbons, even though Gaeta, the last fortress of King Ferdinand, fell into the hands of the Savoy army. This was followed by a ferocious civil war, which the North was later to refer to as 'brigandage'. It is beyond dispute that the 'bands' were endemic in character; but after the annexation to Piedmont, conditions in the South, both social and economic, had deteriorated. The crisis was aggravated by the poverty of the day labourers, by compulsory conscription and harsher taxes. The Bourbon King fanned the flames from the safe distance of Palazzo Farnese in Rome, where he had taken refuge together with Queen Sofia.

Between his two trips to Russia, Verdi had agreed to compose the *Hymn of Nations* for yet another Exhibition in London; the text had been written by the young Arrigo Boito, poet and musician; he had presented himself to Verdi with a letter from Clara Maffei when they were in Paris. Arrigo's elder brother (Camillo, author of the novella *Senso*) was an architect and writer; Arrigo was a cultivated and energetic young man. They both represented modern tendencies; Arrigo was like a colt chafing to take part in a race, and his natural instinct was to laugh at everyone and everything.

Peppina set off for London a month before Verdi; she liked England and her English had improved a little. 'If you can and it does not derange you too much,' she wrote to a certain Maggioni, 'to be so kind as to lend me during my abode in England a French and Italian dictionary.' She liked wandering around the museums and the crowded city. She admired the shops in Regent Street and made her purchases. London was the mecca of the world; one could find everything in its great stores, which was a definite novelty – and unimaginable in Italy. '. . . You must know, if you do not already know, that Verdi is not giving his piece at the Exhibition. You will ask why?' she wrote from London to Corticelli (28 April 1862). 'I haven't got time to tell you why today. The world in general and men (I do not exclude women) in particular are a great dung-heap. The idea is not a poetical one but unfortunately that is the case with most truths.'

She was forty-nine years old. Verdi seemed to be bursting with energy, his grey eyes were velvety and restless, his beard streaked with grey. It was as if he refused to leave his youth behind; he was constantly on the move: from Genoa to Turin, from Turin to Parma, and then to Paris with that meddler Mariani, who was a womaniser – as Peppina knew all too well. After Cavour's death, the Prime Minister Rattazzi had encouraged Garibaldi to take Rome.

But while the government provided the Garibaldini with arms, at the same time they had to pretend to be against all dangerous Roman ventures, especially in the eyes of Napoleon III. Thus when the Garibaldini landed in Calabria to the cry of 'Rome or Death!' they were attacked by the regular army and Garibaldi, a man of honour, ordered his troops not to counter-attack, thus preventing a civil war.

The episode in the Aspromonte in which Garibaldi was wounded and many of his men killed on the field or condemned to death (others went to swell the ranks of the bandits) led to the capital of the new Italian state being moved from Turin to Florence: the intention was to show Napoleon III that Rome's hour would come soon. In Turin there were protests and riots, which were put down by the army. Naples also expected to be chosen as capital – Peppina expressed her puzzled amusement to her friends: how on earth could such an out-of-the-way city become the capital? But Florence was not an ideal site either. Unlike Turin it did not have any government buildings and its topography was medieval, with narrow streets.

At Sant'Agata they were preparing to return to Russia, when it was discovered that Barberina had a 'poitrinaire' illness. Like cancer today, tuberculosis was an unmentionable word. 'She is the only one left to me of four brothers and sisters,' Peppina wrote. 'She will certainly pass on to a better life with the angels . . . only a miracle of God can return her to the earth . . . !' She spoke of a second bereavement: '. . . and maybe some people will laugh but I am still crying as I write to you, it is the loss of my dear Loulou. Four days of atrocious suffering have brought him to eternal rest under a weeping willow in our garden . . .' Mariani had been to stay; 'he would be even dearer if he spoke only 23 hours a day instead of 25.' Piave was now living in Milan. He was married, and had a daughter. His brother had been arrested. Verdi had written to Massimo d'Azeglio, the Governor of Milan and Manzoni's brother-in-law, to help him obtain a post at La Scala. After this favour, Piave could consider himself replaced; the new courtier-friend was Mariani, who had no family and was thus more readily available.

La forza del destino (*The Force of Destiny*) in St Petersburg was a triumph. 'The Emperor was struck by bronchitis and a violent eye-ache and could not come until the fourth performance.' Peppina continued her letter to Cesarino De Sanctis, 14–26 November 1862, recounting how the Emperor himself had summoned Verdi to the imperial box and how the reticent composer had had to present himself in his imperial presence, where he was showered with compliments, especially from the Empress. As if that were not enough, the following day he was decorated with imperial crosses and orders.

In *La forza del destino*, Verdi had touched the romantic chord of the moment; the story and characters belong to the world of the feuilleton (they are not real characters like Violetta, Rigoletto or Amelia of *A Masked Ball* – they are not even heroes like Attila, the Conte di Luna, Ernani). *La forza del destino* is a full-blooded opera which owes its greatest moments to the scenes with the soprano, a character truly felt by Verdi, and the chorus, whose 'Maledizione' seems to lead towards the power of the Requiem. The opera achieved the kind of success we associate today with those musicals which travel all over the world and are seen by everybody. It is worth reiterating the point: operas that entered the permanent repertoire, that were not written for one particular theatre but for all time, were a totally new phenomenon – one that came in with Verdi. Rossini wrote with a specific theatre in mind, as did Donizetti, Spontini and Cherubini; they would then perhaps serve the opera up elsewhere, changing the libretto and a few arias, thus creating another 'uniquum'. *The Force of Destiny* was so successful that Verdi later wrote a pot-pourri of the best melodies, which was to sell like a Beatles album. Since Verdi was writing for the repertoire now, it became necessary to consider the question of what happened when an opera returned to the stage with different singers from the original performance and with conductors other than the composer himself. Thus another new figure appeared – that of the conductor who made it his responsibility to see that the score was respected. Angelo Mariani belonged to this category; he was a great performer – and a very famous one by now. In addition 'Anzulett' was a great communicator – he talked both profusely and intelligently, and he devoted terrific energy to writing letters and diaries. It was he who was greatly responsible for the deification of Verdi as a composer and a man. During his time at the Teatro Carlo Felice, he had performed many of Verdi's operas. He was the lover of Marchesa Teresa Sauli, the unhappy aristocratic wife of a certain Marchese Negrotto, and a friend (some sources say more than a friend) of her mother, Luisa Sauli Pallavicino; Mariani somehow managed to remain on good terms with everyone. He had woven relations with politicians and aristocrats, like Sir James Hudson who had introduced him to Cavour. There was no-one Mariani did not know. He was likeable, always ready to strike up a conversation, he took his work seriously and had unlimited energy. The job of permanent conductor at the Théâtre des Italiens had been dangled before him, and he had sought help from Verdi. In this case he handled things badly, because at the same time he had consulted other people and he thus succeeded in offending his adored Maestro; at times he seemed to cultivate an almost masochistic relationship with Verdi, as if he yearned for chastisement – and he usually did not have to wait long for it.

Mariani wrote to Verdi from Cesena in 1865, calling his attention for the first time to Teresa Stolz, a soprano who had distinguished herself in *William Tell* and *A Masked Ball*; Verdi asked Piave to listen to her in *Macbeth* – his new version. Thus he would discover whether she had the right dramatic temperament or not; he did not trust *Giovanna d'Arco*, which was one of Stolz's pièces de résistance. Angelo Mariani already knew this singer; he was to fall in love with her and, at the end of 1867, she became engaged to him. In 1865 Giuseppina wrote to him, perhaps about this very infatuation: 'I have received your most welcome letter, written in an access and excess of sentimentality, stirred up perhaps by a storm of the blinded god. Let us hope that the pains, the slow inflammation and black mood will have passed by this time, thanks to some sweet-scented note that has arrived at the right moment to act as a doctor . . .'

A tall woman, with a determined, square jaw, Teresa Stolz was born in 1831, the youngest of a family of singers. Although a Czech from Bohemia, she was German in appearance, with thick blond hair often adorned with flowers or jewels, while a Wagnerian tress rested on her candid shoulders. After a period at the Conservatoire in Prague, she had studied under an Italian teacher who had advised her to give up the idea of a singing career. Instead she followed the circuit which was as exotic as it was predictable, from Tiflis to Odessa, Constantinople, Nice, Granada, making her Italian début in Spoleto in *Trovatore* (1864). It was said that when Teresa was in Odessa and Ricci was living with her two seventeen-year-old sisters, the apartments were connected by a wardrobe-cum-door; the visitor could thus find himself in the embarrassing position of seeing a wardrobe suddenly open from which would emerge not some article of clothing but one of the twins – there was no telling which. The twins Frances (Fanny) and Ludmilla (Lidia) were born in 1827 and, by 1843, had moved to Trieste with Luigi Ricci, the Assistant Conductor at the Teatro Grande whose baldness was compensated by a thick beard; Ricci, who was quite

The interpreters of *La forza del destino* (*The Force of Destiny*), Teresa Stolz became the great protagonist of this opera until Verdi wrote *Aida* for her. The opera was written for St Petersburg and became an immense success.

The barricades at Porta Ticinese in Milan during the Five Days (1848) when the Milanese people fought the Austrian army and chased it out of the city. It was a century of barricades and citizens' struggles against the police, the army and the monarchies. Napoleon III's architect George Haussmann found the solution to barricades by designing boulevards too wide to be blocked.

After many years of life together, Verdi and Giuseppina married in Piedmontese Savoy but the union was kept secret. Their witnesses were the coachman who had brought them to the village and the bell-ringer of the church.

ABOVE Giuseppina went twice to Russia in 1861 and 1862; she described the customs of the country in many letters. By that period Verdi enjoyed world-wide fame. When *The Force of Destiny* was about to be staged, the protagonist fell ill and her substitute was so bad that Verdi refused to go ahead. The following year Verdi and Giuseppina returned to St Petersburg where the opera was enormously successful.

RIGHT Giuseppina at the time of *Un ballo in maschera* (*A Masked Ball*) (1858) in a painting made in Naples which her dog Loulou recognised at once.

Filomena 'Fifao' Verdi was re-named Maria when she was adopted by the Verdis. She never lived with her official parents staying first with Verdi's father in Busseto and then moving to Sant'Agata. She was probably Verdi's (but not Peppina's) natural daughter. Maria Verdi was engaged to Alberto Carrara, whose father the local notary and mother, a Demaldè, were all friends of the family. She grew into a fine, elegant lady whose portrait dominates the little sitting-room at Sant'Agata. Her heirs still live in the house.

ABOVE Clara Maffei, 'Clarina', was Verdi's friend since the early days of Milan; in her salon he met 'everybody'. They were probably lovers. She became a friend of Giuseppina late in life and they corresponded, but then she 'betrayed' her for Teresa.

RIGHT Teresa Stolz (1834–1902) as Aida for which she was coached by Verdi himself at Sant'Agata. At some stage in her life, she began to sign her name as 'Aida'.

LEFT The church of San Marco in Milan, during the first performance of the Requiem Mass which Verdi composed for Manzoni. This was the only church which would allow women to sing in a holy place. From a drawing by Pessina, etching by Centenari.

BELOW The same Requiem Mass performed at La Scala; Teresa Stolz had been trained by Verdi personally. The extraordinary success of a religious work was a novelty. From a drawing by Tofani, etching by Baldi.

LEFT Giuseppe Verdi in 1887 at the time of *Otello*. His circle was so secretive about this opera that they referred to it as the 'African'.

RIGHT A photograph of Teresa Stolz. She retired very rich and established herself as one of the . great ladies of Milan society. She survived both Giuseppina and Verdi himself.

Al mio Verdi; coll'affetto e la venerazione
d'un tempo!
S¹ᵗ Agata 8 7bre
1877
Peppina

Giuseppina aged sixty-three by now ill and suffering from bouts of depression, but she was to die at the ripe age of eighty-two. Verdi went to live in Milan where he died in January 1901, the same year as Queen Victoria.

a successful composer and conductor, was to end his life killing himself. The twin sisters made their début in Trieste and, in 1845, followed Ricci to Odessa, with Teresa as well, where the composer took over the artistic management of that theatre.

Giuseppina met the Stolz twins in Trieste where they performed *The Lonely Girl from the Asturias*, an opera that Luigi Ricci had composed for them. The *ménage à trois*, which seemed to be a speciality of the Stolz family, proceeded more or less happily in Milan and Cremona.

In 1847 Luigi Ricci composed *Il Diavolo a quattro* for both singers. The twins and Ricci continued to live together although the composer in 1849 decided to marry Lidia with whom he had a daughter; but three years later, almost as if he had regretted the choice, Fanny gave birth to a son. The boy took the name of Luigi Ricci-Stolz and was to become his aunt Teresa's sole heir, thus inheriting quite a few of Giuseppe Verdi's possessions – as well as Giuseppina's. And Luigi Jr was to become the lead-violinist in the orchestra at La Scala.

At the time of Mariani's meeting, in 1856, Teresa Stolz, who was not particularly bright or intellectually curious, was studying with Luigi Ricci, something which can only arouse our suspicion, with what we know of the habits of this composer and his weakness for the Stolz family. When the young conductor heard Stolz, the stage lacked a first-rate actress or real primadonna; Mariani decided that she should fill this gap. If she was going to make that leap into the firmament of Italian opera, Teresa needed a Svengali, like all the stars of the stage – or Hollywood actresses.

Meanwhile, after studying a great many librettos and plays, the Verdis accepted an invitation to Madrid. *La forza del destino* was to be performed there:

> ... Spain has a beautiful sky, stupendous pictures, imaginative poets and the remains of marvellous architecture left by those Arabs, those Moors whom the Spanish still detest with implacable hatred ... But despite their Poets, their painters and all the dazzling individuals that honour the nation, the Spaniards remain ignorant, proud, cruel and hostile en masse to every form of progress that will make our century famous. In Granada gas-lighting and railways met with violent opposition ...

She found the corrida barbaric and she began to be irritated by the South of Italy as well, which she had loved until then. 'Do

not talk to me of Sicily, of Naples, of Spain etc etc,' she wrote
on another occasion, 'they are lands, peoples, nations that are full
of pride, ignorance and lice!' They found themselves disturbed by
the Escorial, that immense, punitive palace. Verdi's next opera was
in fact to be *Don Carlos*. He felt drawn to the character of Philip
II, to his excesses of mysticism and libertinage. In his mind there
burgeoned the idea of an opera based on the drama of the Infante
Don Carlo, Philip II's son, the subject of Schiller's great romantic
drama, which had already been set to music by various composers
during that decade. It was not in fact the first time that he had
thought of an opera featuring Philip II – who is the protagonist of
Don Carlos. But Peppina was excluded from this choice.

'This evening we sail for France,' wrote Peppina. Verdi had agreed
to compose for the Opéra in Paris. They changed their apartment
once again and went to Avenue des Champs Elysées. Peppina wrote
to her Canon:

> You will say: after 27 days in Paris she has not found 17 minutes
> to write to the poor Canon . . . I have spent these 27 days amidst
> tribulations. The house I am writing to you from is the third
> house we have lived in. The cook who will prepare lunch for us
> tomorrow is the fourth to enter this house in these few days . . .
> Verdi, supremely happy with all the difficulties, all the tribulations
> that I have to overcome and conquer, licks his whiskers, and waits
> in hope that I will beg to return to the hotel.

They had brought with them an English maidservant. After the peace
and quiet of Sant'Agata, however excessive, Paris was exhausting.

> Here everything goes at such a feverish pace, at a gallop . . .
> In Busseto and similar towns one leads a vegetable existence,
> in Paris one's life is devoured . . . in big towns like Paris, the
> arteries and heart of modern civilisation, life is synonymous with
> frenetic activity, with possessing, with enjoying glories, power,
> luxury, pleasures . . . and above all money, money.

Despite all this, they led a more active social life than usual; beautiful
Adelina Patti had visited them, flirting with Verdi; they had seen the
Tamberlicks, du Locle, the librettist of *Don Carlos* (Méry had died in
1865) and the baritone Ronconi, who had sung with Peppina in her
youth. They went to the theatre occasionally.

'*Pregiatissimo Signor Tito*,' Giuseppina wrote to Ricordi on the 23 October 1866, 'Verdi, who is oppressed by fatigue and work, tells me that he forgot to write to you concerning a billiard table which he would like to have installed in his Genoese apartment. Although matters in this Imperial theatre proceed always with a slow and solemn pace, the only eternal being is God, so that the rehearsals and preparations for *Don Carlos*, however long and complex, must come to an end. We long for this end in order to return to Italy and more precisely to Genoa where we would be happy billiarding furiously away after so many months of deprivation.' She therefore asked Ricordi to see that a billiard table, exactly like the one at Sant'Agata should be made by the same artisans and for the same price. Giuseppina even told him what light should illuminate it.

Paris too was on the alert against cholera: 'the disease has not died down completely in Paris, since only today they announced the death of a granddaughter of Lamartine's from cholera. Only in Paris, they do not talk of it regularly in the public papers for commercial reasons, and I do not know whether to approve or condemn them for this!'

Peppina bought furniture in Paris and had it sent to Genoa. There had been problems, but in the end the apartment of Palazzo Sauli on the hill of Carignano, in Strada San Giacomo, two floors looking onto a garden with cypresses, cedars and magnolias, was ready. The palazzo, with a splendid view over the port, just a few minutes from the centre, had only recently been vacated, and, owing to the relations between the ladies of the Sauli family and Mariani, an agreement had been reached immediately. Without consulting anyone, Mariani took five rooms, contiguous and connected, of the Verdis' apartment for himself. It could be considered a reward for his role as intermediary; he would pay them a suitable sum for the sublease. And when the Verdis were not in Genoa, he would be able to keep an eye on the place for them.

Verdi finished composing the third act of *Don Carlos* in Palazzo Sauli. The Genoese piano-tuner Dodero left this account:

I was summoned to mend Maestro Verdi's piano in Palazzo Sauli. I asked him first if he liked life in Genoa. Wonderful, he answered. They say the climate is a little capricious but one simply has to equip oneself with suitable clothes. Today you can go out without a coat, tomorrow with a mid-season coat and the following day with a cape up to your nose; but when the weather is good it's enchanting, especially in winter and spring! But – he added, passing onto practical matters – mind you tune it robustly because this key-board has to express choruses, overtures, songs and griefs of all kinds. Was the Maestro writing another opera? I hastened to ask. And at once he said: What other job do I have?

The laborious work on *Don Carlos* continued in Paris and in the Pyrenees. A few months later, on 12 January 1867, Giuseppina wrote to Ricordi: Verdi had asked her to tell him that 'within two or three days he will have finished the ballet (which he started very late) and the whole opera including the instrumentation. As soon as he is free from his work, he will send you the contract for *Don Carlos* ... The opera, I think, will not be staged earlier than the 15 or 20 of February. If, by some chance for which I dare not hope, the first night were to be anticipated, I shall make sure to warn you to give you time to travel. We shall leave Paris immediately after the first night.' She then went on giving him more details about the location where the billiard table was to be placed and enclosed a drawing. 'This is based on the plan of the apartment sent to me from Mariani in Genoa.'

And while Verdi and Peppina were in Paris, in Italy events were unfolding that were to lead to the annexation of the Veneto. After forming an unpopular alliance with Prussia, Italy found itself repeatedly conquered by Austria on both land and sea. Only Garibaldi ever had the better of the Austrians. 'Verdi is in a very black mood and so am I . . . At this moment, no Italian of any heart can be gay and calm in spirit . . .' At Sant'Agata, where they had returned, they could hear General Cialdini's cannon-fire. As if the sense of national shame were not enough, cholera once again got a grip of the cities of Italy, and in Palermo yet another popular insurrection broke out – yet another volte-face. It was the Sicilian Vespers all over again – under a different name, or even without any names at all.

In what was called the Third War of Independence, the corruption of the military high command, the politicians and the monarchy was revealed once and for all. The new nation wanted to be treated on a par with the others, but could not in fact hope to compete with Germany and France, the two colossals of continental Europe. Germany, led by Prussia, put forward alarming theories on the superiority of the Germanic nation, which was to be forged with 'blood and iron' as Bismarck put it. A musical voice, insidious and fascinating, emerged from these theories, propagated them, and made them his. Wagner was hissed in Paris, but his name was on everyone's lips in the musical world. Rossini had met him, although he was not taken with his Teutonic orchestration. Verdi, who had heard excerpts from *Tannhäuser*, concluded: 'He must be mad.'

Don Carlos at the Opéra was not a success, but Verdi knew that one day it would be recognised as one of his greatest operas; Mariani, who had come up to Paris, was of the same opinion. Impelled by the force and drive of Schiller's romanticism, Verdi had managed to give life to the characters and to capture the full historical tension of the play. Angelo Mariani decided to stage *Don Carlo* (in Italian, the title drops its Spanish 's') on in Bologna, where he would be able to do justice to it, with an orchestra and singers worthy of the masterpiece – something that Paris, as usual, had failed to provide. Verdi was working on this production of *Don Carlo* when he heard some terrible news: 'Verdi's father, an octogenarian who had been ill for the last four years, ended his sufferings and gave his soul up to God on the night of the 14th of this month! Verdi is grief-stricken and, although I hardly lived any time with him, and we were at opposite poles in our ways of thinking, I feel profoundly sorrowful . . .'

But that devastating year held another loss for him. Peppina wrote on 26 July 1867:

We are deep in mourning. Signor Antonio Barezzi, that honest and beneficent creature, closed his eyes in eternal sleep in our arms! He was 80 years old and died after a long sickness on the 21st of this month at 10 in the evening. He is the third dear person we have lost in the space of a few months! You see therefore that the year 1867 is proving an ill-omened one for us! The grief and the heavy labour of *Don Carlos* have altered Verdi's constitution and made it essential for him to undergo a thermal cure and also a period of light distraction. He will therefore set out from Sant'Agata next week and if there is no other obstacle will be in Paris on the 10th or 15th of August, and after a few days' rest, will continue his journey to the Pyrenées, returning to the waters of Cauterets, which he has already tried, to the great relief of his throat. I wish you all the consolations that we lack, especially at this moment.

For some days Verdi maintained total silence, wandering around Sant'Agata, furious, tired, and ill: the death of Barezzi, the man to whom he owed so much, was not to be endured. He took it out on Peppina, the nearest and most readily available victim; not even the little girl who came to play – indeed, who practically lived at Sant'Agata – could prove any consolation. 'The girl I told you about is called Filomena and today, Thursday, a holiday, she is here in my room, playing with her doll. The happiness of childhood . . .' She confessed to her diary, which she had just started keeping:

> There are definitely actions that are repugnant to the conscience of an honest person, but which careful consideration suggest one should do. And maybe women, who do not despise certain little tricks, do such things and are right to do them. So that being a hypocrite, a flirt, and simpering works more or less with all men. Devoting oneself exclusively to one man may be admirable in theory, but is a mistake in practice. I try to raise Verdi's morale because of his indisposition, which his nerves and his imagination make him consider more serious than it is. He often comes to my room but cannot stay still for 10 minutes. Yesterday he came and as usual, especially these days, no sooner had he sat down than he got up again. I said to him: 'Where are you going?' 'Upstairs.' And since he is not accustomed to go up there, I answered, 'To do what?' 'To look for Plato.' 'Oh, don't you remember that it is in the cupboard in the dining-room?' The questions and answers seemed quite natural to me, and my main concern was to see him in peace as he needs to be and to save him a useless journey . . . If only I had not said this! It was a serious matter, premeditated on my part and almost an abuse of power! . . . Alas, I do not know how things will end because he is getting steadily more restless and angry . . .

July 2nd 1867: 'Another outburst this evening over a window left open . . .' The atmosphere between the two was growing more tense than ever, Verdi was hostile towards her, almost as if he saw her in a different light. He grew impatient with her and accused her of being arrogant, of always wanting to be in the right. It was the classic situation when a man discovers another woman. Peppina was on the alert; without Verdi she would be left with nothing, and there was no knowing how many of her 'friends' would drop away once she ceased to offer them the opportunity to meet the rich, famous and brilliant composer. A year later, Peppina confided her worries to her diary (she wrote in French, maybe to protect it from the eyes of Zeffirina, the maidservant who was beginning to gossip about her in the village): Verdi was continuing to torment her and the servants, nothing was working. Even her voice irritated him, its intonation was too sonorous for him, or too faint. One morning he had reprimanded her in front of Corticelli and Maddalena Barezzi! 'Now he is playing the piano with Mariani.' Fortunately there was Filomena. 'I will tell you that we are tempted to adopt a dear girl aged seven: she is a distant relative of Verdi's, and is called Verdi herself.'

Filomena Maria, born on 14 November 1859, was a second cousin of Verdi's, being the granddaughter of Marcantonio, the composer's uncle, and the daughter of Giuseppe and Maria Verdi, poor peasants who lived at Le Roncole. After her brother died of burns, 'Fifao' was taken into care by Carlo Verdi and her aunt, at Palazzo Dordoni. Verdi took charge of her education and then decided to adopt her, with the name of Maria. Maria Verdi was to be the composer's sole heir. As we are dealing with a world of hypotheses and lies – few people have ever succeeded in concealing the truth as thoroughly as Verdi and Peppina – one is tempted to think that Filomena was not simply adopted by Verdi but was his real – and long-desired – daughter. This would explain the otherwise surprising decision to send the girl to live in Palazzo Dordoni with Carlo, Verdi's father, taking her from poor parents who became mysteriously rich overnight, suddenly able to buy various pieces of land.

If there were any truth in this hypothesis, we can be sure that Giuseppina would not have opposed the plan: she was too old to be jealous of the feminine distractions that Verdi undoubtedly conceded himself, especially at that time, and the arrival of a small girl in the house could hardly fail to cheer her up. And in fact she doted on Fifao. If Fifao had been the daughter of a maidservant, of a peasant-girl – as was the case with other illegitimate children of Verdi's – they would have maintained absolute silence, not only because it was shameful to have an illegitimate child, but because Verdi would have had to look after her. The likeliest proof comes from the fact that Maria's second son was the very image of the Maestro.

In May 1867, two months before Barezzi's death, Peppina had gone to Milan alone; it was a specially planned trip. She made her way to Casa Maffei – that famous house with its intellectual salon from which she had always felt excluded, the house which continued to receive letters from Verdi, and from which regular replies were sent out, in a laborious curling hand. She rang the bell and had herself announced by Angiolino, the manservant. She gave him a photograph of Verdi and said, 'Tell the countess that I am this gentleman's wife.'

Clarina Maffei welcomed her with extraordinary affection. She even accompanied her to see Manzoni. Peppina thus met the man whom Verdi had long venerated from afar. But let us see how Clara recounted the visit to Franco Faccio, composer, conductor and a friend of Boito's.

Milan, 15 May 1867

Angiolino came in with a portrait, telling me that the wife of the gentleman (in the portrait) begged me to receive her: it was Signora Verdi. I rushed to meet her, with one of those heartfelt impulses that you know, I clasped her to my bosom, I kissed her lovingly and, both of us feeling overcome, we introduced ourselves. I cannot tell you how good she was, how expansive and happy at having visited me at last. I had the fondest and clearest proof of the affection Verdi feels towards me. She told me so many kind and consoling things, which Verdi has repeated about me . . .

Verdi was not very fond of Faccio on account of certain attacks that had been levelled at him by 'young men'; Clarina Maffei had taken advantage of this visit to talk of him to Peppina. Peppina wrote to her from Locate, on her way back to Sant'Agata: 17 May. 'How wrong I was to tremble at my bizarre boldness, presenting myself to you with just one little portrait, as my herald!'

But her finest moment was when she revealed the whole story to Verdi, who was waiting for her at the station with little Filomena; from the way Peppina recounts it to Clara Maffei, we can divine her state of joyous anticipation. When they were in the carriage, her husband asked her about the family, the furniture, the people she had seen . . . Peppina, pulling his leg, told him that she would have been happy to meet Clarina if only he had given her a letter of introduction. But maybe he was ashamed of her, fat as she was.

As he referred to me with the flattering epithet of capricious (only ever bestowed on young women, and it is some time since I was young) I very very slowly pulled your note from my bag, tossed it onto his lap and as soon as he had glanced at it, he displayed a great row of teeth, including his wisdom teeth! I told him quickly, quickly, at a gallop, how you had welcomed me, how you had come out with me (something extraordinary for you), how silly I had been to wait all these years before meeting you and he kept repeating: 'It doesn't surprise me, it doesn't surprise me – I know Clarina . . .' Wanting to go ahead at full steam, I said with affected casualness: 'If you go to Milan, you must introduce yourself to MANZONI with Clarina. He is expecting you and I went there with her the other day!!' Pouff? . . . Here the bomb was so strong and so unexpected, that I did not know whether I should open the doors of the carriage to give him air, or close them, fearing that in the paroxysm of surprise and joy he might jump out! He turned red, pale, sweaty: he took off his hat and crumpled it so, that he almost reduced it to a pancake. Then (and this must remain our secret) the most severe and proud Bear of Busseto found his eyes filled with tears and both of us, overcome, sobbing, remained for ten minutes in total silence.

Verdi to Clara:

Sant'Agata, 24 May 1867

I am still open-mouthed at Peppina's account of what happened between you and with you. And I am all the more surprised because before my better half set out from Sant'Agata I asked her if she wanted a few words to you in writing. No, she answered, do you imagine that I, looking so large and so like a housewife, want to present myself to a highly elegant lady, to a wisp, to one who lives on enthusiasm etc, etc? . . . You are great devils, you women! But I do love this kind of boldness, which does not embarrass anyone, and if you are happy, I am very happy, and as for us, Peppina is happy; she has done nothing but talk of you in such a tender and friendly fashion that it is as if you had known each other for twenty years. If I was amazed by the first part of the account, I cannot express my sensations on hearing the second. How I envy my wife for having seen that Great Man! But I do not know whether I will have the courage to present myself to him, even if I do come to Milan . . .

Peppina was exaggerating when she described herself as a fat-lady from a fairground. She was no longer the slender 'traviata', the diaphanous heroine of early-romanticism; but her skin remained transparent, her expression ambiguously haughty, and the determination that shone from her eyes was only emphasised by her solid appearance. Her dark, arched eyebrows stressed the intelligence of

her face. She had liked Milan, and she had liked Clarina, with her
house full of portraits and dark landscapes. It was years since Verdi
last set foot in Milan; maybe the magnet of Manzoni might persuade
him to forget the slights he had received there – or that he imagined
he had received. It was true that La Scala – and Ricordi was partly
to blame – had given wretched productions of Verdi's operas, almost
as if they had wanted to ensure that they were a flop. Verdi was
no longer attracted by the salons, and Clarina's was in decline in
any case, now that it lacked the political and patriotic component.
Camillo Boito described the salon in a letter to his brother with a
slightly malicious but clearly accurate eye:

> At midnight I was at Maffei's, where two tiny rooms were packed
> full with about ninety men and women, scholars and simpletons,
> young and old. It was all a din, a crush to compensate for the great
> quiet and terrible silence of those evenings when you came and
> joined the unattractive throng. Amidst that chattering, laughing
> crowd I remained silent, grumpy, bored and lonely, as in the
> middle of a desert . . .

Piave was even harsher about Clarina Maffei in a letter to Verdi, in
which there is a regrettable note of anti-Semitism:

> On the evening of 31 December we went to see the new year in at
> your friend's house . . . It seemed that Israel, under the guidance
> of the erstwhile Member-of-Parliament Finzi, had pitched his tents
> there. There were also the Boitos, the Faccios, the Pragas, the
> Filippas . . . but the lady of the house was brilliant, she told
> everyone about a letter from you, and trumpeted it to the four
> winds. I am convinced that she is too vain, that the heart is the
> smallest item in the make-up of such a butterfly-woman . . .

'Filippa' was Piave's nickname for the critic Filippi, a homosexual,
who championed German music.

Meanwhile in Bologna, Mariani found an enemy in Mauro
Corticelli who was spreading gossip about him. But Corticelli had
the protection of Peppina: indeed, as it was becoming increasingly
difficult to run the houses and business-matters, she managed to
persuade Verdi to take on 'Maurone' ('big Mauro' – he was of an
impressive size) or 'Cappellari' as Sant'Agata general administrator.
Corticelli, a schemer, had Peppina's ear. Here she made a huge

blunder (and it was not the first, nor would it be the last); Maurone was 'a good fellow', she claimed; he was serious and reliable.

In October 1867, Maurone settled in at Sant'Agata. To Peppina's relief – and against Verdi's wishes – he dined with them, making jokes that Verdi found in bad taste; when Anzulett was present, Corticelli would direct his barbs at him. The atmosphere was extremely tense and Peppina confided to her diary how sorry she was to see her husband treating her so badly. Maybe he hated her. But it was Corticelli who hated Anzulett: the latter was a good-looking man of forty-seven, talented and successful; the former was a schemer who had got nowhere and had no money. When they were together at the dinning table, Mariani paid no attention to him and hardly talked to Peppina either: his whole attention was concentrated on Verdi with whom he talked of projects, of music, hunting, travel, adventures ... These were unpleasant hours and Verdi seemed to enjoy ignoring her, playing this ignoble game. Mariani wanted a splendid performance of *Don Carlo* in Bologna. Only at the last moment did he accept Teresa Stolz for the part of Elisabetta di Valois, not having found 'anything better'. She wrote to Signor Tornaghi of the Ricordi publishing house: since she had signed a contract with Bologna, she asked him to send her 'the score of *Don Carlos* so that I may study it more seriously than I did when I was not sure whether it was I who was going to sing at the Italian première ...' (27 June 1867). But during the rehearsals, Anzulett realised that Stolz would sing Elisabetta 'well, very well indeed'. He was teaching her to move on stage, to interpret a queen, a great and fascinating character.

Probably the love-affair between Mariani and Teresa was already under way. Stolz was a woman of strong character, she had charm and knew how to please a man. It was at this time that Mariani began to suffer from strong pains in the lower abdomen; he did not understand the cause, but decided to work less and settle down.

From Bologna Anzulett wrote:

Corticelli is here and comes every morning to wake me. He too has taken up the bad habit of rebuking me because he says I stay up late at the café. He is a real moaner. I have been assured that he is a womaniser par excellence and here in Bologna has a number of young and old lovers. This morning I had letters from the Pallavicinos with the usual greetings to you and the Signora, and among other things they tell me that young Count De Sonnaz has died of cholera – he aroused the jealousy of Marchese Negrotto, the daughter's husband. The fool now takes pleasure in tormenting that poor creature, showing his infernal joy at his death and saying that God has avenged him.

Angelo Mariani won the first round over Maurone, making *Don Carlo* into a total success; even Filippi was unstinting in his praise for both Verdi and Mariani. But when Mariani and Verdi met up again in Palazzo Sauli, there were two new factors: the Verdis' marriage was at a crisis point and Anzulett, 'Fake Head', had brought a fascinating woman with him, a musician and a skilled seductress. Although she had taken lodgings in the nearby Palazzo Corallo, Teresa lived at Palazzo Sauli with Mariani – which is to say she lived together with the Verdis. Peppina consoled herself by joining Corticelli in making spiteful remarks; Verdi remained irascible. Dinners with the five of them were sheer torture: Mauro and Angelo, Teresa and Peppina – and Verdi. Fifao was staying with her aunt. 'If you should have occasion to pass by Le Roncole, I beg you to look in and see how my dear Filomena is; I often think of her and hope she will turn out well . . .' For Christmas there was 'a package with 10 francs for that little devil Filomena . . . mind, she must be a little calmer than she has been recently . . . Maddalena's trip has been decided and Corticelli will act as guide . . .' In fact Barezzi's widow was on her way there with Corticelli: would the Canon not like to join them?

From Milan, Ricordi and Maffei began to put pressure on Verdi to return to La Scala with *Don Carlo*; Teresa Stolz joined in the campaign. His latest operas had been staged shoddily and, in Verdi's mind, disastrously: he wanted nothing to do with La Scala. But for Teresa Stolz, a Milanese production of *Don Carlo* was her chance to make her triumphal début on the Scala stage, the crowning glory for a soprano. They could not persuade Verdi to conduct it, but *Don Carlo* was eventually put on with Teresa in the part of Elisabetta, the desperate protagonist of the opera. She was suited both dramatically and physically to this role. Even Giuseppina, who went to see her on her way through Milan, decreed that Stolz was a truly great singer.

There was friction between Verdi and Angelo Mariani for various motives: Verdi had turned down a prize and expected Mariani to do the same; the hated Corticelli – a kind of Don Basilio – had to mediate. Anzulett, who had always been so faithful, was becoming an object of scorn. If Angelo complained of sickness, it was obvious that he was pretending, maybe it was just piles. Peppina attributed Mariani's imaginary illnesses to too many women; she accused him of intrigues while being engaged to Teresa Stolz – and before that to Sauli. But there was one simple reason why Verdi was slowly becoming hostile towards Mariani: whether he knew it or not, he was in love.

That a man of his age – he was nearly fifty-five – should have been struck by so strong a passion should not surprise us; there is nothing unseemly about it, it is only too natural. It is at that age that men often succumb to their greatest passions, under the influence of Cupid's most provocative and disturbing darts. He was no longer in love with Peppina – perhaps he never had been; certainly there was no longer any physical attraction. In Teresa Stolz, Verdi saw an admirable performer and a determined woman, someone far more coquettish and attractive than Peppina. There is no doubt that Teresina was what we would today describe as sexy: she aroused thoughts of bed.

Thus, at the insistence of Clarina, but actually in order to be close to Teresa, Verdi returned to the city of his first successes and his first great griefs, after twenty years. Many things had changed: a new gallery joined Piazza del Duomo to Piazza alla Scala, many streets had disappeared, many people had died. Clarina Maffei took him to meet Manzoni, with whom he had previously exchanged photographs. Peppina had definitely passed into the background. Left alone, with her correspondence, with Corticelli, she did not even serve as an intermediary.

They were at Sant'Agata on 13 November 1868, when they heard of Rossini's death. Verdi wrote a letter to Ricordi, which was published by the *Gazzetta musicale*: Italian composers should each write a piece of a funeral Mass, an entirely Italian Requiem for Rossini. 'A great name has disappeared from the world!' he wrote. 'His was the most widespread reputation, the most popular of our age, and it was Italian glory! . . .'

Pesaro and Bologna had already planned commemorations; the first such function was held under the artistic direction of Mariani, Rossini's pupil, who had vaguely pledged to conduct the Requiem desired by Verdi. He waited for the scores. On 31 January 1869, the Verdis set out for Turin, and Fifao went to college, according to Verdi's wishes. Depriving Peppina of that little girl, now her only joy, was yet another way of getting at her. Her anguish was intense as she saw the college gates close on the girl's tear-stained face.

Then she left for Genoa while Verdi went to Sant'Agata; restless and quarrelsome, he returned to Milan immediately afterwards to try out the new version of *The Force of Destiny* with Stolz. He asked Ricordi to book him an apartment at the Grand Hotel in Milan. He had ordered Peppina not to join him. At the last moment he changed his mind. She replied to him bitterly; the sense of her letter is one of despair: she had heard from Turin, she wrote to Verdi. Although he had had many distractions, he must have had time to think of that poor child who had been left all alone and who was, she felt sure, suffering. She herself had returned to the sad, ghost-filled rooms of Palazzo Sauli, bitter at heart. She had given the question long consideration and had decided not to join him.

I will thus spare you from having to come mysteriously at some hour of the night to the station to smuggle me out like a parcel of prohibited merchandise. I have pondered over your profound silence before setting out from Genoa, and your words in Turin, your letter on Tuesday and my premonitions all advise me to decline the offer that you make me to come and attend some of the rehearsals of *The Force of Destiny*. I can sense the forced nature of this invitation and I believe it a wise decision to leave you in peace and to remain where I am. If I do not enjoy myself, at least I do not expose myself to further useless rancour and furthermore you will be completely at your ease.

She would never have imagined, after the joyful visits to Clarina and then to Manzoni, that they would have reached this point. 'Therefore accept the fact that my exacerbated heart finds the dignity to refuse and may God forgive you for the most acute and humiliating injury you have inflicted on me.' She would never have believed that one day she would be discarded by the man to whom she had devoted her whole life, she added.

She confessed to Clarina Maffei: 'My spirit is so sadly disposed, I feel so depressed at heart that at times I weep and at times I am almost afraid of myself.' Giuseppina had been hurt; for the first time she had perceived a deep hatred within Verdi. Verdi wanted to be left alone with Teresa Stolz and was irritated by any obstacle in his path. On 27 February, *The Force of Destiny* (which was not conducted by Verdi, but had been prepared by him) was greeted with ovations. It was a return in grand style; and by his side he had a young woman, which made him feel young.

Giuseppina was in Milan, but she stayed in the hotel. It had been a terrible idea to come to Milan; she was exposed to a thousand humiliations. It had been a terrible idea to furnish the apartment in Genoa as well: by now the affair with Stolz was on everybody's lips. 'Since we have the expensive and inauspicious luxury of a vast apartment, I am always having to deal with vexing little jobs!' If only she could find some eccentric Englishman who might want to buy the whole place, maybe out of a love of music, how happy she would be! That was the age when the great magnates were English, not American. She told Clarina that she spent the day by herself, thinking, reading. 'I review men and objects: and in this kind of mental phantasmagoria, you would see me, from time to time, laugh and cry, grow affected, get angry and gradually abandon myself to the endless chain of emotions aroused in me by different thoughts and memories, either sad or amusing.' She thanked her for having been sincere – and repeated the word 'sincere'. So many people in Milan had ignored her, had played up to Verdi's new darling!

In October the Verdi family were at Sant'Agata again with 'little Maria whom I will take back to her college in mid-October. The senior teachers were so pleased with this dear little girl that they awarded her the first prize in her class.' She was as studious as she herself had been at the Conservatoire in Milan. Taking leave of Maria, who was perhaps her last link with Verdi, accompanying her to college once again, 'seeing that severe door close' – all this was torture for Peppina. But she was not the only one to feel abandoned. 'I have not yet recovered from so keen a disappointment, but I am now more resigned and in the course of next week I shall return to Genoa and that for me will be the end of the most perfect theatrical season I have known, one that leaves a truly sweet impression on the spirit and, at the same time, a sense of pain.' Mariani wrote these words to Franco Faccio in October 1867. 'There is no rose without a thorn, but this time, my thorn was extremely cruel.' Peppina, on the other hand, received a cheerful letter from Teresa Stolz: 'All that you have heard about the dear good Maestro concerning me, may not be true ... I kept feeling the tears rise to my eyes with emotion, enough! Now I am happy that it is all over, and that Maestro Verdi was sufficiently pleased with me.'

10
BETRAYALS

Peppina falls in the lake. Stolz breaks faith with Mariani.
Paris invaded by the Prussians, the Commune. Verdi
attends *Lohengrin* conducted by Mariani. The Requiem a
great success. Teresa Stolz moves in and shares their lives.

———————————— • ————————————

Oh infamia orribile tu commettesti!
Un cor sensibile così uccidesti!
Di donne ignobile insultator,
da qui allontanati!
What you have done is shameful!
So to strike down a tender heart!
You have insulted a woman! Get out of here!

LA TRAVIATA, ACT II

As Verdi became increasingly prone to bouts of restlessness,
everything changed in Peppina's life and her role as a devoted
wife came to an end. Her opinions were no longer sought, she was
no longer relied upon to find subjects for his librettos, to employ
the staff, to choose decorations for the house and she ceased to
be the only person in whom Verdi had complete faith. Instead he
rejected her, making her feel that she was no longer necessary. She
was unable to speak to him or to seek the cause of the breakdown
in their relationship because she herself could not even believe it. A
man like Verdi losing his head!

It was all so different and she was often the victim of his
unpredictable rages. Now, at last, he was angry with Mariani who
was the source of all her misfortunes, introducing to the house that
impetuous youth, those mad projects and then that woman. 'Mariani
the loud-mouth and gossip-monger,' as she described him to Escudier
and, on another occasion, to Du Locle: 'We have left the beautiful
Mariani with all his victims.' Giuseppina had come to loathe him,
everything had gone wrong in their lives from the moment he had
ingratiated himself with her husband at Palazzo Sauli, that grandiose

palace in Genoa which, in any case, they had only taken on under the influence of Mariani.

By now Peppina preferred to stay at Sant'Agata, in spite of the weather, at least she felt she was the mistress of the house, of her time, of Verdi's decisions. She liked to hide in that misty retreat far from the madding crowd where she could enjoy the company of her parrot, to which she had taught a few musical bars, her animals and her trees. She had decided to comply with Verdi in everything and now that she no longer had any influence on him, she stopped trying to change him. But there had been a certain amount of worry in the Verdi household because it had been noticed that Corticelli was less than disinterested in Maddalena, Antonio Barezzi's rich young widow.

Meanwhile she had a nasty fright at Sant'Agata: Verdi used to row her in a boat on 'the puddle' as she disparagingly referred to the pond which an admirer had given them. It was excavated in the shape of his initials, a G and a V, connected by a romantic little bridge.

'Verdi was in the skiff and put out his hand to help me down,' she wrote to Clarina.

I was half in and half out, when the boat capsized on top of us with me right underneath. Verdi, thanks to God Almighty or his own presence of mind, feeling the boat lightly touching his head, by putting his arm up vigorously was able to shift our sepulchral covering. Somehow, and I don't know how, he regained his feet and, with amazing strength and speed, plus the help of Corticelli, managed to pull me from under the water where I couldn't move because I was so dangerously tangled up in my voluminous silk skirts and was also almost unconscious, so that I could do nothing for myself. I can't describe how terrifying it was or the desperate panic of my poor sister who ran off shouting for help. I had passed out, and came round in Verdi's arms, he was up to his neck in water and I thought he must have thrown himself in to rescue me.

Verdi made light of the drama; there had been absolutely no danger of them drowning because the water only came up to his neck, he wrote to Clarina. 'Whilst it would have been better if the lake affair hadn't happened, there was no risk to our lives.' All the same one wonders if the thought of leaving her to sink into the depths of that pool like a mature Ophelia crossed his mind.

On one occasion Mariani was conducting Cherubini's *Requiem* and Rossini's *Stabat Mater* at Pesaro, when he received a letter full of invective from Verdi, which would have been inexplicable were it not for the fact that Teresa was with him and not at Sant'Agata. Mariani answered: 'Signora Stolz begs me to send her very best wishes to you and your good signora Peppolina – there are never roses without thorns – and on the subject of thorns, please remember me to Mauro.'

He hoped that Verdi would join him and Teresa at Pesaro. 'You only have to write to me and I will arrange whatever you want and make sure that there are no problems. If I let you down, you can beat me.' Verdi's reply to this and other letters was hostile. 'Please don't write me such difficult letters because you humiliate me.' He continued with some comments which can only have been intended to cause friction or start a fight.

Verdi had persuaded himself that Mariani wanted to prevent the *Requiem* for Rossini being played because he was looking for an excuse to quarrel with him and to diminish him in his own eyes as well as Teresa's, so that he would be able to say that Mariani had betrayed his art and friendship. In fact if anybody were to blame for the failure to perform the Requiem, it was Ricordi and Scalaberni, the Bolognese impresario, while Verdi himself was less in favour of the project than he ever admitted. Mariani did not understand this behaviour and, in a way, he was experiencing the same kind of torment as Giuseppina, without knowing the reason why.

Furthermore, he was suffering physically. The problem with his bladder, which Giuseppina ridiculed and Verdi discounted, was in reality a tumour from which he would eventually die in agony. Anzulett or 'Fake-Head' complained, when writing to a friend that, although he had put on weight, not even his fiancée believed that he was ill: 'I will not talk of myself and of my health for fear of appearing to attract attention to myself. I live a quiet life and try to get better – but all the same, I admit that this situation is beginning to worry me . . .' Peppina wrote to a Genoese friend Teresa del Signore as follows: 'Mariani replied . . . he is always talking about his changeable health but nobody takes him seriously.' Five months earlier however she had written to Stolz in a different vein (13 December 1869): 'Mariani seems genuinely and seriously ill. Underneath all the embroidery, one realizes that the illness from which he is suffering is the old curse of haemorrhoids which, thanks to his exhaustion after *Lohengrin*, have become so painful and inflamed, that an operation may be necessary.'

Here there is a little mystery. Verdi had not received Mariani's letters which were copious and full of arguments, excuses and extravagant promises of love and affection. If Verdi claimed that he did not receive them it would have been the truth because this kind of deception was not part of his character. Why was it that these letters which are available to us today, never reached him? Peppina used to watch the post arriving after which it was probably checked by their secretary before distribution. Therefore it must have been Corticelli who did not deliver Mariani's letters to Verdi. Corticelli loathed Anzulett because the latter had always diminished him in the eyes of Verdi and Maddalena with his jokes and behaviour. He had also usurped his place at the card table and at billiards. Moreover as Mariani was hated by Peppina, Corticelli wanted to please his patroness by impeding him in every way he could. It cannot however be discounted that she was perfectly aware that the post did not reach Verdi, although one would like to think that she would not stoop to such a low level as to intercept it herself. Corticelli had increased her malice; he was a kind of domestic Iago who liked to create difficulties, to stimulate the jealousy of Peppina, to make the difference between the married partners more acute. He had gained the trust of his employer, becoming her sole support and confidant. As she became increasingly more isolated and lonely, Peppina needed him.

In January 1870, after a hard life, her mother Rosa died in the house that Peppina had bought for her in Cremona. She had been widowed when she was very young and also penniless, neither loved nor helped to any great extent by her husband's family, she had not succeeded in remarrying but had survived only through the help of her eldest daughter, who after many adventures, had had the luck to find Verdi. 'Dearest Signor Canonico. I am in Cremona! You can well imagine that I am here for a very serious reason (my mother has died). She passed to a better life almost without sickness or pain, just like a lamp which runs out of fuel . . .' Giuseppina had received a telegram with the news. 'I wanted to see her once more even though she is dead, in order to touch her forehead with great grief. I knelt before her poor corpse and prayed for the soul of one whom I will never see on this earth again.' Giuseppina went into deep mourning and tried to organise the lonely life of her sister Barberina who was always sickly, apparently hovering between life and death, but she must have been intrinsically strong, because she would outlive Peppina by many years. Barberina who was often a guest at Sant'Agata, was looked after by a good maid, Maria Alini, who lived with her for many years. Perhaps, after all, Barberina did not really live alone, but had some responsibilities such as, for instance, looking after Peppina's secret daughter and her own illegitimate son. This could be the reason why Cremona was such an important reference point in the later lives of the Strepponi family.

It was winter and therefore Giuseppina returned to Genoa rather than Sant'Agata. La Stolz and Mariani had come back together from Turin where the soprano had sung in *Don Carlo*. Mariani was now a star performer, applauded by the press while La Stolz was still someway off becoming a primadonna. Anzulett continued to conduct at the Carlo Felice Opera House where La Stolz, Verdi and Peppina would go and listen to him, all three of them together in the same box. The exchanges between Mariani and Verdi had lost their cordiality, their original warmth and joviality; Verdi assumed a despotic attitude which Anzulett masochistically accepted while Peppina was contemptuous of him because of it. She despised his weakness and wanted to see Mariani elope with Teresa, marry her and vanish from the scene altogether. 'That Teresa that should go off with Mariani if only Mariani had a mind which follows his instincts and wasn't his own worst enemy. Shake the hand of that friend of ours who could well become one day . . . no, no it's not God's will!' That she regarded this Fake-Head who had ruined her life as her enemy, is all too obvious. Later she wrote to Clara Maffei: 'Mariani hasn't married nor will he marry La Stolz, or at least that's our opinion . . .' Alarmed, she sought refuge in her friendship with Mauro Corticelli whilst Teresina calmly bided her time. In the eyes of society as well as those of Anzulett, she was officially his fiancée.

In the first letter Peppina wrote to Stolz she showed the devious side of her character in a pretence of friendship.

> . . . what I want above all is to hug you again and to be with you a bit longer than is possible, because I wish you well, my admiration for your honest and sincere character is increased by the fact that I don't find you in the least theatrical. I blush in spite of my mature age when reading the eulogies that you bestow on me with such generosity. I don't deserve them at all, except that of being a loyal and reliable friend and when I say friendship that is a very rare thing.

There is more than one way of interpreting that . . .

After witnessing Teresa's long afternoons with Verdi at the piano, Peppina commented: 'Having got to know you at close quarters, I can only think the world of you. So, if you hadn't written to me before, even if you have no reason to do so, it's a sign that you weren't able to . . . My health is improving, but slowly, slowly. Talking is still very painful . . .' Peppina suffered from a bad throat and preferred writing to speaking.

The Verdis left for Paris where they stayed at the Hôtel Bade in the Boulevard des Italiens. Verdi went to hear Adelina Patti whom he liked very much and who was performing in both *Rigoletto* and *La traviata*. Peppina had become too depressed about her own looks to enjoy such entertainments; she described herself: 'Talking about girth you will find that mine deserves some respect and, added to that, my hair is going grey, so you can easily imagine a matron who would not look out of place as an abbess.'

Emanuele Muzio also joined them in Paris. He had returned from Cairo where he had conducted *Rigoletto* for the Khedive, who was passionate about opera and who had asked him to discuss with Verdi a new piece for the theatre which was being built in Cairo. They paid very well in Egypt, Muzio emphasised. Verdi found him the post of Musical Director at the Théâtre des Italiens to which Mariani had aspired for some time. There was talk of an Egyptian story, based on ancient texts, reworked by the Khedive himself. The framework of the libretto which Verdi immediately recognised as a superb plot, had been prepared by Mariette, an archaeological writer and friend of the Khedive. It was given to Ghislanzoni to render in Italian and put into verse. In fact Giuseppe Verdi was to write almost all of it as is proved by letters and notes on the manuscript, even some in Giuseppina's own hand. We have already said how Verdi instinctively searched for texts which would give him a means to express his own emotions. The conflict between Aida, the young enslaved daughter of a king and Amneris, the monarch in whose house Aida lived, reflected the situation which he himself faced. The slave Aida who holds the heart of Radames was a metaphor for Teresa Stolz; while Peppina in the Amneris role, smoothly treats her as a friend, confusing her rival for an ally.

Verdi, in this opera, wanted to conquer not the public but Teresa. He wanted *Aida* to become a vehicle for their glory: he had decided to dedicate the score to the woman he loved. He was by now obsessed by Teresa and only in her company, only thinking about her, only composing for her, could he find respite from his otherwise uncontrollable irascibility. We can only imagine the humiliation that Giuseppina, who had been his companion of so many years, his legal wife with whom he had shared so many hard times, must have felt; he had only dedicated *Jérusalem* to her and that was in any case a reworked version of another opera, and, at that, not one of his best. But in the introductory pages, next to the title '*Aida*', screamed the words: 'To Teresa Stolz'.

Verdi was more than happy to compose *Aida*; usually when he worked on an opera he became ill. On this occasion he neither had need for money nor for success, the motivation was only Teresa and nothing else. He wanted to dazzle her, to conquer her, to launch her and to link her to him. He aimed to seduce her with *Aida*, that disdainful woman with the cold expression and green penetrating eyes. After a short stay at Sant'Agata with Teresa, the three of them returned to Genoa where they went to the theatre for a performance of an opera buffa. It was called *Une folie à Rome* and it was by Teresa's nephew Luigino Ricci with Mariani conducting. Just imagine Verdi going to the theatre to see a farce! Nobody except Teresa Stolz could have made him do it.

Maria joined them from Turin and Verdi took the young girl to see the city both on foot and in a carriage. 'Filomena (now called Maria) has been at college for three months. She works hard and behaves herself well. She has already won five medals and looks like becoming a well brought-up girl. When I come to Naples I will show you her picture. She is not beautiful but she's nice and looks intelligent. What a pity she's not really mine!' Verdi took her in a gig to a sweet shop in Piazzetta Luccoli, where she looked through the window and pointed her finger at the cakes; the handsome man and the child walked inside the shop like any normal father and daughter the world over. One day they went into a printers. 'The nice little girl was with him,' a diarist records. 'He ordered himself some visiting cards. First he wrote on a piece of paper G. Verdi and, in making the order, said: "This is for me." Then he wrote on another sheet: Madame Josephine Verdi, adding, "this is for my wife and be quick because we have to leave for Paris." The little girl asked the Maestro: "And nothing for me?" "Wait until you are a bit bigger," replied the great man.'

Peppina described her as follows:

She has an intelligent face and that's it. Today I'm waiting for her father and mother who are more or less nothing but peasants but not at all stupid! They come to hear from my mouth the details about their little marvel and, jokes apart, although maybe not a marvel, she is a little girl who is anything but ordinary. She works hard but since I don't like the usual snobbish education, we chose a school where they concentrate on proper tuition . . .

It was the Verdis' saint's day – but that year Giuseppe and Giuseppina celebrated it together with false gaiety. The atmosphere was tense, a greeting card arrived from Alessandro Manzoni which Verdi showed her and friends who had come to lunch; one of these described the episode in a letter:

Lunch finished, Verdi remembered that card but he couldn't find it any more. Eventually he can only say: 'If anybody has played a conjuring trick on me, kindly stop it!' At that very moment Signora Strepponi discovered that Manzoni's card had been left on the shelf below the mirror; she took it and, giving it to the Maestro, said: 'Please understand that there are no thieves among your guests.' Turning to everybody, the Maestro immediately replied: 'That's all very well, but I confess that I would become a thief in order to get Manzoni's autograph!'

After three months of ménage à trois, the engagement between the soprano and Anzulett was considered to be over, although not officially because it had never been formally announced. Tormented with pain, Mariani left for Bologna where he consulted a doctor in whom he had a misplaced trust. Bologna was a way of distancing himself from Palazzo Sauli. He was unaware that he had a malignant tumour in the bladder but to be disbelieved and, worse still, to be derided about his suffering, caused him even greater agony. He was mocked for having the prosaic condition of haemorrhoids by both Peppina and Corticelli who were pleased to make Verdi smile – and also La Stolz.

The ex-fiancé described in a letter to his friend Carlino del Signore how things had developed: 'It was because she intended to break our engagement off that, on 10 December 1868, we parted in Bologna promising that we would marry after she finished working the following spring.' So he had gone to Ravenna in order to obtain his marriage licence when he found out that she had been contracted to perform in Venice. Therefore Stolz, he said, was still accepting new commitments. 'She came to Genoa in the spring of last year. You know what my health was like at that time and I certainly told her but she didn't understand . . . I returned to Bologna, she went to Florence and wrote to me a few times like one writes to anybody, saying that she was having a good time there . . . I was hoping that she would not take other jobs and that after Venice we would be able to get married.'

They had met again in Florence but he found her totally changed. 'I asked her to marry me immediately so that she could come back with me to Bologna. She replied that she didn't want to talk about it . . . So I escorted her to Bologna and she went on without me to Sant'Agata.' The lady had then told him that:

> she had to follow the dictates of her heart which were ordering her to go to Milan and she repeated this harsh judgment to me with terrible cynicism. You know all the rest and also what happened in Milan involving both her and the Maestro. But those were only comedies in which each player ended with his own partner, and I was the only one left out . . . I still thought that the Maestro was a real friend and that the lady of Prague had a warm and affectionate heart.

But Teresa Stolz no longer had any need for the conductor. In fact Mariani, who was desperately ill, was probably by now a useless companion for such a vigorous and ambitious woman. At this point all that he needed was a hospital and some care and affection. Teresa had much more to gain from intimacy with Verdi which gave her position – and wealth. At the time, in fact, she was moving house in Milan to the very fashionable Via Agnello. She earned huge sums after her successes at La Scala because every opera house wanted to hear her sing. She had enough money to invest and, predictably, had decided to purchase land near Sant'Agata. At one point she had even considered a big farmhouse a few minutes from Busseto. Verdi wrote to her about this proposal – an act which was very rare because Verdi had hardly ever written to a singer. Teresa was a guest of her sister in Florence but those letters which have survived are formal and disguise a secret correspondence about which we know nothing.

Since he was failing to recover, Anzulett was reduced to lighting a candle to the Virgin Mary of Loreto who was famous for her miracles. 'I was in Loreto (don't laugh) because, not feeling any improvement in my physical suffering from my medicines, who knows whether

the Madonna can't make me better? You will laugh, but that's
how it is!'

It would be impossible to understand the illogical hatred which
Peppina nourished for Anzulett without reproducing the letter which,
it is clear from her letterbook (in which she kept copies of the letters
she sent), she herself wrote for Corticelli to sign. A web of hints, a
confusion of rage and fury, it is also vulgar which is sad because
that was something which had always been absent from Peppina's
behaviour. But, because of her hostility towards Mariani, nourished
by her jealousy for Stolz, Peppina debased herself to the same level
as Corticelli. Such an able and subtle writer wrote, forgetting that
streak of irony which had made her remarkable and instead let her
pen be guided by fury:

> Your immense vanity always forces you to pretend as though
> you want to appear like one of the most despicable sycophants
> in the Pope's court! Verdi handed me your unctuous letter with
> a dismissive smile. You only go to Loreto in order to make people
> talk about your faith and devotion to the Virgin Mary, but you
> can tell that to the husbands and womanisers and to the women
> with whom you no longer bother to be what you were a short
> time ago.

Here she is again repeating the same complaint that he had not
married Stolz. 'But how could you be such a hypocrite as to want
everybody to believe that you went to the Madonna so that she
would cure that wonderful bladder of yours, that eternal subject of
discussion with everybody? You can burn this letter so that posterity
will not find it among those that you keep in order to boost your
vanity.' How wrong Peppina was, because Mariani kept the letter;
it was eventually discovered years later and finally set the record
straight for him. Although the early biographers of Verdi continued
to diminish poor Anzulett, whom they accused of stealing money
from Stolz, it was ultimately the letters of Peppina herself which
established the truth and consequently condemned her attitude.

Verdi asked for 150,000 francs on deposit at the Rothschild Bank
in payment for *Aida* which he had by now been banking on for four
months. It was an immense amount of money but he himself would
have commissioned and paid the librettist as well as a conductor.

However, the Franco-Prussian war delayed the exchange of
contracts. Following victory against Austria, the German army

was ready to attack France in the first of the three world wars which they unleashed on Europe in less than a century. There was a heavy price in blood and tears to be paid for the Germany which Bismarck united. The mighty Austro-Hungarian Empire had been a strong bastion against German aggression. The Krupp factories manufactured artillery with which, in a few months, the Germans defeated the French army at Sedan where Napoleon III himself was taken prisoner. The following day, on the 3 September 1870, Paris rose up and the Third Republic was proclaimed.

The Prussians were at the gates of Paris by the beginning of October. The people resisted for four months during which many died in the bombardment and dogs, cats or animals from the zoo were eaten in order to survive. In 1871 the Governor of Paris surrendered to the Germans and the King of Prussia was proclaimed Kaiser. The First Reich was born. Verdi wrote to Clarina: 'This disaster for France causes both of us complete desolation in our hearts.' He recognised so clearly the menace of 'the hard, intolerant Goths, contemptuous of anything non-German, a strong and barbaric race'. And how prophetic his words were. 'And what of us? . . . I would have preferred a more generous policy and that we should have repaid our debt to the French. One hundred thousand of our men could perhaps have saved France.' In fact only Garibaldi and his army of volunteers had moved to aid France. 'We will not avoid a European war and we will be devoured. It won't happen tomorrow but it will happen. An excuse will soon be found. And what about the Adriatic which they have already designated as the German Sea?'

The new French government had retreated to Versailles where it was to sign an armistice with the Prussians, but although it had surrendered, Paris rebelled. When the Prussians advanced, the populace retreated to the centre where they set up defences. 'May God assist France and allow her to retain her ancient position amongst the nations of Europe,' wrote Peppina, '. . . it is a nation with spirit and deserves what it always has been, that is to be the heart and soul of Europe.'

Mariette, the Egyptologist, who had gone to Paris to collect the sets and costumes for *Aida*, advised Cairo that the première would have to be postponed because they would not be finished in time. Verdi was therefore forced to postpone the opening at La Scala for which he had already started to prepare. Under the contract, *Aida* was supposed to appear in Egypt first and then in Europe. France exploded in a dreadful civil war and the costumes, not to mention

Mariette himself, were in great danger. 'Victorious Prussia means officially proclaimed German rule,' wrote Verdi to De Sanctis: 'The loss of the French lowers my morale to such an extent that I am completely dumbfounded.'

The rebels organised themselves into an assembly in Paris known as the Commune which did not recognise the government of Versailles. It was the first Socialist experiment in the history of the world. On 28 May those very same French troops who had surrendered to the Prussians, entered Paris and, after desperate struggles at the barricades, handed over the capital, the Commune and the revolution to the First Reich. It was a massacre; over and above the 20,000 Parisian men and women who died on the barricades, 38,000 more were executed and 7,500 were condemned to be deported. 70,000 people who had been evacuated were forbidden to return to the capital. The repression was appalling.

While the Prussian troops marched towards Paris, the Italian government, realising that Napoleon III and his army would be unable to intervene and defend the Pope, ordered its troops to occupy Rome. 'The events which happened today in Italy have moved me and exhilarated me despite the great catastrophe which has befallen France,' wrote Tenca to Clara on 15 September 1970. 'Ah! to be able to say that today we are in Rome and that we are striking the final blow against the temporal rule of the papacy!'

Verdi and Peppina, however, were disappointed by the behaviour of the new regime. All that carnage had been caused by industrial power and technocracy which fed the newly flourishing business of war. 'I will not speak about the war. I will only say that I don't believe in progress any longer, if it is personified by machinery designed to destroy humanity . . .' she wrote.

On 2 October 1870 the Romans, who had been faithful papists until the day before, voted to be annexed by the Piedmontese state. At last Rome had become the capital of Italy.

Work continued feverishly at Sant'Agata. 'It's useless for me to talk about *Aida* and Egypt. Verdi (who must have written to you about all his plans) works and works . . . and reads the newspapers, looking in vain for news which could give hope for an end to this barbaric war,' Peppina wrote to De Sanctis. 'The Canonico is not very well and nor is my sister; but these poor wretches would give me a shock if they ever said that they felt perfectly well! Maria is here for her holidays and will go back to college at the end of the month. She is always such a dear child. Corticelli is still fat and round and the nicest man I know . . .' From these lines it would seem that life went on as calmly as usual, but, Verdi would appear accompanied publicly by La Stolz in Milan, Genoa and Parma. Bruno Barilli, the writer, tells us:

> One day a wise old man, a familiar and well-known person who held the role of solemn sage, tapped my shoulder. On that baking-hot summer's day you could hear an earthenware salesman shouting his wares to the skies: 'My son,' said our authoritative friend pointing at one of the arcades which opened out into the harsh light of the Piazza Grande, 'through that narrow gap I just saw Verdi with La Stolz on his arm. Amidst this infernal heat these two pilgrims unexpectedly appeared before my eyes.' The same repetitious and lonely cry which we are listening to now, also echoed then under these arches and Verdi appeared startled by it and dropping his companion's arm, removed a little notebook from his pocket to jot down those four notes.

This cry reappeared in the prelude to the third act of *Aida* which describes the wind in the reeds by the Nile, the hot and oppressive night amongst the papyrus . . .

Whilst he waited for events to allow the opera to take place in Cairo, Verdi asked Ricordi to negotiate with Teresa Stolz because he wanted her to play the part of the protagonist on the opening night at La Scala. Ricordi however was astonished by the request for 40,000 liras in gold for just three performances. Even Verdi commented that if all singers were so greedy, the impresarios would have to close their businesses. As soon as Ricordi received the letter, he cunningly wrote to Verdi as though he thought that he recognised Mariani's hand behind this request, 'He is ruining the career of Signora Stolz!'

In fact it was nothing to do with Mariani and La Stolz herself proposed even more extravagant terms when she was approached by Cairo, by which time she was in any case no longer with Anzulett. The latter was rehearsing *Lohengrin* at Bologna for the first occasion on which an opera by Wagner was performed in Italy. Of course this was immediately interpreted as an act of revenge although the performance had actually been booked two years earlier. Worse was to follow; *Lohengrin* belonged to the publisher Lucca against whom Verdi remained perpetually hostile. 'La Sciûra', Giovannina Lucca, who cared deeply about the performance of 'her' operas, considered Mariani to be the best conductor in Italy. Once a great friend of

Peppina, 'La Sciûra' Lucca used to say that Verdi had not shown his face in Milan for twenty years because he feared that she would hit him with her umbrella. A great musicologist, she wrote long and interesting letters to Wagner which were just as ungrammatical in German as they were in Italian.

The preparations for *Lohengrin* which were so different from his usual repertory, affected Mariani's health at a time when he was already in poor physical condition. Wagner was satisfied with the performance and so *Lohengrin* became well-known and acclaimed with the Italian public. Mariani wrote to Wagner (in October 1871): 'It is my wont to stage all the works with which I am entrusted, with the maximum care even more so when they stand above the average and are of the calibre of *Lohengrin*. You can be absolutely sure that all your instructions will be accurately followed.' The Italians talked of nothing else but Wagner, so much so that two camps became ridiculously divided. Verdi supporters would not recognise Wagnerians and vice versa. As always with this kind of rivalry, it grew out of proportion. Like many others, Arrigo Boito, a supporter of modern music, rushed to Bologna: Wagner's music was revolutionary.

On 19 November, crippled by pain and full of morphine, Mariani had gone to the station to meet a friend when he encountered Verdi who was also in Bologna to listen to this novelty. Poor Mariani with difficulty, bowing deferentially, tried clumsily to help with the baggage, but Verdi would not let him and cut short any possibility of conversation, simply ordering him not to tell anybody about his presence because he did not wish it to be known that he was in Bologna. Nevertheless, that evening Verdi was at the Teatro Comunale, hidden at the back of a box between the bulk of Corticelli and another character, Luigi Monti, Ricordi's Bologna agent. Verdi, with the score on his knees covered in notes, had his presence betrayed by Monti who leapt to his feet while the audience were applauding, shouting 'Viva Verdi'. The public took it up and, as a result, there was prolonged applause for Verdi. Monti intended to fan the flames of the musical controversy and increase the rivalry between Verdi and Wagner, but Verdi had only come to hear *Lohengrin* for genuinely professional reasons. In fact his ear did not remain deaf to Wagnerian invention despite the comments that he scribbled on the score. Humiliated by such vulgarity, Verdi refused to acknowledge the public even though the mayor of Bologna begged him to take a bow before the applauding crowd. Meanwhile poor innocent Mariani had been so intimidated by his encounter with Verdi at the station that he was nervous and produced what was by his standards a poor performance. They would never meet again and it is sad to see Verdi in such a bad light and in the company of Corticelli.

He then turned once again to *Aida* which meant to La Stolz. All the singers were being coached by Verdi himself and – in the case of La Stolz – that meant at Sant'Agata. The Cairo première, in which Teresa did not perform, was on 24 December 1871 while the La Scala opening took place on 18 Februrary 1872 which was much more important to Verdi because it signified the zenith of his career so far, particularly in financial terms. One impresario wrote that *Aida* was a gold mine.

He was not yet sixty and at the height of his powers. Gossip about La Stolz was now on everybody's lips and she was treated as *maîtresse en titre*. Giuseppina wrote to Nina Ravina, a new friend (19 January 1872): 'This time I only want to go to La Scala once and I don't expect to come back again except for *Aida*. I don't go out very much and I have made a point of avoiding new acquaintances . . . Milan is so noisy, with so much coming and going.' Milan was also much changed, having assumed the air of a capital city. 'But I only want quiet.'

Verdi, accompanied by La Stolz, left for Parma where they would perform *Aida* together. Peppina could not fail to notice the repetition of her own experience in the days of *Nabucco*. The Maestro arrived in his own city with the interpretess of his music and triumphed. Many years had passed since the great success of the young composer. That had been another world for Verdi and the famous primadonna.

Immediately the performances were over Verdi and Teresa returned to Sant'Agata into which by now the soprano had infiltrated herself. This time Peppina asked Teresa to leave her husband alone. There was a packet of letters from Stolz kept by Verdi which somehow Peppina must have discovered either in his writing desk or in his dressing-room or one of those places into which nobody is supposed to poke their noses and on which she had written: 'Sixteen letters! In such a short time! What activity!' She allowed herself to unleash venomous sarcasm on Mariani who in the meantime had also conducted *Tannhäuser*, saying that he misunderstood the complications of the plot and at the same time considered himself to be some kind of Jupiter flinging olympic obscenities at Juno.

Verdi was preparing for the third premiere of *Aida* – this time in

Naples and with La Stolz, of course. Peppina wrote to De Sanctis from her sick bed, where she had been leeched, begging him to find her an apartment: 'a nice drawing-room, two pretty bedrooms, large and well lit. Especially beautiful for Verdi because he will want to have his piano there ... Also Signora Stolz asks you to keep an eye open for a nice furnished apartment for her in a detached house. The apartment in Toledo Road, which primadonnas normally take, would not suit her, being too noisy ... She will require a chef or a cook.' She heard that they wanted to organise a reception in honour of Verdi: could they be spared! 'It would aggravate his already bad mood, unfortunately bad enough.'

Their worst expectations of Naples, described by Peppina as an earthly Paradise inhabited by thieves, were as nothing in comparison to the experiences of the choir and orchestra. All the same, at one time, Peppina had loved the place. Verdi had been attentive to her in the very different circumstances of the joyous *A Masked Ball* when Loulou was alive. Then Vincenzo Gemito, the sculptor, produced a bust which gives Peppina an exhausted and defeated appearance. Her head is bent and her face deeply lined. All the same Verdi gave her a bracelet with the inscription 'To my dear Peppina, 1872'. Perhaps he was stricken with remorse, or perhaps he recognised that she was adapting well to the new status quo of *ménage à trois* not yet fully recognised by Peppina. It was a most important gesture reassuring her at a time when she felt rejected. Later it would be the symbolic object which, shortly before her death, she decided to leave to her sister.

New characters emerged on the scene and the old ones died. 'The death of Mazzini has given me at least the comfort of seeing the entire country united in its gratitude and esteem for him,' Clarina wrote to Tenca, their relationship was also on the point of break-up.

When the Bologna season ended, Angelo Mariani returned to Genoa. He knew he was no longer wanted as a sub-tenant of the Verdis and had taken another apartment which he was too ill to move into: 'Since I returned here I have spent most of my time in bed. I get up with great difficulty solely to go by carriage to the theatre because, as you know, I'd rather die than let everyone down.' He continued to conduct at the Carlo Felice. Disgusted by the behaviour of Verdi and La Stolz, Luisa Sauli, their landlady, had asked for more rent and consequently lost all four of her tenants because Mariani would soon die and the Verdis moved to another grander but less attractive palazzo. Mariani wrote on 23 January 1873: 'The bleeding continues and they calculate that I lose as much as eight or nine ounces of blood daily.' And on the 28 May: 'My sufferings have become so intolerable that I am robbed of what little intelligence God gave me.' His doctor didn't visit him, he had no morphine and he was alone, 'like a dog'. He spent almost all his time in bed writhing in agony.

It was really too much that her ex-fiancé should continue to occupy the apartment in Palazzo Sauli, said Teresa Stolz. It was only because of 'the past and new affection' that he had for the mistress of the house that he could remain there. Thus we are able to tell that the old flame between Mariani and Teresa Sauli had been rekindled. In a short time Anzulett would breathe his last tortured gasps in her arms.

Under Peppina's influence Verdi had given orders that Mariani should be evicted using legal means; eventually he realised that the conductor, despite being much younger than him, was really dying. '. . . Here I am abandoned by everybody . . . that is to say that I must die here, alone like an animal and alone I will die. The pain that I suffer is so great that to be honest, I no longer have the strength to endure it . . . even if I am resigned to it, mine is a death that is too agonising,' he wrote on 4 June to the only friend who had not deserted the sinking ship. Nine days later he drew his last breath.

We don't know how Peppina reacted to the news of Mariani's death but it is easy to imagine how a sense of guilt might have become a spectre which would make Genoa unbearable. We don't find a single word about Mariani in her correspondence with the Canon. Instead she wrote giving him news of the various illnesses of La Stolz and, 'This time the beautiful sky of Naples has not been kind to anybody. And what about the Emperor Napoleon? What an unexpected death! Peace be on his soul which was great, despite everything . . .'

After the Neapolitan interlude Peppina no longer had any doubts about reports of Verdi and Teresa, or rather she continued to torment herself over them. She wrote to Cesarino De Sanctis asking him to speak with La Stolz who had remained in Naples in order to find out whether there was any truth in the gossip. 'I would be curious to know if it has reached the ears of S, the talk that's going around about the affair . . . which you have told me is discussed so much in Naples . . .' Poor Cesarino replied: 'I haven't got the courage to go and ask Signora Stolz.' She goes on: 'If by any chance you hear something said about this scandal and silly chit-chat and find anything out, it will be quite enough if you answer by writing on a piece of paper

"She knows that" Meanwhile Verdi, also to Cesarino, not realising how often Peppina wrote to him: 'By the time you receive this, Donna Teresa should have left Naples, but if not give her my best wishes and tell her that she will find my letter waiting for her at Ancona.'

Zeffirina the maid at Sant'Agata played with the men just like Donna Teresa, Peppina said, unburdening what she had been longing to say. Verdi had always called Teresa 'Donna'. Peppina, on the other hand, always maintained the formality of 'Madame Stolz' or 'Signora Stolz' and always addressed her using the formal third person. She received Teresa at Sant'Agata as she often came over from her sister's house in Florence to study with Verdi. Alas, Sant'Agata was a convenient halfway house. Perhaps Peppina was still not aware of the local gossip which pointed to the Cappello Hotel in Cremona as the rendezvous between the Maestro and the soprano who – as though always in the world of opera – used to arrive in disguise. La Stolz pretended to have business in Cremona, by alleging she worked in textiles, an idea which Verdi might have had because Peppina's savings were invested in woollens. On the other hand Verdi had every excuse to take himself off to the market in Cremona because of his agricultural acquisitions.

Peppina did not mix her metaphors about friendship and loyalty in her letters to La Stolz who was using the name of 'Aida' in her letters. She felt betrayed not only by Verdi, who obviously had to lie to her, but also by that woman with her well-groomed blonde hair. She had infiltrated Peppina's nest like some kind of cuckoo, she even looked like a cuckoo with her rapacious beak of a nose. 'I hope that you will never have to struggle with the sorrows of life and, in particular against disillusionment and pain in your heart . . .' wrote Peppina. These words full of significance, were almost menacing. 'Here we are at Christmas when the Christ-God appears to redeem humanity and to show by His example to her, that greatest virtue of all; not only to forgive but also to love your enemy. I wish you anything you want, certain that you would only want those things that are worthy of you . . .' But she failed to forgive her. 'I really need your affection. But understand, I mean love for me alone with all my vices and virtues.' She thanked her for her good wishes: 'If you say that you wish us long life and happiness, I believe that you mean both of us.' By now she saw guilt, sin, in every furtive glance; she was annoyed by the sight of the young, by their amorous behaviour which is often the reaction of older people who have passed the age of passion.

Verdi and Peppina quarrelled continuously, which is not evident from their letters although it appears in descriptions which have now reached us. Verdi told friends of the awful depression into which his wife had fallen and of how the vivaciousness had disappeared from her correspondence and was replaced by bitterness. The subtle happiness of her earlier correspondence had vanished. 'I love to feel secure when you hold my hand,' she wrote to Stolz using those tones that she had developed to cope with the latter's unexpected and prolonged presence, 'the touch of a sincere and loyal lady who does me so much good.' She demonstrated her need for affection to Clarina Maffei. She loved very few people and she needed them now that she had lost Verdi. She had rejected so many friends, even the most faithful including Piave and those from Busseto; except for Barberina whom she could dominate, no Strepponi ally remained in the neighbourhood.

More seriously, Peppina lost her profound faith in God thus losing the support and spiritual security which religion had given her. She believed that she had paid too much for the man who had treated her so badly and certainly she had if we consider of the cost of having surrendered her children. Notes and comments have been found in Giuseppina's notebooks: she felt she had an attachment to her religion. 'All in all we must call on a Supreme power and man has always tended to humanise Him and to give Him a comprehensible shape.'

Teresa was happy, she had become a force that impresarios had to recognise. She could make Verdi do whatever she wanted and she led him around the Milanese drawing-rooms capturing friends who, at one time, had been also Peppina's. Even the friendship with Clarina Maffei who had recently left Carlo Tenca was usurped so that only Corticelli remained faithful to Peppina. 'Naturally I find that you feel the need to hear repeated that one wishes you well,' wrote Peppina. 'Independent witnesses are necessary for our mortal nature which cannot see into our hearts.'

Invited from one end of the peninsula to the other, always travelling by train, Verdi heard the news of Manzoni's death and announced that he would compose a Requiem Mass for the man whom he considered his true spiritual guru. Manzoni, the author of a book which had moved him so much, who had been a liberal and a patriot, had been a devout believer as by now Verdi himself had also become. What Verdi had gained through his friendship with the Canon of Vidalenzo was the faith which Peppina had lost. That is the faith which we find in the Requiem, it describes an understanding and forgiving God.

Verdi did not go to the funeral of Manzoni who died on the 22 May 1873 but he accompanied Clarina and Ricordi to the cemetery a few days later. Peppina wrote from Genoa to Clara Maffei in a tearful letter:

> In a few days, I think Verdi will actually make another trip to Milan but I will stay in Genoa. He has many things to arrange for his Mass . . . It's true when one reaches a certain age, one lives on memories. We all have happy ones and sad ones and fond ones but, alas, not everyone is lucky enough to keep affections and friendships intact, or at least the illusion of having had these pleasant things which make life good . . . I tell you with deep disappointment, I don't believe in anything any more and almost nobody . . . I have endured so many and such cruel disillusions that I have become fed up with life. You will say that everyone has experienced the stony road of disillusionment, but that means that they are stronger than me, they have retained some hope and a little faith in the future . . . Also my religious fervour has disappeared and I cannot quite believe in God even looking on the marvels of Creation! Thanks to anybody who, remembering Verdi, does not forget me. I note with an invisible pencil the names of those very few people who, claiming to wish me well, I can find the faith to believe in. My friendship is worth nothing but if you don't ignore it, I have the honour to claim myself to be, your affectionate Giuseppina Verdi.

Her husband on the contrary enjoyed a second spring – and a summer as well – of joyous vigour which excluded her. He had begun to compose the Requiem; a new project gave him the excuse to spend precious hours with La Stolz who would be the ideal protagonist: he used the extraordinary 'Libera me', the finale he had composed for the Requiem for Rossini which is the key for the soprano who is *prima inter pares*, amongst the contralto, the tenor, the bass and the chorus. On 22 May 1874, the first anniversary of the death of Manzoni, Verdi himself conducted his Requiem at the Church of San Marco, in Milan, which was the only church to permit women to sing in a holy place. The success of this religious composition was unexpected and over the next few years Peppina followed the Requiem circus led by Verdi and Stolz, between stops at Sant'Agata and Genoa.

They moved to an apartment with twenty rooms at Palazzo Doria. This palace was truly regal, built for the same Andrea Doria who had brought Genoa from a French alliance into that fatal Spanish embrace. Both Charles V and Philip II had in fact been guests in the very same rooms which received the composer, his wife and, often, La Stolz as well. While Peppina became feverish and bronchial through the effort of organising the house, Stolz was on tour amassing money, as the former wrote with a certain bitterness. All the hard work fell to Giuseppina's lot whilst the younger and more beautiful Teresa basked in all the limelight. But, repeating the experience of Peppina and many others like her, Stolz was beginning to lose her voice. She had taken the waters at Recoaro before singing in Venice and Cremona where Giuseppina had sung on so many occasions previously. Teresa had visited Barberina to whom, like a true primadonna, she had given a signed photograph of herself as though she was trying to steal her rival's sister.

After Milan she had continued via Florence to Rome. She had to honour a contract with Teatro Apollo, also a scene of Peppina's past triumphs. She then performed in *La forza del destino*, but her voice cracked during '*La vergine degli angeli*' and she rushed from the theatre in tears. However with Verdi by her side she felt secure, safe and confident although she was unpopular with many. That this cloud of blonde hair, on an ignorant head, should have at that point stolen her husband increased the taunting jealousy in Peppina. She insisted on knowing everything, on persuading everybody to tell her the gossip that she already knew perfectly well, but which she wished to have confirmed perhaps in order to contradict Verdi. All the time she continued to write to Cesarino De Sanctis about 'that affair'. She was in a black mood and full of irritation, also because of a maid who was completely inept. She described her depression to Clarina: 'There is a grey veil over my spirits and I don't believe in anything any more. This lack of faith sometimes makes my life very difficult to bear and makes me long for complete solitude so that I can have what I really want, rest.'

Verdi spent the spring in his Milanese hotel far from Peppina. In Milan he felt liberated from the weight of worrying about her, her silences, her scenes. Verdi was preparing for the European tour of the Requiem and rehearsed in Teresa's apartment in Via dell'Agnello while Peppina had gone to stay with her sister in Cremona.

Peppina, by now always suspicious, began to think that Verdi wanted to take Teresa with him to Paris leaving her at Sant'Agata, which would have been a public declaration of the end of their relationship. '. . . I am so tired both physically and mentally that it even exhausts me when I try to put it into words,' she wrote to Barberina; 'it has now been decided that they will give six performances in Paris and that Verdi will at least take charge of the rehearsals.'

The Verdis left for Paris together on 10 April but La Stolz was also staying at the Hôtel de Bade. This was a most painful period for Peppina because Verdi did nothing to hide his need to be with the soprano. Giuseppina wrote to Clara Maffei on 16 June: 'By now the fourth performance of the Mass has taken place, and I wanted to escape in order to write a few words to you and at the same time to my poor sister, angels both of you . . . There is no point telling you about the Mass and its truly enormous success which both the composer and performers (in order of merit) have achieved . . .' Then she changed her theme and talked of shopping:

> They use and abuse much too much *jais* in Paris because the fashion for it should last a long time, so you were right to give it up. You should see the hats! They are like mobile gardens. I can't possibly tell you more about this wonderful Paris, because apart from the Requiem Mass, which is a highbrow occupation, and putting my rags in order, which is lowbrow, I live like a goose. My head is in a whirl, I am tired without having done anything.

She paid visits and the day ended with her being exhausted without having achieved anything. She complained to the Canon: 'It looks as if France is in a muddle . . . I won't conceal from you my fear of German tenderness and embraces.'

The ménage next moved to London for more enthusiastically received performances. Peppina, in a better humour, writes: 'The journey into the area of *oui*, of the *yes* and of the *ja* has been truly pleasant.' Verdi wrote from England to Ricordi asking him to reserve for them and also for Stolz, hotel rooms in Vienna. Peppina and Verdi needed a suite with a sitting-room, two bedrooms and dressing-rooms while Stolz required a bedroom, a sitting-room and a room for her lady's maid. Meals would always be eaten in the Verdi suite by all three of them.

The fact that Verdi himself wrote directly to Ricordi on such a mundane matter, indicates that Peppina had refused to do it and that his relationship with Stolz had become so well known that he no longer bothered to hide it. So much so that, on 22 August *La Rivista indipendente* promised to publish the 'true life story' of Signora Teresina Stolz. It was in four instalments which all of Italy followed and it recounted the adventures of 'Teresa Stolz, German in origin, about forty-eight years old, with a proud appearance and very bad manners', how she was dragged from obscurity by the late Maestro M. [Mariani] and how this 'courtesan' launched herself into the arms of Verdi who behaved like an adolescent notwithstanding his fame; she could lead him around by the nose. With obscure phraseology and in a rather vulgar style, the review kept its 'bombshell' for the third instalment. It described how 'the ripe and appetising soprano' and the Maestro felt that they should not live under the same roof. One day, when Verdi had lost his wallet, containing at least 50,000 lire and had begun to accuse everybody, his valet, thinking that he might find it elsewhere, went to La Stolz. The wallet had in fact fallen into a fold of the sofa, which the magazine described as a place for gymnastic exercises of a certain type rather than for conversation. The fourth and last instalment described Signora Strepponi in Vienna where she had hoped to spend time together with her husband, feeling irritated by the persistent presence of La Stolz. If only Verdi had kept his eyes open, he would have realised that the middle-aged Teresa Stolz had not only lost her voice but was causing him to lose his dignity. *La Rivista* promised further instalments. But in fact nothing followed the first four articles, certainly because silence had been purchased in the best traditions of this kind of Italian journalism.

The Verdis were at Sant'Agata when the articles appeared whilst Stolz herself was singing in Florence and Trieste. Giuseppina wrote to her to say that she did not believe what the magazine said and that there was no need to worry. In truth by then she was terrified that Verdi might leave her, thus she metaphorically threw herself at the feet of Stolz, assuring her of her love and alleging that the singer would always be welcome at Sant'Agata. It was not such an unlikely possibility because Verdi could easily have abandoned her or have established her in Palazzo Dordoni which Peppina had bought from him two years earlier for less than the original cost price. Now why should Verdi, who was tight-fisted, sell the palace in Busseto for less than what it had cost him thirty years before? All this notwithstanding the fact that Peppina claimed to have bought the residence in Busseto from which they had both fled, as a memorial for posterity. And in any case, if not from Verdi himself, where else would she have found the 18,000 lire purchase money? It was therefore Verdi that had bought the house, which they had both loathed, in the name of his wife, as a possible lodging for someone he did not wish to live too close to him. He was irritated by Peppina; so much so that the following comment had slipped from her pen: 'It didn't seem to me to be a convenient day to visit a lady who is neither your wife nor your daughter nor your sister.' She was hurt by her husband's obsession that made him unable to let even half a day pass without seeing La Stolz. 'These words slipped off my tongue and I immediately realised how they would displease you. But, of course, your bad mood hurts me because she is neither ill nor performing,' she wrote to Verdi. 'I would have thought that you could last twenty-four hours without seeing the aforesaid lady ... I still don't know whether you are or not ... I only know that since 1872 you have spent so much time and thought on her that no woman could fail to interpret it as partial.' She intended to be frank with him, instead she had been thanked 'with harsh, violent and hurting words! You are unable to control yourself ... If it is [a love-affair]. ... let's part once and for all! Be honest and stop humiliating me by your excessive attentions to her.'

Peppina went down with bronchitis and remained in bed until January 1876. She failed in her intention of leaving Genoa where she had no good reason to live except for the climate (but after the enlargement of the harbour and the opening of the Ansaldo ship-yard, the air was no longer what it once had been) and where she was tormented by the ghost of Mariani. 'Since fate has decreed that what made my life happy has been irreparably destroyed,' she wrote with resignation to Verdi, she would at least have peace of mind if he were to leave his assets to Fifao-Maria rather than making everything over to La Stolz.

Peppina made a heart-felt appeal to Verdi begging him to let her leave Genoa; then she said the Palazzo Doria didn't suit her, it was a tiring and lonely lodging and allowed him to keep her at arm's length whilst he settled himself in the Hotel Milan. She suggested taking an apartment in Milan where he had friends. There were certain things that they must discuss. In Milan she would be exposed to his intimacy with La Stolz and her popularity in the drawing-rooms. But she did not want to lose him completely and was ready to pay the price for remaining reasonably close to him.

Another spectre joined the long list of those who had played a role in their lives: Piave, by now paralysed, died. Peppina did not

go to his funeral, instead she went to Paris with Verdi; as usual
they stayed at the Hôtel de Bade and as usual Stolz was there.
Verdi wanted Paris to witness an exceptional performance of *Aida*
and everybody involved gave of their best including Waldmann, a
fine-looking woman who was making her farewell appearance. A
local Italian duke had fallen in love with her and she was keen to
retire with a title. The couple returned to Sant'Agata after what
was for her a long and tormenting stay in Paris, but a triumph for
him. Peppina's consolation was Filomena Maria who sat her final
examinations in Turin before announcing her engagement to Alberto
Carrara who, according to Verdi, was not a genius but a good man,
his mother had been a Demaldè from a Busseto family who were
all friends of the Verdis. Peppina went to collect the girl from her
college and rejoined Verdi and La Stolz at Tabiano. That the latter
were by now a couple had to be recognised by both the long-suffering
Peppina and Maria. Worse was to follow because Stolz had decided
to retire. By now she was rich, she felt she possessed Verdi's heart,
she was socially powerful in Milan and she probably hoped that
Peppina, who was so ill and depressed, might soon die so that she
could become the third Signora Verdi. Even Peppina confided to her
diary that she longed for death, if it would realease her from a life of
intense suffering. Verdi no longer had any need for her and she knew
it. When Peppina ordered him to chase La Stolz out of Sant'Agata
(as Illica wrote to Signora Mascagni) Verdi had threatened suicide
if Teresa even left the house. The decision was taken to spend some
time apart from each other following the months together in Paris
and Sant'Agata and after the press attacks, the gossip and the scenes
created by Giuseppina. Verdi could not in any case marry Teresa
while Peppina was alive and the legal separation would have caused
an intolerable scandal.

Teresa was about to leave for Vienna and St Petersburg for which
she would be paid a fortune; it was the most elegant means of keeping
out of the way. Giuseppina and Teresa exchanged letters.

From her Russian 'exile', Teresa wrote to '*Gentilissimo*' Signor
Giulio Ricordi (no longer to a mere secretary – 23 November 1876).
She was in Moscow where she sang 'in *Aida* which was performed
five times always with great success, then I sang in *Roberto* and for
the third opera we did *Don Carlos*. This had to fight against the
little success it had enjoyed some years ago in Petersburg but the
Muscovite public understood at once its fine music and appreciated
it a lot . . .'

Stolz embellished her letters with gossip about Adelina Patti whom Teresa loathed because she had flirted with Verdi: Patti had sung so badly; her divorce from the Marquis de Caux for a tenor who left a wife and five children, was a scandal. *Aida* and the Requiem conducted by Faccio, were making a fortune, she went on. Her letters were full of unpleasant hints about her colleagues and against those she hoped to diminish in the eyes of Verdi.

With Stolz far away peace returned to Sant'Agata. They had decided to be more discreet and certainly the parting, which lasted months, cooled Verdi's passion. He dedicated himself to the countryside while keeping an eye, from a distance, on the various performances of his works. Meanwhile the two principal protagonists of unity, Victor Emanuel II and Pope Pius IX, died. 'Dear Clarina,' wrote Verdi from Sant'Agata on 19 June 1878:

> I can't tell you whether we will go the Exhibition or not. Peppina doesn't want to know about it. It's the first time that she is not tempted by a journey to Paris. I can't tell you anything about myself; I live a solitary life here away from human company, and I don't know anything about anything. You will tell me that no one forces me to lead such a monotonous life and that I have the means to live differently. It's absolutely true, but the bad thing is that I would not be any better off even if I did differently.

On her return to Milan, Stolz received a letter from Peppina on 20 November 1875 saying that she might have had enough of receiving so many letters from her. After she had rested for a while in Milan, would she please write to them giving some news of her trip. She wanted to know whether it was true that Verdi was wanted at St Petersburg to conduct four performances of the *Mass*, that the Opera Director Gospodin Kartsoff offered 6,000 roubles for each of the performances.

Teresa had become an intimate of the Maffei household, in fact the affectionate correspondence with Clara stopped: once again Peppina felt betrayed. But Verdi wrote to Clarina pretending to know little about Teresa in Milan: 'Give me news about the esteemed Signora Teresa, I haven't heard a single word since the Mass at Bologna. I well understand that luxuriating in a capital city in a comfortable apartment, making and receiving calls, going to theatres and concerts as I read in the press, she doesn't often think about the old Maestro . . .'

Tenca had returned to Clarina's side. 'I would often meet Stolz when leaving the house in the evening because she obviulsy goes out at the same time to get some fresh air. She looks rather fat and she is happy with the cure she had at Tabiano. She will go for a few days to lake Como and then she will take herself off to complete her cure at Sant'Agata. It seems that she will spend all of September with the Verdis . . .'

Verdi had been invited to conduct his Requiem in Germany from which he had felt excluded because of Wagner's opinions about Italian music. He would be able to return to Teresa's side. He left with Peppina who had studied German at home and travelled to Cologne where the Requiem was an enormous success. Even this journey was a calvary of humiliation for Peppina who had hoped she would find peace again.

Her aunt Giovannina died at Lodi and left her a pair of diamond earrings, the only piece of jewellery she ever received from her family. Peppina had been generous with her relations and likewise with institutions as well as individuals. Like Verdi she did not publicise her generosity and also like him she gave voluntarily and without being asked. Perhaps because of this, Corticelli, who was her housekeeper, her confidant, ally against Mariani – Pinocchio's Cat to her Fox – had not told her that he was bankrupt. Corticelli had helped himself to the savings of Antonina Belfanti, the cook at Sant'Agata, who was a simple person and who was easily led by the nose. He had also cheated Maddalena Barezzi, another simpleton according to Peppina. Maurone had even taken his own initiative in replying to Ricordi without consulting anybody; Angelo Carrara and then Verdi had investigated and then decided to sack him. It had been a great disappointment for Peppina to discover that the friend of many years was not 'a straight guy' and that she had completely misjudged him. Corticelli fled to Milan because his own family in Bologna would not have him in the house. He took lodgings in the Albergo dell'Angelo and six months later, attempted suicide in Milan's canals.

On learning of this, Peppina wrote to La Stolz:

Any observation or recrimination would be out of place in the face of the catastrophe which could have resulted in the death of that disgraced wretch. Compassion is the only sentiment that I can feel in such sad circumstances and this compassion makes me ask you to go and see him on my behalf. I don't know anybody in Milan who is his friend except perhaps Mr Brosovich whom I have not met but you know well. Assuming this is correct, please call on him and beg him to see Mauro on my behalf in order to find out if there is anything I can do for him and I will do anything within my means. Please be completely open in your reply.

Stolz was always taking the waters. Instead of going to fashionable places like Salsomaggiore or Montecatini, she went to little Tabiano, frequented by the Verdis and where she received another letter from Peppina. This time, she wrote saying that she had decided against taking the cure that year because she had so much to do. Poor Peppina! she had terrible liver spots as well as bad knees, but she ended her letter in a happy key, as if by now she had accepted the situation: 'You don't need me to give you news of Verdi because he gives it to you himself!'

On 11 October 1878 Maria Verdi, Fifao, married Alberto Carrara, the son of the notary, in the chapel of Sant'Agata and everybody was in tears including the Canon. They had wanted that beautiful, well educated girl to marry locally, somebody from amongst the local people. They had not wished for her what Maria had probably wanted.

'My responsibilities are certainly not over with the marriage of little Maria who today has become Madame Carrara, having married the eldest son of an old friend who lives a short distance away. So we have the consolation of seeing that dear and good creature settled in a proper and Christian manner before we die,' she wrote to Cesarino De Sanctis who was by now almost blind and up to his neck in debt to Verdi.

Teresa Stolz had kept away from the wedding, but thought of visiting Verdi and Peppina. 'Yes, dear Peppina, I had the great desire to pay you a visit to bring in person every good wish on your saint's day but, having thought and rethought about it, I decided not to impose myself with one of those inconvenient surprises.'

Luckily she kept away but Verdi soon found a way to spend time together both officially and secretly by organising a concert at La Scala with Stolz and Waldmann who had come out of retirement to help the victims of the flooded river Po. He too re-emerged from his retreat at Sant'Agata.

Milan accorded him an unforgettable reception by which he was greatly moved; after the performance a crowd surrounded his hotel and shouted for him to appear. The orchestra of La Scala serenaded him from the street with the overture from *Nabucco* and the prelude from Act III of *La traviata*. Peppina watched from behind the curtains: the city at last adored him and honoured him as they had never honoured anybody before. There would never be any further misunderstanding between Verdi and Milan.

Verdi forgave Milan and he forgave Arrigo Boito with whom there had been disagreements in the past. It was from then onwards that *Otello* began to be discussed. Two years earlier Peppina had written Verdi a calm letter, her last. Subtly she underlined how she, the silent observer of his genius, knew how to respect him and nobody else. It was as if she was trying to ingratiate herself with him by flattery and appeals to his vanity. There was something antipathetic in this chain of praise and recrimination – that she was the first and only one to have recognised his greatness. 'Let us allow the ladder of applause to reach the sky as long as you take me with you. You will find that I will not bother you but I will only tell you in a passionate and low voice how much I love you and respect you whilst the others are silent.' He should not abandon her nor should he forget her who would be his companion for ever. 'Don't be tired my dear *Pasticcio* and remember, however little money remains, it will always be more than your heirs deserve ... I have always loved you madly and always will and at times when I am in a bad mood, it is a kind of love-fever, not understood by any doctor, including Todeschini. What nonsense I write!'

She was again in Milan at his side, small, a bit shrunken, but round despite those attacks of pain. In fact, he had temporarily returned to her. By now this was all she wanted, it was everything for Peppina.

EPILOGUE

O cielo! Muor!
Violetta?
O Dio, soccorrasi!
Èspenta!

Oh, Heavens! She is dying!
Violetta?
Oh God, she needs help!

She is dead!

LA TRAVIATA, ACT III

From now on, during the last fifteen years of her life, Giuseppina renounced any activity or interest which did not involve Verdi. She surrendered her own personality and, in so doing, showed a typically feminine trait by constructing a protective zone around her consort. At the same time she demonstrated a very human frailty by appropriating many of his achievements for herself. Therefore the last years of her life were nothing more than a period full of regrets, depression and deep introspection.

'How my feminine vanity was humoured by the master hand and my yearning as an artist and as an Italian was enormous because Verdi was persuaded to take up his pen again, but my pressure does not weigh on the scales of yes and no however much you and others might believe the contrary,' she wrote to Ricordi. In short, she no longer had any influence on Verdi.

Her health had begun to deteriorate; her lungs and breathing which had always given trouble, functioned badly and she was often unable to speak for days on end. However the possibility that this might have been psychosomatic cannot be excluded. Verdi hated to listen to her sad silences as he watched her wanderings, dressed in black like a phantom in the mist of Sant'Agata, a stark contrast with the terrible scenes of a few years earlier; the deafening screams, the invective and the recriminations. He would leave her in the stuccoed rooms of the Palazzo Doria and stare morosely out to the sea whilst she, lost in silence, could only communicate in long letters.

Sant'Agata had become morbidly sad. Somebody, out of spite, had killed the black swans which La Stolz had given Verdi; they were discovered poisoned near the pond. A few years later, whilst the eighteen-year-old maid was serving coffee, a shot was fired and the head of the girl was blown to pieces. The story was suppressed and nothing emerged from behind those secretive walls. The house closed its shutters around the mystery, one of several. 'I dream almost with longing of the other world,' she wrote to her sister (in 1880). Giuseppina became increasingly introverted, having reconciled herself to what seemed an unjust situation. But she continued to take cover behind falsehood: she had never had children; how lucky were those that did have them! 'Happy you,' she wrote to one lady, 'who have had the fulfilment of having brought up your daughter successfully. I can imagine how nice that must feel for an affectionate mother. It is an emotion that I have not experienced but which I would have enjoyed deeply. I envy you it and the thought of it warms my heart.' In fact this is not completely untrue because Giuseppina had not brought up either of her two daughters; as we have seen, one had been farmed out to a family and had died, the other was in a mental hospital.

As a biographer one tries to discover what is behind a phrase in a letter or to see through a crude deception and in these instances, one needs to refer to one's own experiences in order to understand that of one's subject. After all, life does not offer many alternatives and each of us experiences the same bitter defeats. In the good deeds and more often in the bad ones, one finds oneself in sympathy with one's subject like joint conspirators in a plot, so much so that, after months of research, study and delving in correspondence, a bond of friendship is formed.

In evaluating letters and documents, I have tried to keep my distance from Verdi, that giant personality who might have distracted me: when there is a genius around mere mortals have to make sacrifices, not only his contemporaries, but also the biographer.

This story epitomises the century, a century during which from an economic, political and cultural point of view, Europe ceased to be the centre of the world. A century of enormous change which saw Great Britain become hugely wealthy, the mistress of oceans and continents. Italy had become the caricature of a modern state: the new craving for colonies, to pretend to be as powerful as France or Great Britain, created the *Bella Figura* mentality which would cause marble façades to be erected in front of slums. Our century invented fascism, and the fascism which was embryonic to nineteenth-century Italy, while France, whose revolution began in the eighteenth century and overlapped the nineteenth, eventually succeded in creating a balanced state.

One can catch a glimpse of the France which Giuseppina and Verdi knew by examining his reaction to current events. His comments were as prophetic about France as they were about Germany. Verdi was to support the protest against the Dreyfus affair as well as subscribing to the monument for Napoleon III, 'the only Frenchman who loved Italy'. But then Verdi was a great man with clear vision.

We have seen the extent to which Giuseppina's political and historical opinions were not her own; in fact a singer had everything to lose from revolutions which would depose monarchies and redistribute wealth. But when she started living with Verdi she shared his credo, his ideals, his utopia, although in the end he was disappointed by the unification of Italy, even angered by the opportunism of the Italians. The world changed around Giuseppina who accepted her lot with suppressed bitterness. The machine-age arrived, the polluting era of heavy industry and the masses.

When Giuseppina and Verdi took themselves to Milan for the opening of the new production of *Simon Boccanegra*, the Industrial Fair was projecting Italy into modern times. The new Galleria Vittorio Emanuele, a Gothic-industrial piece of architecture containing shops, restaurants, and cafés, would become Milan's icon, with its great iron frame clad in glass. Verdi was fascinated by it; to him it represented progress and was the expression of a new Italian force in the world.

Giuseppina buried herself in her sorrows, her place at Verdi's metaphorical table was taken now by Arrigo Boito, a cultivated young man who stimulated the old Maestro. Not only had she ceased to become Verdi's intellectual stimulus but she was no longer the lady of the house, both roles having been taken over by Teresa Stolz who remained Verdi's faithful consort until he died and Teresa herself had become a fat old woman.

Giuseppina did not even wage war on Boito as she had on so many other intruders. She accepted him and the 'marriage' with La Stolz. She had miscalculated over Corticelli, Mariani and Teresa;

she had not understood with the latter that once physical passion had subsided, the real bond with Verdi was music. Teresa brought Verdi's notes to life while Giuseppina could no longer even summon up her own speaking voice.

Although her influence on Verdi was by now a thing of the past, Giulio Ricordi asked for her help on behalf of Boito who, on one occasion, had annoyed Verdi by his indiscretion. 'I do not know Boito at all well, but I think I have understood him. A nervous nature, highly excitable: when he admires somebody, he is capable of boundless enthusiam and, by contrast, sometimes also of excessive dislikes.'

She would have set up a meeting in Milan on the question of the '*African*' [*Otello*] and showing her great tact she continued:

> I want to say and I feel that one can say 'all's well that ends well'. Don't write or speak to Verdi of fears, indecisions. I should add: don't ever tell him that I have written to you on this subject. I think this is the best way to avoid suggesting in his mind that there is even a remote idea of putting pressure on him. Let us allow the current to flow straight down to the sea. It is in the open spaces that certain men are destined to meet and so to understand one another.

Giuseppina hardly ever went to Milan now and almost all the Milan she had once known was changed; the Sunday soirées at the Casa Maffei had been displaced by the Monday evenings of Teresa Stolz who had moved to Via Bigli. La Stolz received and entertained the most illustrious singers of the day in her salon decorated in the Egyptian style in memory of her triumphs in *Aida*. The epoch of the Belgiojoso, of the Maffei, of the great beauties, had disappeared.

So had Tenca, who died in 1883 after a long illness. Indeed they had all died, Arrivabene had died, Carcano too, dear Escudier had died (thereby avoiding bankruptcy), the manager of Palazzo Doria had committed suicide, Muzio was dead, Clarina had succumbed to meningitis and Verdi had rushed from Montecatini to embrace her but arrived too late. The lady-in-waiting of the Countess, who had sent the Maestro a telegram, saw him appear in the dawn-light just after Clarina had expired. Her description of the old man with his head pressed against the door frame, and his entire body convulsed with sobs, remains unforgettably tragic.

Giuseppina witnessed the slow development and production of

two great operas, *Otello* and *Falstaff*; she saw *Simon Boccanegra* and *Don Carlo* magnificently rewritten; she was present as a great love song was composed, a score which perhaps still is hidden amongst the mysterious archives of the villa at Sant'Agata. She was also a witness to the composition of the Ave Maria and Te Deum.

'Verdi works excessively in an alarming way but without physical ill effect. He has nerves of steel, his mind is clear, lucid, powerful, energetic as a young man's. He has re-arranged *Simon Boccanegra* and it will be performed at La Scala during the current season with him conducting, but only in the rehearsals of course!' (Genoa, 17 February 1881) She admired him from a distance but she was no longer a close source of information about him. She allowed Verdi to go and take the waters at Montecatini with Stolz, to see his Milanese friends, but she remained at Genoa sullenly in that enormous apartment; they had moved onto a different floor of Palazzo Doria. And even when she was allowed to join him, Giuseppina was treated by Verdi and his circle as a passive consort. On one occasion she read in the Montecatini newspaper: 'We saw Verdi accompanied by his consort Signora Strepponi and also by Teresa Stolz the one time celebrated performer.' She too had been a celebrated performer, once, a long time ago, she remarked angrily.

Having decided not to accept that secret separation at Busseto and having agreed instead to live those final years apart but still as Verdi's legitimate wife, Giuseppina put Palazzo Dordoni-Cavalli, which he had given to her, up for sale. It was bought by the Sivelli family and she kept the proceeds, although they were not strictly speaking hers. The interest from this money was destined for the poor in Busseto who would receive it on 11 November every year, the day when their rents fell due.

She continued to spin like a top, following Verdi from Sant'Agata to Genoa, to Paris, occasionally to Milan, but only when he required her presence on opening nights. She always dressed carefully, observing the new fashion. She also threw herself headlong into religion, into the faith that she had abandoned a few years earlier and she was generous with the poor. In a letter to Maria, who had become pregnant for the second time before even reaching her twentieth birthday, Peppina recommended that she should be resigned to her fate of modest consort. She had brought her adopted daughter up as a proper lady, as opposed to a *traviata* which she herself had become through force of circumstance, so often the fate of penniless young women. She had been reproached for this throughout her life and had wanted to forget it by inventing for herself a world of intolerant respectability. 'Let life go by as it does for everybody, it is the fate of every living person, you cannot avoid it. What is important is always to be able to plunge, to know (as you are able to do now) in your feminine heart as if you were in holy, pure sanctuary. It has been my constant wish, my burning desire from the moment I consented to take in hand your education.' Then she made some indiscreet remarks: perhaps Maria, a handsome woman, had been in doubt about the choice of her husband. 'It would not have been difficult perhaps to find you a richer husband, to give you a more glamorous position. But it would have been impossible to have found instead a more honest and affectionate man nor to place you in a kinder family or one of greater integrity.'

She described herself to a friend showing how she could be the victim of moodiness: 'I am sometimes a jester and deep down I am always full of melancholy and mistrust.' She continued writing that her nature was 'at times, I would say, almost an excess of energy, of high spirits which are followed by periods of depression, of demoralisation, of a need for solitude and silence.' Peppina was ill. In a letter to Ricordi, 1 December 1881 (recommending the umpteenth young soprano), Stolz also wrote: 'Our mutual friends the Verdis will arrive neither today nor tomorrow because of the bad indisposition of Signora Peppina. We hope they will be able to come on Saturday or Sunday (this is at least what the Maestro writes).' Thus we know for certain the existence of a private correspondence between Verdi and Stolz.

Giuseppina was obviously enduring a bout of manic depression. 'Now and again one seeks the cause of these apparent peculiarities, one prays to God to grant strength to an oppressed mind or one begins a dialogue between the two "I"s which are within each human being.' Here Giuseppina is in advance of Freud; as was the custom then, she would have asked for help from a priest 'the light in the darkness of the spirit: the veil is torn, one takes a deep long breath: the crisis is over.'

In the second week of February 1883, Wagner died in Venice: 'How sad! sad! sad!' wrote Verdi. In March of that year, Giuseppina reflected on how death levelled everyone. 'Alas! Whether great or small, there are few enough handfuls of earth needed to bury them forever and to give them that peace which I believe he never enjoyed not even when he was honoured by kings, by the nation and overwhelmed with wealth.' She was certainly speaking of Verdi.

At the same time, a request arrived from the New York Metropolitan Opera: could Verdi write a new opera for that season? He refused without consulting Giuseppina. Who knows how much Verdi, who was so attracted by what was new, so full of admiration for the great achievements of engineering industry, would have loved that city.

Giuseppina unwound with Canon Avanzi; while her voice no longer resounded through the house, in her letters she screamed. April 1884: 'Really, with the retired life that I now have, my letters would be some small comfort in my solitude.' She observed political events from a distance. 'The changes of ministers, the integrity of a few, the bad faith of many who sing in all tones of the patriotism which they don't have ... In almost everyone, a hypocrisy, a dishonesty, a corruption which grows and threatens to draw like an immense river.'

She felt for the poor, for what was happening in the new nation. These were years of misery for the peasants of the Italian South who resorted to emigration, some to France but in even greater numbers, to the United States and Latin America. For many years New York had the largest Italian population of any city in the world. The Sicilians brought the Mafia with them, whose existence was never acknowledged in their homeland until almost the present day. As a result, emigration favoured the State through the huge sums of money which the emigrants returned to their families, which every year was equal to half the Italian foreign debt.

Giuseppina who was by now old regretted the happy times of her youth, the salons, the toasts in her honour, the theatre, the love affairs. 'I live alone always turning my thoughts back to childhood, which I wish could have lasted forever, not only because of my inward feelings, but also for my outlook which I know all too well. It is not even possible for God to eradicate the past. May He make the future better. I am sad hearted and my mind is full of dismal thoughts.'

At the beginning of 1886 she was ill, perhaps more mentally than physically. Verdi was worried: 'Peppina continues to improve but slowly,' he wrote to a friend. 'The coughing is less and her appetite, which had disappeared, is restored. She got up again at lunchtime, today. 1885 was an awful year and this one has started just as badly. Thank Todeschini for his kindnesses and many good wishes to him also from Peppina.' (Genoa 9 January 1886.) A month later Peppina herself wrote to Canon Avanzi saying that she had nothing to impart: 'I have always been indoors and I haven't even been able to receive those few people who occasionally come to visit us. La Stolz has been here for the last few days full of joyful health.' To the same friend, 4 February 1886: 'She left today for Milan where she certainly won't dedicate herself to reflections on the misery of mankind or on the world to come. She achieves happiness in this way, may God keep her there for a hundred years!' How Giuseppina loathed that balloon of an ex-soprano!

Verdi was well, he was in excellent spirits working on *Otello* which after so many doubts and delays, was pouring from his piano. But while Verdi was bursting with creativity, Giuseppina suffered and coughed in solitude. A month later she wrote to a friend asking his help in packing up her belongings; when the shipment was finished it only remained for her to 'roll up my enormous knees with all my heavy and useless self! How exhaustion and melancholy invade the body at my age!' (9 February 1886.)

Verdi rushed hither and thither, 'he is well, he runs and he is strong and may God keep him thus for a long time!' (24 December 1886.) 'Verdi is well,' she wrote to La Stolz, 'and it is with pleasure full of tenderness that I say so.'

By now Verdi and Teresa were setting up their own apartment in Milan but Giuseppina rose above it all, at least maintaining her dignity and pretending to give instructions for a house which would not be hers. 'Since you have been kind enough to take charge of it, that is how we would like the apartment in Milan to be arranged.'

From time to time, however, she found moments of tenderness and pity in Verdi. He wrote to her from Sant'Agata where he had arrived unexpectedly, causing confusion among the servants who shouted to each other: 'Il Padrone! Il Padrone!' (like the last act of the *Marriage of Figaro*).

He sent her a kiss, reminding her that he, the writer, was a man who was surprised at finding himself so old; he was seventy-one and he could hardly believe it! Giuseppina commented on all this to her sister who suffered mainly from hypochondria:

I have not written to you for some time since I am always either in bed or on the sofa because of a catarrh which I can't get rid of. I often think of you and the good news from you has greatly cheered me. May Almighty God give us both better health. I cannot summon the energy to swallow down even the occasional bite of food and so my strength diminishes. One must resign oneself to God's will. Have you received the 100 lire which should cover your future expenses? Today is All Saints but for me every day seems a struggle. Take good care that you make the most of every single day and forgive me if through lack of strength I only rarely write. Best wishes to Maria. A hug and a kiss from the bottom of my heart, your affectionate sister.

Maria was the housekeeper-companion whom Giuseppina had found for her sister.

In April she had her stomach cysts removed by a young surgeon from Reggio Emilia called Azio Caselli. Peppina recovered well and her gastritis and stomach upsets disappeared although she continued to be tormented by bronchitis.

Verdi was working in Genoa. 'Boito has been here for a few days and I have been a bit worried from time to time because the authors let out sounds of anger and savage shouts from the music room,' she wrote in the autumn of 1886 to De Amicis adding a final flash of good humour, 'but don't worry, it is only Othello's contempt clashing with Desdemona's protest and the unjust suggestions of Iago.'

Throughout 1886 she was always hoping that, 'my constant catarrh will leave me when the violets blossom again'. The violet was the opposite to the *traviata*'s camellias, the flower of Marguerite Gautier and of Violetta Valéry; the timid violet had been the name which Giuseppina had suggested to Verdi and Piave in order to describe the inner purity of a *traviata*. It remained a symbol which would be with her until her dying day. It represented a characteristic of nineteenth-century sentiment, of the romanticism of the time translated in the language of flowers.

Giulio Ricordi tells us that when he went to Sant'Agata to be briefed by Verdi about *Otello* which the latter had just completed,

Signora Verdi, who was never present at these very rare auditions, left us and went to her own room. I stayed alone by the piano, in front of which the Maestro was seated with his hands shaking nervously, turning the pages of the manuscript and mouthing Boito's libretto through silent lips. In one passage, giving in to an irresistible impulse, Verdi attacked the opening bars of the fourth act and that wonderful masterpiece flowed out with sublime and inspired notes. Now we hear that sweet prayer of Desdemona! . . . A slight creak makes me raise my eyes and I notice that the door between the two rooms is partly ajar. Through the crack I see the soft features of the Signora, pale and beautiful, expressing a feeling of almost ethereal ecstasy!

When Giulio Ricordi left, moved to silence, he entered Giuseppina's room: 'She was seated as usual in her little armchair and was maintaining or trying to maintain an expression of complete calm, but suddenly she looked up at me,' and exclaimed in Lombard dialect which she and Ricordi both spoke, '"Eh! isn't he great my Verdi?"'

Milan was in chaos on 5 February before the opening night of *Otello*. The Mayor had ordered all the streets around La Scala to be closed to traffic all day. As a result, from first light the crowds thronged Via Manzoni. Giuseppina and Boito remained hidden in a box until Verdi called his librettist up to the stage to share the enthusiastic applause. When they left the theatre, the crowd mobbed Verdi's carriage, unhitching the horses, and dragged the composer all the way to the Grand Hotel Milano. The La Scala orchestra played until five a.m. below the balcony of the room where Verdi and Peppina were staying, flowers were not spared and Boito said that the enthusiasm was insane. Peppina admitted being touched by the demonstration and the affection shown for Verdi. Milan had witnessed his first success and now it was seeing his latest. But she was annoyed to read in a newspaper: 'We observed an old woman in a box in the third row, absorbed by the spectacle: the wife of the Maestro! . . .' She commented: 'They might have been kinder in describing me!' She wrote a description of the events to the Canon: '*Otello* had a splendid opening after so much effort, attention and forethought, it had a terrific reception and even an exaggeratedly bombastic ending to the whole evening.' She was almost nauseated by the excessive demonstrations of enthusiasm by the people of Busseto who suddenly seemed to have forgotten the past. The bitterness of both Verdis towards Busseto was not yet extinguished.

After *Otello*, Verdi had become not only a national institution but also a hero of literature; the libretto was by Boito, based on Shakespeare. But Verdi felt that his music was out-of-date, and that he was overshadowed by the advance of younger men, of whom there was no shortage. He recognised new promise for Italian music in Puccini, even if his lyric tone was too symphonic. He also admired Ponchielli who unfortunately died young but who had maintained 'the Italianness' of national music which others were 'Germanising'.

Falstaff was born in an atmosphere of silence and mystery with the nickname of *Pancione* (Big Belly). Verdi was cajoled by Boito and Ricordi into writing it but Peppina had no influence on its evolution. If Verdi described *Falstaff* as an opera buffa, it certainly was not. *Falstaff* reflected the deep sadness of the Old Maestro who felt decrepit and mocked by the universal and cruel 'disease' of old age which strikes everybody.

She welcomed the new year in a letter to Barberina: '1888 arrives with an exceptional cold spell everywhere as well as threats of war and all kinds of disturbances. We are therefore steeling ourselves to meet whatever ills mankind and the elements might wish to give us!' In her reply Barberina complained of the wind, the ice and her own illnesses as well as those of her sister. She had received her allowance from Giuseppina and thanked her for it. But, after sending money to Angelo Uttini from Sorbello, Giuseppina unburdened herself on the Canon: 'These relations who crop up ever more numerously like funguses after a storm, all want to commute a once and for all gift into an annual subsidy in perpetuity.' Then she was back in Genoa, which she could just bear if Verdi was with her; people, famous people, would come and visit them at Palazzo Doria. She wrote to Marietta Carrara, '. . . I must stop because, just now, Carducci is coming in with another poetess and I rush to catch a glimpse of him being most curious also to see the young poetess!' Carducci was the most celebrated poet of their times. 'Now they have left, Carducci is small, ugly, he is simple, almost timid . . . !' Verdi had gone to open the door himself and had escorted both Carducci and his mistress onto the terrace where he showed them the plants he cultivated and the panorama of the port. Carducci asked Verdi if it was true that he was composing *Falstaff*, he replied that it was so but that he was only doing it for himself. Peppina added that by now Verdi was only composing for his own amusement and that he occupied himself mainly with his flowers. Peppina commented sarcastically that the short Tuscan poet had granted the passport to Parnassus to his twenty-two-year-old mistress.

Rehearsals of *Falstaff* took place in Milan in January 1893. Peppina wrote to her sister:

> The busy bodies, the fans, the friends and enemies, the genuine musicians and those who pretended to be genuine musicians, the critics and the malicious gossips, all emerged in swarms from far and wide. The demand for seats was as though the theatre was as big as a parade ground . . . I attended a rehearsal yesterday evening for the first time and, if my opinion is anything to go by,

it seems to me like the advent of a new genre or more the birth of a new art, music and poetry. We will see what the general consensus and the respectable public will say.

The irony is not lost but this opinion from a seventy-seven year old lady is very clear-minded. It also reveals that poor Peppina was hearing the Opéra for the first time. In fact *Falstaff* came off and with what success, at La Scala on 9 February, signalling Giuseppina's farewell to Milan. It was *the* great musical event of the season and Puccini, Boito, Mascagni, Giacosa and Boldini were all present in the theatre.

Giuseppina's last visit to Paris was in 1894, for performances of *Falstaff* at the opéra Comique and also of *Otello*, plus the usual ballet which was de rigueur for a French audience. *Falstaff* received a clamorous ovation and the audience rose to its feet in homage to 'the old Maestro' as by now he called himself. Giuseppina wrote to her sister: 'Again this battle has been fought and won in triumph! *Falstaff*, performed yesterday evening, before a seduced and subdued audience drawn from the most exalted members of the arts, the sciences and the aristocracy. The enthusiasm was completely unreserved.' Verdi was weighed down with medals and honours by that France which had alway recognised his greatness and had always respected him. The Verdis were received in the Elysée Palace by the President himself, France having once again become a Republic.

In the last year of her life, Giuseppina received a request. She found herself in Genoa where she was invited to write something in celebration of the birth of Donizetti. But she, who could express herself so well and who wrote so many letters every morning, only sent a few dispassionate lines in memory of the Maestro, saying that in the course of her

very short theatrical career, I have almost always sung the operas of the great author of *Lucia* and *Lucrezia Borgia*. Later Maestro Donizetti wrote *Adelia* for me, to be performed at the Apollo, in Rome. It was then that I got to know him personally and I was able to understand more of his personality than just his genius, to admire his mind which allied together with his goodness and his tremendous culture, form a complete artist, a truly great gentleman. (16 April 1897)

Who knows if we can trust this assertion, had she in truth met

Donizetti before 1840? Were those words not once again part of a
fabric of misleading evidence, of mysteries designed to confuse her
contemporaries, herself and those who lived later? By now she was
very sick, feeling ill every day.

They were about to leave Sant'Agata to return to Genoa. On the
evening of 11 November, Giuseppina felt ill with a severe pain in her
side. The doctor was called and acute pneumonia diagnosed. The
fever disappeared on the evening of the following day and her pain
ceased so that she began to feel relatively well and to speak again.
But by the morning of the 14th things had deteriorated and she
knew that the end was near. She exchanged a few whispered words
with Verdi who gave her the last violets of the season which he had
picked from the garden. 'Smell them,' he said to her. 'Thank you,
but I cannot smell anything because I have a slight cold.' She died
at 4.30 p.m.

In addition to a telegram from the King, others arrived from
Mascagni, Puccini and Sardou, in tribute to a woman of many
qualities, of humour and determination.

She left precise instructions for her funeral: 'No flowers, no
speeches, no representatives. I came into this world poor and
without pomp and I want to go to my grave also without pomp.'
After making her last wishes in which she left her entire estate to
Verdi, she wrote: 'And now goodbye my Verdi, as we have been
together in life, so may God Almighty reunite our souls.' She wanted
to be buried with a precious envelope which she had sealed at the end
of 1846. What did this sealed envelope contain that was so dear to her,
so precious, and so secret? The house was turned upside down but the
envelope was never found. Both La Stolz and Giuditta Ricordi stuck
their noses into her papers and even the staff had their turn. All to no
avail, nothing more could be done, the envelope proved impossible
to find.

Although Verdi had not invited anybody to the funeral, from three
o'clock on that cold, misty, sombre morning, the country roads in the
neighbourhood were filled with muffled figures. A little after six a.m.
the funeral cortège arrived at Sant'Agata where the body, dressed in
black, had been laid out on her green bed with a rosary in its hands
and beside it the reliquary of her father's and, on the sidetable, the
bust of Giuseppina. Along the little bridge over the Ongina, outside
the gate of the villa and on the country roads still shrouded in the
semi-darkness, people waited with candles and torches illuminating
the vapour of their breath as they murmured comments to one

another. The crowds were asked not to approach too near the house. The Maestro's image was visible through the windows of his room next to Peppina's where the body lay, a powerful, spectral presence, a character out of Ibsen.

An awning had been erected in front of the church of Busseto and above the portal: 'For Giuseppina Strepponi-Verdi, departed to a better life, 14 November 1897, aged 82 years. Obsequies.'

The offices of death were recited without musical accompaniment, followed by mass, the absolution and the blessing of the coffin. The funeral carriage with no wreaths, at the express wish of the departed, was escorted by the mayors of Busseto and Villanova and, by a long and tortuous route, reached the railway station. 'We arrived in Fiorenzuola at about midday,' recounted the lawyer Martinelli, a family friend:

> They put the coffin on a wagon, the wreaths were placed in an adjoining compartment. The Fiorenzuola band was there but was asked not to play. A huge crowd was at the gates of the station. We had seats in a saloon car which had been prepared for Maestro Verdi; with us were Commendatore Ricordi who had left his wife behind in order to be with Verdi, also the mayors of Villanova and Busseto, Dott. Lino and Alberto Carrara.

Boito, the Erba family, Maestros Giordano and Toscanini, were all waiting at Milan Central Station. This is the first-hand account of Amilcare Martinelli:

> Commendatore Ricordi full of kindness and grief advised us that he had arranged for the obsequies to be kept completely private. But we had hardly put our heads out of the train when we saw the huge square and the station packed with people, a sea of heads. The extremely polite mayor immediately presented himself, followed by Arrigo Boito and an array of other ladies and gentlemen ... The crowds swelled continuously all along the way, down Via Moscova and before four o'clock, we arrived at the grandiose Cimitero Monumentale.

Lino Carrara, that young man who was the image of Verdi, entrusted the body to the mayor of Milan: 'Mr Mayor,' he said between sobs, 'in the name of the communes of Villanova d'Arda and Busseto, I entrust to you as representative of this illustrious city, the remains of Giuseppina Strepponi Verdi. And I am sure that, just as the poor lady loved Milan with great affection, so the Milanese will hold sacred the veneration of her memory. And now may you, beloved Giuseppina, rest in peace.' Giuseppe Verdi had the following entry placed in the newspapers: 'Deeply grieving, Maestro Verdi is unable to reply individually to the innumerable, compassionate condolences sent to him upon the loss of his dear companion Giuseppina; deeply moved and in gratitude to all.'

They had spent fifty-three years together. All her life Giuseppina suffered from bouts of manic depression which struck her indiscriminately whether she was destitute or living in complete security. The stress of her early years, the traumas and privations she endured, had weakened her and made her cynical. She had succeeded in suppressing her maternal instincts so that she had not experienced filial warmth and perhaps she regretted it. She camouflaged her life beneath a mantle of false assertions and hypocritical respectability which ill-suited the fresh girl from Lodi, daughter of a bohemian composer. But the role of consort to a ruling prince had been imposed on her. Giuseppina had guided Verdi down many paths, not all of them successful . . . the initial failure of *La traviata* was a shared defeat. It was she who had been booed in Venice, but it was because of these boos that Giuseppina received the constant, obstinate and determined support of her Verdi; once she had been recognised and had become acceptable, Verdi had stopped fighting for her, he was no longer interested in her. Perhaps Giuseppina's excessive devotion and admiration for him had suffocated his love. Nevertheless at times theirs had been a good union: she was his secretary, ambassadress, teacher, draft-reader and business manager and above all his inspiration. For her he was a rock, her only anchor. She always gave way to him. She encouraged his dislikes, his obstinacy. That was how it was until Verdi decided to take everything away from her, all of her roles. It was a mortal blow; not so much because of La Stolz herself, but more because Giuseppina's resources were exhausted. She could no longer rise to the heights demanded by an ageing genius in his final years. Verdi had always had companions who eased his way through life – Muzio, Piave, Mariani, Boito – the last two in particular had been effective intellectual substitutes for the by-then superfluous Giuseppina. So far as the others were concerned, it had really been Peppina who, for the same reason, had supplanted

Muzio. But, with or without Verdi, hers had been a full life, a life which had spanned the century and which had evolved during the time of Europe's greatness.

Giuseppina did not forget the poor in her will and one reads the following inscription in the little church of Sant'Agata:

1897
Giuseppina Strepponi
wife of Maestro Verdi
to the poor of Sant'Agata
who were supported and comforted
by her in life, left on her death
an annual allowance
in perpetuity of considerable size
in favour of fifty families.
The beneficiaries have in recognition made
this small offering of stone
in memory of her kindness
praying for Christ's mercy and the blessing
of mankind on the good lady.

+

Blessed is he who dying
has in his honour the tears and prayers of the poor.

In her will she left Teresa Stolz a bracelet studded with diamonds and bearing the inscription 'Souvenir'. It was the symbolic hand-over of her own role, a bitter declaration of surrender. She bequeathed to Verdi that other cherished bracelet which he had given her in Naples, the last act of affection and recognition he had shown her. She asked that on his death, the bracelet which bore the inscription 'To my dear Peppina 1872' should go to her sister if she were still living, otherwise to Maria Fifao.

Teresina Stolz remained at Sant'Agata, at last mistress of the house. Soon afterwards the letters which Verdi could now write to her began to appear, full of intimate affection, calling her 'Dearest'. 'Happy times, but too brief. Oh, well, when will they return? Oh, the life of an old man is certainly unhappy!' He remained deeply in love with Teresa, that little woman — by now matronly — who kept him happy for the rest of his days. 'I am in a good mood and I give you not one but two kisses.' But some of these writings went back to

1880: 'Content, happy, most happy! I wrote on Monday and spoke of many things. Goodbye, goodbye and always goodbye.'

Without the envelope and without the jewels, nothing of Verdi's remained with the body of Giuseppina except that violet picked in the bleak garden of Sant'Agata by a hand which clearly understood that it had torn out that symbolic flower, that *violetta* which had united them for all those years.

ACKNOWLEDGMENTS
AND BIBLIOGRAPHY

———————— • ————————

I would like to thank those who have helped me in the course of this work
– in alphabetical order:

A. F. Angelucci Luisa Bormioli Bertogalli, Maestro Brussard of G.
Ricordi Archives, Julian Budden, David Cairns, Marisa Casati of the
National Institute of Verdi Studies, Maestro Marcello Conati of the
Parma Conservatoire and Institute of Verdian Studies, Adriana Corbella
of the Theatre Museum of La Scala and assistant of Maestro Tintori,
Maestro Claudio Desderi, Prof. Marcello De Angelis, Professore Gabriele
Dotto of G. Ricordi Archives, Dott. Adriano Dugulin, keeper of the civic
museums in Trieste, Martine Kahane of the Bibliothèque de l'Opéra, Prof.
Guglielma Manfredi, Prof. Corrado Mingardi of the Biblioteca della
Cassa di Risparmio of Parma and the Monte di Credito su Pegno of
Busseto, Mimma Guastoni of G. Ricordi & Co., Hugh Myddelton, Prof.
Pierluigi Petrobelli, director of the National Institute of Verdi Studies,
Dott. Giuseppe Pintorno, Andrew Porter, Prof. Harold Powers of the
Faculty of Music at the University of Princeton, Cav. Lav. Dott. Guido
Rignano, President of G. Ricordi & Co., Maestro Egidio Saracino, Dott
C. Schmidt, Sandro Sequi, Maestro Giampiero Tintori, director of the
Biblioteca Teatrale Livia Simoni at Museo Teatrale alla Scala and keeper
of the Scala Archives and Madame Wilds of the Bibliothèque Nationale
de France.

FOR USE OF THE COPYRIGHTS:
I would like to thank the Studio Fotografico Dalmazio, Obiettivo Due di
Busseto and Foto Saporetti for permission to reproduce photographs. I
also thank Prof. Mingardi for the photograph of Verdi's daughter which
appears here for the first time; and the Biblioteca della Cassa di Risparmio
of Parma and the Credito su Pegno of Busseto for the same; the Museo
Teatrale alla Scala, the Museum of the Risorgimento in Milan and the
Bibliothèque du Musée de l'Opéra for permission to use their material and
Maestro Claudio Desderi who found marvellous images from his father's
library; Maestro Desderi's father was the Director of Turin Conservatoire.
For the photographs of the portraits at the Museo Teatrale alla Scala, I
thank Adriana Corbella in particular, the Museum and the photographer
Saporetti.

My thanks for the letters I reproduce in part or in their entirety are due to the Bibliothèque Nationale de Paris, the Cassa di Risparmio of Parma and the Credito su Pegno of Busseto. Also, I thank G. Ricordi & Co for permission to reproduce previously unpublished letters of Giuseppina Strepponi Verdi, Barberina Strepponi and Teresa Stolz.

I would like to emphasise the helpful attitude of institutions like that of the Biblioteca Teatrale, Livia Sironi at the Museo Teatrale alla Scala, the Archivio Comunale of Brescia, the Milan State Archive, the Monte di Credito su Pegno of Busseto, its director who trusted me with original letters and papers, who read and annotated my manuscript and to whom I am sincerely grateful; the Civico Museo Teatrale of Trieste, the Bibliothèque Nationale de France, the Bibliothèque de l'Opéra in Paris, the British Museum Library, the London Library, the National Institute of Verdi Studies in Parma which is in need of financial support, the Ricordi Archives, the library at I Tatti which belongs to Harvard University and its director Prof. Walter Kaiser; at the same time denouncing the attitude of some Italian State archives which often behave as if they were the personal plaything of some lazy clerk.

I apologise to all those institutions and individuals whom I have been unable to contact, even after many attempts.

For my general comprehension of the subject I used the *Bibliografia Generale delle Antiche Province Parmensi* edited by Felice da Mareto (soggetti II, Parma 1974) which was provided for me by Prof. G. Manfredi of the Parma Accademia Belle Arti.

I would like to thank Gregory Dowling for his help in translating part of the manuscript that was originally written in Italian. I also thank Hugh Myddelton, who translated part of the tenth chapter and the Epilogue and revised other chapters. Allegra Mostyn-Owen also gave me a hand in revising some passages.

I thank my general editor, John Curtis, for the dedication with which he nursed this project and followed it through all its hiccups.

INTRODUCTION

In this chapter of intent and presentation, I have summarised information which I obtained from various sources, books, letters and manuscripts: for theatrical customs, John Rosselli in *L'impresario d'opera* (Turin, 1985) and *Sull' ali dorate* (Bologna, 1992) besides his manuscript source 'Agenti teatrali nel mondo dell'opera lirica italiana nell'Ottocento' (Firenze, 1982) and *Il cantante dell'opera – storia di una professione* (Bologna, 1993) besides *La sagra del bel canto* by Giovanni Baroni (Lodi, 1930).

For the history of La Scala, *La Scala racconta* by Giuseppe Barigazzi (Milan, 1990) and *Le carte dell'impresario* by Marcello De Angelis (Florence,

1982) besides *Guida al Museo Teatrale alla Scala* (Milano 1989) from which I drew on the visual side.

For political history *Storia dell'Italia moderna* by Giorgio Candeloro Vol. III and IV (Milan, 1964) and *Mémoires de Marie de Flavigny d'Agoult* [Daniel Stern], (Paris, 1900). The important statistics about operas staged in 1842 come from an essay by Augusto Pierantoni (Rome, 1889). In the quotation from Stendhal, Via dei Mercanti corresponds to today's Via Orefici and Corsia dei Servi is Corso Vittorio Emanuele.

CHAPTER 1: LODI'S WERTHER

Little is known about Feliciano Strepponi and his music seems to have disappeared but I found some scores of his at the Bibliothèque Nationale in Paris. The libretto *L'Ullà di Bassora*, melodramma comico in two acts by Felice Romani is kept at the Biblioteca della Cassa di Risparmio of Parma, in Busseto.

Mercede Mondula *La moglie di Verdi* (Milan, 1938) and Elena Cossulani in *Giuseppina Strepponi* (Lodi, 1984) give scant information on Feliciano and Rosa Cornalba; some extracts of the reviews taken from contemporary newspapers in this and the following chapters, come from these two volumes. Others from the original sources. Concerning the impresario Bartolomeo Merelli *Memorie di un ottuagenario dilettante di musica* (Bergamo, 1908), is an autobiographical tale written in the third person by an old and by then poor impresario.

On Milan: *A Popular Description of Italy* by Josiah Conder (London, 1832) and *Sketches* Vol.IV (London, 1830) by Lady Morgan; also from *Sull'ali dorate* (op. cit.). On Giuseppina Strepponi: Massimo Mila *La giovinezza di Verdi* (Turin, 1974) is an excellent and intelligent book used throughout the first chapters of this book. Also Frank Walker's splendid work *The Man Verdi* (London, 1962) and Carlo Gatti *Verdi* (Milan, 1950).

On Italian history: Massimo d'Azeglio *Ricordi* (Milan, 1905), Harry Heander *The Age of the Risorgimento* (London, 1983), Francis Haskell *The Italian World, The Age of Romanticism* (edited by John Julius Norwich, London, 1983), Giovanni Baroni *La sagra del bel canto* (Lodi, 1930) and Charles Santley *Student and Singer* (London, 1892) are other texts which I have used for this context.

CHAPTER 2: AGENTS, LOVERS AND IMPRESARIOS

I have consulted the previously mentioned *Giovinezza di Verdi*, *Le carte dell'impresario* and *Verdi* by Mary Jane Phillips-Matz (Oxford 1993): the chronology in this latter work is admirable.

For the correspondence: F. Abbiati *Giuseppe Verdi* four vol. (Milan, 1959) and letters from the Archive of the Museo Teatrale alla Scala. For history in this chapter: Vol. XXVIII of *Storia d'Italia* di Indro Montanelli (Milan, 1971).

It is important to see faces and places: *Verdi nelle immagini* by Carlo Gatti (Milan, 1941) and, also by Gatti *La passione verdiana di Trieste* a publication issued ten years later by the same Comune, besides the material and costumes at the Victoria & Albert Museum.

For theatrical ways: *Il teatro italiano – il libretto del melodramma dell'Ottocento* Vol.III edited by Cesare Dapino (Turin, 1983), *La vita di Rossini* by Stendhal (Paris, 1850), not always accurate as Rossini himself observed – not that he complained, he was delighted by the praise – is an excellent guide to the habits of the time.

On Milan: Gaetano Afeltra 'Addio Milano Bella' (*Corriere della Sera* 20 March 1993) and *I salotti di cultura nell'Italia dell'Ottocento* by Maria Iolanda Palazzolo and Franco Angeli (Milan, 1985), and the op.cit. *Le carte dell'impresario*, as well as Gino Monaldi 'Bartolomeo Merelli' in *Musica oggi* Milan, August 1924.

The Souvenir book of the ballerina Taglioni is kept at the Opéra Garnier in Paris. Giuseppina's dedication reads: 'A Madame Taglioni, regina delle Silfidi e modello di grazia e di gusto. Giuseppina Strepponi 28 ott 1831.'

CHAPTER 3: PRIMADONNA ASSOLUTA

Also in this chapter I used the texts on Verdi which I have mentioned above plus *Filosofia della musica* by Giuseppe Mazzini in 'Scritti editi ed inediti' (Imola, 1910); and *Problemi del Risorgimento* – La musica nel Risorgimento by Raffaello Monterosso (Milan, 1948).

In particular, in this context, I have made use of letters from the Dossier Strepponi in *Le carte dell'impresario* (Florence, 1982) and from the Biblioteca Nazionale of Florence (but the Fondo contains about 15,000 letters!) besides other letters to Lanari from the Archivio di Stato of Florence which are to be found in photocopy at the National Institute of Verdi Studies in Parma.

Again, for information about Merelli, the op. cit. *Memorie di un ottuagenario dilettante di musica*; the letter from Maffei to his wife from *Quartetto milanese ottocentesco, lettere inedite (di Giuseppe Verdi, Giuseppina Strepponi, Clara Maffei e Carlo Tenca*, a wonderful book published by Edizioni Archivi (Milan, 1974) from which I often quote. At the Museo Teatrale alla Scala I have looked up *Storia del teatro Regio di Torino* edited by A. Basso (Turin, 1976) besides *Dizionario biografico dei più celebri poeti ed artisti melodrammatici* by F. Regli who was the editor of *Il Pirata*, a musical journal (Turin, 1860).

From the op. cit. *The Man Verdi* by Frank Walker I have taken some letters of Giuseppina and Verdi's; I have paraphrased other letters which were not used by Walker and are part of his Bequest to the Institute of Verdi Studies in Parma. The mezzo Carolina Unger was born in Austria, 1803–77, and sang at the première of the *Missa Solemnis* and of the Ninth by Beethoven.

Sinforosa's birth has been registered in the Registry of Introduction 1839 and was marked A- Part 1 n 209 under the name of Cirelli Sinforosa; see op. cit. Phillips-Matz and De Angelis.

CHAPTER 4: THE ENCOUNTER OF HER LIFE

In order to compile this chapter I have studied the op. cit. *La giovinezza di Verdi* by Massimo Mila who was my remarkable colleague at *La Stampa* (I am still flattered by the mere memory) in whose company I saw various Verdi operas. Also by Mila, *Il melodramma di Verdi* (Bari, 1933) and Franco Abbiati *Giuseppe Verdi* Vol.II (Milan, 1959) besides the op. cit. by Gatti.

The details on the origins of the family of Giuseppe Verdi have been uncovered by Mrs Phillips-Matz in full in her biography of Verdi (op. cit.); other details on the librettists come from *Il teatro italiano – il libretto del melodramma dell'Ottocento* Vol. I, edited by Cesare Dapino (Turin, 1983).

The Roman reviews from *Due secoli di musica al Teatro Argentina* by Mario Rinaldi (Florence, 1978). The Argentina had been built in 1732 by the duke Cesarini Sforza; it had been designed by Marquess Girolamo Teodoli, it was thus called after the residence of the cardinal bishop for the Argentine which stood beside it. In 1861 the theatre, which had been bought by Principe Torlonia (along with the Apollo) was restructured by an architect called Carnevali.

The letter (partially unpublished) by Giuseppina to Lanari of 20 August 1841 is at the National Library in Florence, as is the one from Genoa of the 28 January 1842 and 25 March 1842 from Milan; I took them from photocopies at the Verdi Institute in Parma.

The reminiscence about Nabucco from *Racconto autobiografico a Giulio Ricordi*, dictated by Verdi to Folchetto, a journalist whose real name was Jacopo Caponi; it was published in the Italian edition (Milan, 1881) together with *Vita anecdottica di Giuseppe Verdi* by the French musicologist Arthur Pougin (1834–1921), the first serious biographical attempt on Verdi written by a foreigner.

La Scala Racconta op.cit. (Milan, 84) is a source of documents and news. I have also used Massimo Mila's *L'arte di Verdi* (Turin, 1980) and *Il melodramma di Verdi* (Bari, 1931).

From the newspaper *Piccolo Sera*, Trieste (5.3.1965): Giuseppina's obstetrician for the birth of Adelina was Theresia Slammig.

On Donizetti, I have read Herbert Weinstock *Donizetti and the World of Opera* (London, 1963), besides E. Saracino *Donizetti e le donne* (Milan, 1974), *Donizetti a Roma* by A. Cametti (Rome, 1907) and *Lettere*, edited by Guido Zavardini (Bergamo, 1948).

CHAPTER 5: FAREWELL TO THE STAGE

We have reached the year 1842: from the magazine *Aurea Parma*, XXV, Jan.-Mar. 1951, Vol. I, the letters with Dr Giacomo Tommasini edited by Enrico Benassi. Gossip from E. Ciccarese *Giuseppe Verdi: la donna, la colpa, la traviata*, (1893), *La storia d'Italia* edited by De Agostini Compact, for the chronology (Novara, 1991) and *La storia dall'Illuminismo ai giorni nostri* by V. Calvani and A. Giardina (Milan, 1988). Keeping up with what was happening, from the letters and news from the First Copialettere: *I copialettere di Giuseppe Verdi* published and illustrated by Gaetano Cesari and Alessandro Luzio with a preface by Michele Schello (Milan, 1913) is mentioned and used in this and the following chapters.

Cirelli is mentioned in a letter written by the tenor Napoleone Moriani, from Vienna, from the Casati Collection, *Lettere di Napoleone Moriani* ca 364 (11189), ca3645, ca3633, 11204, ca3644. Camillo Cirelli was born in Brescia on 20.12.1778 and died in Milan in 1855; he had married Elisabetta Pinotti whose sister was the wife of the celebrated singer Luigi Lablache. Elisabetta was three years younger than her husband; they had an only daughter, Giulia.

On the Salon at Casa Maffei, see: *I salotti di cultura nell'Italia dell'800* by M.I. Palazzolo (Milan, 1985) and the op.cit. by Mary Jane Phillips-Matz. I have taken from *Interviste ed incontri con Verdi* by Marcello Conati (Milan 1980) the details of Escudier's visit in Milan (26 May 1845) and also in this chapter I have used *Due secoli di musica al Teatro Argentina* op. cit. by Mario Rinaldi.

CHAPTER 6: THE ROMANTIC AGONY

The European revolutions are in full swing when Giuseppina arrives in Paris and Verdi in London; I have consulted *The Age of Capital 1848–75* by E.J. Hobsbawm and *The Age of Revolution 1789–1848* by the same author (London, 1975).

Mary Jane Phillips-Matz, with her spectacular labour of some thirty years, has guided my chronology. I am endebted to David Cairns for the article by Berlioz on Giuseppina's singing and the quality of her voice (which, as already stated in the text, had a Callas ring to it. Indeed Verdi not only based the musical characater of Abigaille on her tonality, but also took inspiration for Lady Macbeth's). *The Memoirs of Hector Berlioz* edited and translated by David Cairns (London, 1969) have been an excellent guide through the French séjour of my protagonist. In this chapter I also dip into *Lettere di Gioachino Rossini* edited by Enrico Castiglione (Rome, 1992); Rossini too had difficulties with Moriani, as we can read on 3 April 1841, '*Farete bene (per ora) di evitare i confronti con Moriani.*'

For the French salons the best book is of course the op.cit. *Mes Souvenirs 1806–1833* by Madame d'Agoult and also *Déclaration à genoux de Sainte-Beuve* 2.12.1842.

Massimo Mila, Frank Walker, Carlo Gatti and, for this chapter, Francis Toye, with *Verdi* (London, 1931), have paved my way in the intricacies of the composer's movements.

I have also dipped into the volumes by Julian Budden *The Operas of Verdi* (London, 1984 paperback edition), but also from Budden's excellent preface for the CD of the opera *I Masnadieri*, 'Verdi's opera for London' and G. Monaldi's *Verdi nella vita e nell'arte* (Milan, 1913). The stories about

266 **THE REAL TRAVIATA**

Grisi and her husband, Count de Candia, are at the Biblioteca del Museo Teatrale alla Scala.

The letter from Giuseppina to Giovannina Lucca Strazza nicknamed La Sciûra (Milanese dialect for the Signora), is from the op.cit. *Quartetto milanese* and the article 'La Strepponi insegnante di canto a Parigi e un giudizio sconosciuto di Berlioz' is by Marcello Conati. Giuseppina's letter to Pietro Romani, Lanari's principal *maestro concertatore*, is at the Biblioteca Nazionale Braidense in Milan. The orchestra conductor Romani (1791–1877) was one of Lanari's best friends and, in a certain period, often corresponded with Giuseppina.

On the French political events: *L'Histoire de la France*, Vol. II by André Maurois (Paris, 1947); and on Maffei: *Il salotto della contessa Maffei* by Raffaello Barbiera (Milan, 1925), while Verdi's letter to Escudier and Giuseppina's invitation come from two originals at the Bibliothèque Nationale de France.

Other details on Peppina from the op.cit. by Elena Cassulani *Giuseppina Strepponi* is too shy with the truth. What I refer to as Palazzo Dordoni and what Verdi called Palazzo Cavalli, today is Palazzo Orlandi – and can be visited. It was bought by Verdi on 6 October 1845 for 22,000 lire. It was originally built for Count Dordoni at the beginning of the 19th century and was considered the most modern building in Busseto when Verdi bought it.

CHAPTER 7: A GENIUS OBSERVED

In this chapter I have been guided by those texts which I have often mentioned in this context to which I add *Verdi* by Claudio Casini (Milan, 1984), *Carteggio verdiano*, by Franco Abbiati, Vol. IV, *Verdi, A Life in the Theatre* (London, 1987) by Charles Osborne; and the magazine *Aurea Parma* (Year LX, Vol. III, Sep.-Dec. 1976). On Giuseppina's travels *A Popular Description of Italy*, in 3 volumes, and the Vol. II of the op.cit. by Josiah Conder and Murray's *Hand-book of Tuscany, Lucca and Florence* (London, 1858).

Her letters: ca 6922 ca 6080 collez. Casati 866, at the Museo Teatrale alla Scala and Emilio Radius *Verdi Vivo* (Milan, 1951) and Vol. II of the op.cit. by Julian Budden.

Giannetto Bongiovanni *Dal carteggio inedito Verdi-Vigna* 1941, *La vita privata di Giuseppe Verdi narrata al popolo* by G. Bragagnolo and E. Bettazzi (Milan, 1905) and *Viva la libertà!* by Anthony Alabaster (London, 1992). As for Verdi's total lack of antisemitism in an era and a class intensely antisemitic, Corrado Mingardi brought my attention to *Il vessillo israelitico* monthly review, XLIX, February 1901 (Casale, 1901).

CHAPTER 8: A RESPECTABLE LADY

Charles Osborne *Verdi* (London, 1978) and *Letters of Giuseppe Verdi* (London, 1971); Corrado Mingardi *Con Verdi nella sua terra* (Busseto, 1991).

The meeting chez Rossini with the King of Portugal comes from *Rossini, Verdi e la Strepponi* from the Museo Teatrale alla Scala. And again, by Marcello Conati the op.cit. *Interviste e incontri con Verdi*.

A copy of the marriage certificate of Verdi and Giuseppina is at the Museo Teatrale alla Scala 3831/1 3. (Maestro Tintori took the photocopy himself.)

For a description of what was Rimini a hundred years ago, I consulted the op.cit., *Italy* by Josiah Corder. The delightful caricatures of Verdi, Giuseppina and Loulou at the San Carlo come from *Ricordi napoletani* by Melchiorre Delfico (Napoli, 1862). About the new cafés and inns that were opening in Milan: 'Tra un bagno e l'altro l'Italia fu fatta' by Arturo Guatelli (*Corriere della Sera*, 12.7.1993) and also from *Carteggi Verdiani*, edited by Alessandro Luzio, Vol.I (Rome, 1935). On Verdi's movements: Paul Hume *The Man and his Music* (London, 1978) *Verdi e la Fenice* (Milan, 1980); *Nuovi inediti verdiani (carteggio di Giuseppe e Giuseppina Verdi con Giuseppe De Amicis, Genova* 1861–1901 by Leonello Sartoris (Genoa, 1991) besides *Lettere inedite di Verdi* and *Le opere verdiane* (Milano, La Scala e il museo teatrale, 1929), *I copialettere di Giuseppe Verdi* published and illustrated by Gaetano Cesari and Alessandro Luzio with a preface by Michele Schello (Milano, 1913.) At Sant'Agata there are 7 volumes of the Verdis' Copialettere or Letterbooks 'which they kept from 1847', Pupa Carrara Verdi told me. At one stage I was allowed to look at some: I found a letter from Rossini (21 July 1846) and another from Berlioz, both written to Verdi. Another letter from Berlioz was addressed to an unknown person but was clearly sent on to Verdi because it recounted how people were reacting to Verdi's presence there.

The baby born on 14 April 1851 was abandoned at the Ospedale Maggiore of Cremona and was identified as Santa Streppini. Phillips-Matz thinks she might have been another of Giuseppina's daughters or one of Barberina's. As I say, I doubt that at this point in her life Peppina could conceive at all. Besides in May, less than a month after Santa's birth, we find Giuseppina trotting around Florence. Such a worrying journey would have been impossible for one who would have been considered to be an elderly mother.

Another baby, born one year before and abandoned at Cremona's hospital with the name of Giuseppe Maggino, was probably one of Verdi's illegitimate children and lived in Busseto. He worked for the Barezzi family who told him about the real identity of his father. His mother was a maid at Palazzo Dordoni.

CHAPTER 9: ENTER STOLZ

The letters of Giuseppina to Don Giuseppe Avanzi belong to the Cassa di Risparmio of Parma which bought them from Dott. Quirino Peroni whose great uncle was the 'Canonico'; they were made accessible in all comfort, silence, a photocopier at my disposal by Prof. Corrado Mingardi. They are at the magnificent Library of the Cassa di Risparmio of Parma and Credito su Pegno of Busseto. In one of its finest rooms, the Committee of the Monte di Credito decided to award a grant to the young Giuseppe Verdi.

An annotated correspondence with Giuseppe De Amicis (Genova 1861–1901) was edited by Leonello Sartoris (Genoa, 1991), *Verdi a Genova, note e ricordi personali* transcribed by Ferdinando Resasco (Genoa, 1906). G. Morazzoni *Verdi, lettere inedite* contains some notorious fakes (Milan, 1929).

I have also consulted Aurea Parma, Vol. III Sep-Dec. 1970.

Other letters from Giuseppina's Letterbooks from *Carteggi Verdiani* edited by Alessandro Luzio, Vol. III and IV (Rome, 1935) and I quote from Giuseppe Garibaldi *Memorie* (Milan, 1982). Giuseppina's letter to Mauro Corticelli is the CA6107 at Museo Teatrale alla Scala.

Those letters to Cesarino De Sanctis come from the published Letterbooks. And some quotations from Ghislanzoni's *Il libro serio* (Milan, 1879). I have taken the details of Camillino's death from the op.cit. by Phillips-Matz. Other texts state that he died on 17 February 1864 in Siena, specifying that he still needed to take two exams to get his degree. But Matz saw the death certificates. That he died of cholera is my own deduction.

I thank my sister Flaminia for transcribing many letters from the original, a slow work, which spared me a lot of time. I have also seen Giuseppe Tarozzi's *Di quell'amor* (Milan, 1980).

CHAPTER 10: BETRAYALS

I have consulted many famous texts for this final chapter including Walker's and Toye's, to Osborne, Gatti, Abbiati and Mila. From some episodes which show the Verdis at home in Genoa, the op.cit.: *Verdi a Genova, Note e ricordi personali* transcribed by Ferdinando Resasco (Genoa, 1906).

Mariani's letters are scattered all over the place, there are many in Ravenna, those I reproduce in part come from Umberto Zoppi's *Mariani, Verdi e la Stolz* (Milan, 1947) and Zoppi's *Documenti epistolari* which leaves no doubt on the relationshiop between Stolz and Verdi. Verdi who appears on the Piazza Grande in Parma, under the Farnese arcade, comes from *Il paese del melodramma* by Bruno Barilli (Rome, 1904).

Giuseppina's letter to Teresa who is travelling belongs to the private collection of the Ricci Stolz Picchio (which is on sale) and is dated 10 November 1875. New texts for this chapter: *G Verdi, l'uomo, il genio* by G. Marchesi (Milan, 1952) and Ferruccio Botti *Giuseppe Verdi* (Alba, 1941).

EPILOGUE

In this final part of my tale the letters of Giuseppina to the Canonico Avanzi from the collection of the Biblioteca della Cassa di Risparmio of

Parma and the Credito su Pegno of Busseto were very important. The letters of Barberina Strepponi come from the same source.

For details on Giuseppina's burial, I have consulted *Verdi e la religione* di Ferruccio Botti (2nd edition, Parma, 1940) but Abbiati Vol. IV is more reliable; for the fashion of the time, the Victoria & Albert Museum.

'La moglie di Verdi' op.cit.is my source about the episode of the violet. Giulio Ricordi wrote the article in the *Gazzetta musicale di Milano* edited by himself (no. 46 year 52; 18.11. 1897 – CA 774/9 also at the Museo Teatrale alla Scala). There is another article on Giuseppina's death and funeral in the musical journal *Il Trovatore* di Trieste (20.11.1897) from which I draw some details; it was sent to me by the Director of the Civico Museo Teatrale, C. Schmidt.

Miss Velleda's acount about Verdi at Clarina Maffei's death comes from *Quartetto milanese* op.cit.

INDEX

INDEX
283

The Imagination of Genius
HENRY JAMES

'Kaplan is thoroughly at ease with the 19th-century
European culture in which James made himself
so preeminently at home. He is also naturally
authoritative on James the American, and one of the
strengths of his book is that it conveys the creative
tension between these two overlapping elements . . .
Kaplan is equally good on James's sexual identity
. . . His comments on the novels are intelligent and
perceptive, sensibly brief . . . no further biography of
James is necessary'
Alan Judd in The Sunday Telegraph

'Excellent . . . a compelling portrait of a life of
extraordinary sweetness, self-repression and loneliness
. . . The real triumph of Kaplan's book is the extent to
which it makes one care for James'
Caroline Moore in The Times

'It never flags, but glides, like its subject, to a polished
end . . . One of the many strengths of Kaplan's
biography is the way in which he identifies what made
James run'
Roy Hattersley in The Sunday Times

'A good up-to-date one-volume life of Henry James
was long overdue; Kaplan has done the job splendidly'
*Miranda Seymour
in The New York Times Book Review*

'May even be superior to Edel'
James Buchan in The Spectator

SCEPTRE

Love From Nancy
CHARLOTTE MOSLEY

Nancy Mitford died in 1973 before she could write an autobiography. But she was one of the great letter-writers of this century, and her sparkling correspondence to her famous family and to a wide circle of brilliant friends sheds an extraordinary light on their lives and the times in which they lived.

'This enormous, rich selection of Nancy Mitford's letters shows that the vitality and peculiarity of this comic genius bubbled up in all her relationships . . . the letters are a trove of perfect one-liners, of fantastical stories confected to entertain the recipient (and the writer), of wincingly accurate assessments . . . She knew that her letters were probably her best work, and this book makes us think she was right'
Independent on Sunday

'These letters, vivid, spontaneous and sparkling with gossip, observation and comment, pulse with the authentic flavour of Mitfordspeak . . . Charlotte Mosley's editing of this enthralling correspondence is flawless'
Daily Mail

'A marvellous book'
The Times

$\int$

SCEPTRE

Queen Victoria
GILES ST AUBIN

Described by her contemporary Charles Greville as 'the most interesting mind and character in the world', Queen Victoria remains a fascinating, often contradictory figure. This masterly new portrait is above all a study of her personality, focusing on her family life, her relations with Ministers and servants, her tastes, beliefs and character traits, to give a fresh understanding of a remarkable woman and a great monarch.

'Long, thorough and penetrating . . . a wise, witty, insightful, detached perspective on the whole period . . . This new portrait of Victoria is as much a triumph of organisation as it is of erudition'
Anthony Curtis in the Financial Times

'It is good to have a biography as thoroughly researched, as fair-minded but not unsympathetic, and as well-written . . . an admirable summary of all that we know about the Queen'
Steven Runciman
in The Times Literary Supplement

'A meticulously accurate biographer . . . those who are already experts on Queen Victoria will still find much in this book to interest them'
Hugo Vickers in The Times

'Passes the three tests all biographies have to meet: it is well-written, scholarly, and it is psychologically penetrating'
Glasgow Herald

∫

SCEPTRE